DRAWING HEAT
THE HARD WAY

DRAWING HEAT THE HARD WAY

How Wrestling Really Works

Larry Matysik

ECW PRESS

Copyright © Larry Matysik, 2009

Published by ECW Press
2120 Queen Street East, Suite 200, Toronto, Ontario, Canada M4E 1E2
info@ecwpress.com / 416.694.3348

LIBRARY AND ARCHIVES CANADA CATALOGUING IN PUBLICATION

Matysik, Larry
Drawing heat the hard way : how wrestling really works / Larry Matysik.

ISBN 978-1-55022-899-1

1. Wrestling. 2. Matysik, Larry. 3. Wrestling promoters — United States — Biography. I. Title.

GV1195.M38 2009   796.812092   C2008-907565-X

Editor: Michael Holmes
Cover design: David Gee
Front cover photo: ECW Press Archives
Back cover: Brock Lesnar, Courtesy of Mike Lano
Photo section: Rachel Ironstone
Typesetting: Mary Bowness
Printing: Transcontinental   1   2   3   4   5

PRINTED AND BOUND IN CANADA

ECW PRESS
ecwpress.com

For Pat and Kelly,
who both get my vote for the Hall of Fame

"So what if it's an illusion? It works."
— *Mark Linn-Baker to Peter O'Toole in* My Favorite Year

Contents

INTRODUCTION

RING THE BELL

My editor, Michael Holmes, is to blame. He said he thought I could write something special simply by recalling what I have learned about professional wrestling from interacting with astute and insatiable personalities — people like Sam Muchnick, Bruiser Brody, Dave Meltzer, Terry Funk, and, yes, even Vince McMahon.

He told me to think of the countless characters I'd met and all the experiences I'd had while working in this multi-faceted business. Prodding me (and feeding my ego), Michael mentioned the roles in which he believed I'd excelled: announcing, booking, and promoting.

Flattery works.

He reminded me of the detailed conversations we've had about wrestling's intricacies, and told me, "You can write a terrific book with all of this."

It was nice of Michael to show confidence in my writing — and in the lessons that I've hopefully absorbed after more than a few years dealing with wrestling at every level. After penning *Wrestling at the Chase*, and then *Brody* with Barbara Goodish, I was tossing around various ideas for other projects.

Michael's suggestion probably made more sense than a murder mystery set in the world of pro wrestling (although that idea is still alive, in my mind anyway, so please don't laugh). At least the prep work for this one would be familiar territory.

But then Michael upped the stakes considerably by pointing out that pro wrestling was much, much more than it appears to be on the surface. Dig deep, he challenged. For every snob that snickers, there is someone with a doctorate who prizes wrestling's garish fun. For every bitter former employee who vilifies the industry, there is another past participant who prizes the uncommon experience. The audience for wrestling is as diverse as society itself. And incredible amounts of money are generated by it — not to mention countless hours of TV.

No matter what the so-called experts say, one heck of a lot of people like wrestling.

Business to its owners, career to its practitioners, and practically religion to some of its followers, the sport seems to demand that someone explore how it all operates, how it all fits together. There is plenty wrong with wrestling — like most anything else — but there's quite a bit that's right, too. Why does it work? How? Michael wanted me to write about that — to get to the heart of the business.

The best way to learn wrestling, Sam Muchnick believed, is by osmosis. He was probably correct. There are so many little tricks to the trade, countless necessary details, and the critical components known as psychology and politics. By keeping eyes, ears, and especially the mind open, by thinking about it the hard way, allowing opinions, experiences, and ideas to soak in and blend with new and personal observations, everything starts to make some sense.

It's like the great Lou Thesz once told me, "You travel down this road long enough, and you start to figure out how it works." Well, at least a little in my case.

The notion Michael had was the seed that grew into the book you now hold in your hand. Let's hope nobody turns it into a foreign object to hurl at either author or editor.

My hope is that what follows will feel like a conversation with an old friend — so let's sit down together and relax and see how it all really works.

CHAPTER ONE

IS IT REAL?

"Is it real?"

When it comes to professional wrestling, everyone thinks they know the answer — but the question is not that simple. Still, it's what the bright, pretty, maybe thirtyish woman asked me at a recent book-signing, so I had to come up with some kind of answer.

It went like this. Perhaps two-dozen fans were in front of me, wanting to discuss *Brody: The Triumph and Tragedy of Wrestling's Rebel*. It was in St. Louis, where professional wrestling has always enjoyed a special relationship with both the public and the media, and I was being treated like some sort of big deal. Why? Because I had been the protégé of beloved local promoter Sam Muchnick, the master who taught me the ins and outs of this incredible business; spent more than a decade on TV as the host of *Wrestling at the Chase*; worked nearly ten years with Vince McMahon and the World Wrestling Federation; and wrote a book called *Wrestling at the Chase* that renewed interest in this crazy industry, both in St. Louis and across the country.

The marketing for *Brody* provided me with the opportunity to visit bookstores, do signings, and take part in discussions. The people gathered around me that particular evening ranged in age from 12 to probably 75. There was an engineer, a teacher, some junior high students with their parents, a card dealer from a local casino, a retired hardware store owner, and a nurse — and everyone had a story. I'd listen to questions, tell the appropriate tale, and ask for their thoughts. It was, simply, fun.

When the subject of today's wrestling came up, most of the

people around me said they didn't watch, or didn't like it. Somebody compared John Cena to David Von Erich. ("They're both so hot!" one middle-aged woman laughed.) Somebody else asked how Ric Flair had managed to compete for so long. From there, the questions flew at me, fast and furious: What would have happened if Bruiser Brody and Hulk Hogan had battled? Is it steroids that make Batista look *that* big? Was Triple H as tough as Harley Race or Dick the Bruiser? Is Vince McMahon anything like Sam Muchnick was? Was Trevor Murdoch really from St. Louis?

Trevor Murdoch?

And they said they didn't follow today's wrestling. . . .

It all reminded me of visiting the Press Club with Sam years ago. A distinguished attorney began chatting about wrestling. Of course, he wouldn't admit that he was a fan. "My son loves to watch your show," he said. "I was really surprised that Bulldog Bob Brown gave Jack Brisco such a tough match last week."

Sam nudged me and whispered, "Closet fan."

The eager group in front of me wasn't closeted at all. Their connection to what they used to love and never missed was just more intense — and to some extent romanticized. Though they didn't want to admit it, they found something to enjoy in today's wrestling as well. The thread connecting everything was there, and it was strong.

Now, in my experience, there are always a couple folks who hang around the fringes at a wrestling book event. I get a kick out of reading their reaction to different names or memorable events. Generally, this type is a bit shy about revealing that they have an interest in something as controversial as the mat game. But there they are — eyes sharp, observant, giving little smiles now and then.

That pretty much describes the attentive but quiet lady who eventually asked the *big* question. I made eye contact, smiled, and asked her, "Are you even old enough to remember Bruiser Brody? It was almost 20 years ago."

The woman laughed and said, "Oh, I remember all the people you've talked about. I'd watch with my dad. Those are great memories."

Some of the others brought up memories of trying figure-four leglocks on their kid brothers, or getting something resembling brainbusters from their older sisters. One remembered going to old Kiel Auditorium and getting autographs, including mine, when he was an eighth grader. I shook my head and denied being that old.

But I still hadn't answered her question: "Is it real?"

"That depends which answer you want," I began. "Because it's almost *too* real on a lot of levels. Is it predetermined who wins? Yes. Are the wrestlers trying to maim one another? No — at least not normally. Is it entertainment? Sure; but what isn't? Is it a demanding business, where people can get rich or go broke? Most definitely: those of us who have been on the inside, as wrestlers or promoters or announcers, can earn a living — or lose one."

I was on a roll. "Is it a show? Absolutely. Do wrestlers get hurt, or worse? Unfortunately, too often. Are lives changed, for better or worse? Yes. Does it have the respect it deserves from the media and parts of the public? No, not even close to what it deserves.

"The term is a 'work.' Professional wrestling is a work — just a work. I guess that means it resides in some never-never land between real and not real. But now, here's *my* question for *you*." Everyone became quiet. "If it's just a work, why does wrestling hook us? Why are we here tonight? If it's just a work, why do we care?"

Maybe, I suggested, just maybe, wrestling is more real than it seems.

***

About one month earlier, Barbara Goodish had come from her home in Florida to join me for the St. Louis launch of *Brody*. Barbara, of course, was the wife of Frank Goodish, better known to the public at large as either Bruiser Brody or King Kong Brody. Brody was a controversial figure, unique within the business, totally independent and a rebel in all senses of the word when it came to dealing with promoters. He was also, more importantly, a tremendous drawing card, both in North America and Japan. That meant he could afford to be a rebel — because he made money. He was also my friend. Tragically, he was murdered in Puerto Rico in 1988.

Today, he's become something of a mythical figure, his growing legend shrouded in mystery.

Barbara has always been a very private person. Writing *Brody* was not easy for her, but she was a natural storyteller. Promoting the book in public, however, worried her. My wife, Pat, assured her she'd do great. And Barbara *was* a gem in St. Louis. At the St. Louis Wrestling Hall of Fame, where we signed and met readers, a couple hundred people turned out. Barbara was amazed.

"They were so polite and kind," she said later. "They were so knowledgeable. They knew so much about Frank. I couldn't believe when they asked if he really knew The Undertaker when he was just starting out."

The next night, Barbara and I made an appearance at an independent wrestling card Herb Simmons was promoting in tiny East Carondelet, Illinois. Herb was a great friend to both Brody and me. After the Muchnick era ended, when I was working for Vince McMahon in the World Wrestling Federation, Brody and I presented numerous independent shows, and Simmons was often our licensed promoter.

World Wrestling Entertainment (today's incarnation of the WWF) dominates the scene, but comes to an area only once or twice a year, so there is a hunger for small wrestling cards like the ones Simmons presents. Tying in the appearance of Brody's widow and the former *Wrestling at the Chase* announcer, Herb's program drew a jam-packed, enthusiastic crowd to the small hall. There were lots of familiar faces — people who'd been coming to events since they were teenagers, plus lots of new fans who were too young to have ever seen Brody perform.

Included on the bill were a few grapplers, most of them semi-retired, who might well have made it to the big time had it not been for the fact that opportunity was drying up in the late 1980s. But working for Herb, Brody, and me, they had been stars in their own realm.

Barbara was enchanted meeting Ron Plummer (Ron Powers), Joe Zakibe (The Assassin), Roger Bailey (colorful manager Big Daddy), and Rob Phillips. She had heard Frank talk about and praise these youngsters "back in the day," and she'd listened to both Frank and me lament the fact that none of them were getting the chance to move up the ladder. It was melancholy and moving to talk with them after many years. Mickey Garagiola, my former TV sidekick, stopped by to say hello and reminisce about how much he'd liked Brody.

In the dressing room, we worked out a little angle to spice up the evening. Barbara, Mickey, and I would be introduced along with the local favorites. All of us would be at ringside watching the main event, which involved 350-pound Jim Hoffarth, who was wearing a mask and dubbed "The Big Texan." Tired of the praise heaped on the favorites, Big Texan would grab the microphone, call everyone old, then dump Powers out of his chair, take the chair to the ring, and use it as a weapon on his opponent.

This, naturally, would enrage Powers, who was known as Brody's protégé, and so he would charge to the ring, while others tried to restrain him. We'd need to get a chair to Powers so he could whack Big Texan, laying the groundwork for a later "come out of retirement" bout between the two of them and sending everyone home happy. Ideas were bouncing around with no pressure; there was plenty of laughing. It was fun to be back in action, even at the grassroots level. Barbara was just taking it all in.

Finally Ron said, "Why not have Barbara give me the chair? After all, she was Frank's wife and the people here tonight know it."

We all looked at her. Barbara's eyes got as big as saucers.

"Me?"

Everyone nodded.

"If you want me to, I'll try. I just hope I don't mess it up."

Big Daddy told her he would lead her to the right place at the right time.

When the moment came, Ron went berserk, fought through the restraint of Assassin and Phillips, and jumped into the ring. The audience was on their feet, screaming.

And suddenly, there was Barbara Goodish hoisting a chair and sliding it into the ring for Powers. Whack! Right on the head of Big Texan, who fell like a chopped-down tree. The fans blew the roof off the place. They actually began chanting, "Bro-dy! Bro-dy! Bro-dy!" as Powers embraced Barbara.

So simple, so effective.

And yes, it was just a work — one that hooked everybody.

The next morning, as I drove Barbara to the airport, we rehashed the evening's events. Barbara said she had never been around the dressing room and certainly had never been involved in booking a finish or working an angle. She had seen some of her husband's matches and had heard his stories, but that was different. She found what was going on, the energy in coming up with ideas, fascinating.

"You know, Frank would come home sometimes and his head would just be gashed, simply horrible slashes where he had bladed to bleed for some match," Barbara recalled. "I'd be shocked and ask him why he did it. What would make him do something so dangerous? Frank would say, 'You had to be there. You had to be in the moment. You had to feel it.' And Larry, I understand now. You lose yourself in the moment. The crowd, the wrestlers, the excitement. I finally understand what Frank meant."

Losing yourself in the moment, entertaining two hundred or twenty thousand — it's all the same.

Was it real?

Who cares?

CHAPTER TWO

VINCE

World Wrestling Entertainment rules the professional wrestling landscape, worldwide. And one man rules WWE: Vince McMahon.

Without question, Vince McMahon *is* professional wrestling today. That's the truth, that's a fact, that's real. Except for the youngest of fans, whose innocence means they probably have no idea what's behind wrestling's gaudy image, everyone knows that the buck stops with Vince McMahon.

McMahon's vision has shaped modern wrestling. Even his undeniably weak, outgunned competition (which should be flattered even to be called that, given its inability to make an impact) mimics Vince. And should McMahon's vision change, as it does every so often, he has such influence and power that he can simply educate the audience (or *sell* them) on another style of his choosing. McMahon has always maintained that he is first and foremost a TV producer who just happens to do wrestling. It's that philosophy that has given him complete control.

To many of us who grew up in the business, this is both a good *and* a bad thing. Most, probably, would say it is more bad than good. Honestly? The heated emotion and vitriol that a simple mention of his name regularly elicits is often triggered, or at least made more intense, by old-fashioned jealousy. Yes, Vince brought the wrestling business to its knees; but seriously, think of what he has accomplished.

Of course, emotions cool, things change, and people — now, more than ever — need jobs. Still, for many, hearing *anything* good about McMahon is a bitter pill to swallow. The way McMahon changed the professional life of the countless men and women once involved in the industry can be heart-wrenching. But the fact remains: with or without him, a transformation was imminent. Wrestling relied on TV, and TV itself was undergoing a revolution.

Wrestling had been a tasty pie, split into a number of profitable pieces. Promoters once thrived across North America. The rise of cable TV, with national channels and less local syndicated programming, meant the way wrestling had been promoted would change forever, and McMahon knew it. A brilliant businessman — even if his ethics occasionally come into question — he ended up with the entire delicious dessert for himself. McMahon merely kickstarted the inevitable, and when all was said and done, he was the one left standing. In this new environment, only the fittest survived.

But does that make Vince McMahon the Antichrist? Or does it merely reflect the foresight of a sharp businessman ready to face the realities of today's rough-and-tumble world?

What is it about Vince McMahon?

His on-air performances are among the best ever. As a TV heel, McMahon is simply remarkable, and in front of the camera he has what is commonly called "it." Natural but charismatic, emotional and explosive — how much is the real Vince, and how much is a work? Does he even want that question asked? The answer is impossible to discern, at least for everyone but himself and those closest to him. That gives him an advantage — one he likes.

Years back, he blew up at Bob Costas during an HBO interview. Later, I asked Costas if he thought McMahon was working or shooting. Bob thought about it, then offered, "I think some of both. He probably knew what he was doing, but he was enraged."

The scary part is when one of McMahon's in-character statements reminds people of their own experiences doing business with him. With McMahon, the line between work and shoot is blurred. Is that blurring just a work, too? Well, kind of. And so when Vince tells Randy Orton and Jeff Hardy to shake hands — explaining that he himself has shaken hands with people and not meant it — there are those in the business whose guts twist because they know that McMahon is speaking the truth.

When "the evil WWE Chairman" raves on *Raw* about breaking people, it's hard not to remember that he really *has*. I will never forget what McMahon told me more than 25 years ago: "Wrestling is a rotten business, with rotten people, and the only way you succeed is to be more rotten than the other guy." He's clearly followed that principle.

Vince McMahon has also taken crazy, physical risks in the ring, apparently to "prove himself to the boys," though truthfully that was never necessary. In the end, he's taken bumps and bled, many believe, because he wanted to prove himself to *himself.*

In his office, McMahon can look at you and make you believe — yes, really believe — that what you say matters. He can be a mirror, building the confidence and belief of anyone he speaks to. His charisma is part of that ability; so is his positive energy. And Vince understands his power. He has never hesitated, after devastating someone on a deal, to say, "It's just business." Minutes later, he's perfectly capable of asking, "By the way, how's the family?" That's just Vince.

He can be charming, personable, and persuasive. Ask any TV executive he has ever dealt with. He can also be mean, cruel, and vindictive. Ask the talent he's tried to break (and likely has broken and/or humiliated). Sometimes it seems he simply enjoys playing mind games and screwing with people.

Let's also measure McMahon's power by how those within wrestling talk about his business. Back in "the day," people would talk about "New York" or "St. Louis" or "Dallas." Even when the territories disappeared, people still talked about either "New York" or "Atlanta" — meaning Ted Turner's World Championship Wrestling. Talent wanted to work "in New York," or maybe "in Japan." Insiders would gossip about what Atlanta or Dallas was doing.

Now, nobody bothers saying World Wrestling Entertainment or WWE. They say *Vince.*

"What did Vince do on *Raw* last night?"

"How many buys did Vince get for that pay-per-view?"

"Vince is trying to bury that guy."

Someone else might be the face of the product — John Cena or Triple H or The Undertaker. A few years back it was Stone Cold or The Rock or Hulk Hogan. But who chose those faces? Who pushed them? Who created them?

It was, and is, Vince. He has the vision; he makes the big decisions. He's all-powerful, but how did he get there? And what has he done since getting there?

Vince represents the third generation of McMahons in the business. His grandfather Jess, who was also active in boxing promotion, was considered a powerbroker from the 1920s to the 1940s. Vince Sr. succeeded him and had his own remarkable career. Rest assured, while growing up, the young McMahon had plenty of history and experience passed on to him, by osmosis or otherwise.

Through his father, Vince became familiar with how the National Wrestling Alliance, led by St. Louis promoter Sam Muchnick, essentially kept order in a business that featured characters and behavior born of its carnival roots. After World War II, when the NWA was formed, wrestling became an industry chopped into approximately 30 different small companies around North America. Relations developed with promoters in Mexico and Japan. Not every office was always technically aligned with the NWA, but all of them generally accepted that the NWA was the controlling force in their rambunctious world.

Muchnick is generally, and correctly, credited with the amazing accomplishment of holding everything together for three decades. He was deeply involved in the formation of the NWA in 1948, and soon became the guiding light for the cooperative organization. Each promotion, whether member or independent, had its own TV show and its own style of wrestling. What Muchnick presented in St. Louis, for example, was more firmly based in legitimate athletics; he limited extreme angles, focused on match depth and importance, and maintained a strict adherence to running a professional business. Ric Flair once said, "We were pretty straight in St. Louis."

Memphis, which never paid well and had many small towns on its circuit, could not afford the type of high-talent wrestlers that Muchnick did. Whatever the reason, the money was not there to pay those high stipends. Therefore, that territory relied on gimmicks and kinky booking ideas to turn a profit. New York was basically on the same page as Muchnick, and so was Minneapolis — Toronto, too, except in the period when promoter Frank Tunney was listening to The Sheik. Houston was somewhat similar to St. Louis. Other promotions landed somewhere in between — the range ran the gamut, from lots of blood and violence to almost cartoon-like productions. Without the Internet or national TV to inform fans, each promoter was free to run his area in the way he deemed most likely to make money.

Muchnick always felt that the World Wide Wrestling Federation, guided by Vince Sr. with Bruno Sammartino as champion, did more kicking, punching, and power moves than the NWA, with tacticians like Lou Thesz, Gene Kiniski, Dory Funk Jr., and Jack Brisco on the throne, but in reality, the difference was not all that pronounced. He also noted that a WWWF challenger usually got his first main event following a long run of TV squashes, while NWA challengers earned their title shot after winning a main event or two against other leading contenders. McMahon Sr. also liked to book immediate rematches for his crown if a bout drew a good crowd. When St. Louis had a hot title duel, Sam would usually delay the rematch for a few months, letting it percolate while another contender got a shot. In letting a contender earn a rematch, Sam believed anticipation was built; Vince Sr. liked to ride the hot hand. Still, the actual differences were minor — just a matter of taste — because both booking methods drew money. Even today, however, it's clear McMahon's son remembers the booking to which he was exposed: Vince, too, tends to schedule immediate return bouts.

Human nature suggests that when folks get something good, they want more. Wrestling promoters were even greedier that way (and less reputable), but Muchnick, as the sounding board of the NWA, did a pretty good job of keeping them in check. Just as booking is part persuasion, NWA chief Muchnick often had to convince promoters not to step onto each other's turf in the hopes of stealing a lucrative market. Navigating the business through a few tricky lawsuits and an FBI-led congressional investigation, Muchnick's hand was immeasurably strengthened because he clearly had friends in high places.

Bob McGlynn, a local lawyer who knew Muchnick from political ventures and his involvement with the Cahokia Downs Race track, once told me Sam was "always on the fence, would never come down for one side or the other — at least in public." Assuming the assessment is accurate, staying neutral was clearly an effective tactic. Irv Muchnick, Sam's nephew, described his uncle's place in the wrestling world as "Switzerland."

Muchnick was a mediator; he established stability where none had existed since the 1920s and 1930s, when a group of promoters (led by Tom Packs in St. Louis and Paul Bowser in Boston) nicknamed "The Trust" effectively called most of the shots. But that group had died away, broken down — in large part, when Muchnick unseated Packs in St. Louis and made new, stronger allies.

Trust: now that's a funny word in any business, and it's even stranger in wrestling. But the sharks trusted Sam Muchnick as much as they'd ever trusted anyone. Sure, at times they balked, griped, and talked behind his back. But Sam was a wily operator, and his sources let him know who was complaining about what. He owned St. Louis. Never a territory town, it was instead a mighty stand-alone market that featured top talent from all over. And he never tried to expand his reach through his role as chief of the NWA. His honesty earned a grudging respect among a tough clientele. When disputes inevitably arose, Muchnick always tried to finesse a resolution that was, in his own words, "in the best interest of wrestling." Sam's belief was that a business that was healthy overall would benefit every player in the game, including himself.

Nothing if not fair-handed in booking the champion, Muchnick protected the titleholder from the unreasonable demands of local promoters as much as possible, and he somehow smoothed rifts that opened during the development of the American Wrestling Association. The AWA was created by Verne Gagne, primarily because he wanted to be the champ and, for whatever reason, couldn't get Muchnick and his NWA compatriots to award him the honor. He went his own way, gave his company an impressive-sounding name, and made himself his own kingpin.

Yet Sam maintained a smooth, cordial relationship with Gagne. Later, Verne even became a partner in the St. Louis Wrestling Club, of which Sam was the undisputed boss — with never less than 51% of the stock of a sub-chapter S corporation. Sam would chuckle about Gagne's empire in the privacy of his St. Louis office: "The AWA is a stationery organization," Muchnick would say, grinning over his play on words. "Verne prints stationery with 'AWA' on the letterhead." Sam was right on the money. No independent promotions belonged to the AWA. Verne had partners in some key Midwest cities (Verne had controlling interest and usually hired someone to be the "front man"/promoter) and through his own TV led fans to believe it was a viable association like the NWA.

Of course, nothing in wrestling, even a territory office, is ever as transparent as it seems.

Omaha, for instance, was with Gagne's AWA, but had its own TV show for some time and ran a satellite territory of smaller towns while utilizing the AWA champion and some of Gagne's talent. Omaha belonged to the famed Dusek family; nobody really knew what portion might have been controlled by Gagne.

Similarly, Pittsburgh was tied in with the World Wide Wrestling Federation. It had its own TV show and ran weekend shows in smaller locations around Pittsburgh, plus the Civic Arena once a month. Bruno Sammartino actually purchased Pittsburgh from Vince Sr. in 1966. Long before that, Vince cohort Toots Mondt had a hand in Pittsburgh; the connection with big boys from New York was always tight. But the WWWF was never a real alliance, not like the NWA. It was a federation in name only. The organization (known legally at the time as Capitol Wrestling Corporation) had survived various incarnations over many years. It became known as a "Federation" with the crowning of Bruno as titleholder in 1963 following a power struggle with Sam and the NWA that focused on the availability and booking of the NWA champion, Buddy Rogers, who had ties with McMahon.

Vince Sr. did, however, keep up a good rapport with Muchnick, and relatively quickly rejoined the NWA, even though he recognized another champion. The trade-off was that Vince Sr. called *his* king the World Wide Wrestling Federation Champion, while the NWA titleholder was billed as the World Heavyweight Champion. In fact, Vince Sr. rushed to embrace the NWA and benefit from their generous assistance when well-heeled Eddie Einhorn, a TV producer who later owned the Chicago Bulls and White Sox, attempted to start a rival promotion in the Northeast in the early 1970s.

The NWA was essentially a cooperative of independent businesses of varying size and success. Outside of the championship belt, the NWA owned nothing. The AWA was a small business that did not belong to the NWA but maintained cordial relations. The WWWF was just a bigger small business that *usually* belonged to the NWA.

Although the NWA attempted to provide a common ground for promoters and wrestlers, there were those who misrepresented the Alliance to further their own aims. Sometimes this was relatively innocent. A good example lies in the fact that the NWA *never* officially recognized a World Tag Team Champion. Sam, like everyone else, looked the other way when a member promotion featured that billing, rationalizing that each territory must be allowed to pursue its own business without interference. Some overzealous offices, however, incorrectly invoked the NWA name in areas that lead to varying degrees of legal warfare.

When the WWWF broke away in the '60s, Sam finessed the situation, smoothed over any ill will, and maintained friendships with both Vince Sr. and Toots Mondt. Why wouldn't he? Wrestling was booming, and so many towns were running regular shows that no single champion could appear often enough in any location. Most cities with populations of 100,000 or more featured live wrestling at least once a month. Having three so-called world champions was actually fortuitous and, from a publicity standpoint, gave magazine writers plenty to debate. Sam's practical handling of what could have become nasty laid the groundwork for the return of Vince Sr. to the NWA fold.

Besides, Vince Sr. was a dignified personality who projected the image of the kind of solid businessman Sam loved. Far too many promoters seemed like carnival operators and were ignored by the "legitimate" business community in their own towns. Sam was never that way. He'd earned the respect of the media and his community. And those who followed suit, like Vince Sr. or Toronto's Frank Tunney, had Sam's respect.

Under Tunney, Toronto probably came closest to St. Louis as a stand-alone market, though the respected promoter also ran several strong cities around Ontario. At different times, Tunney had deals or arrangements with Pedro Martinez from Buffalo and Ed Farhat (The Sheik) from Detroit before finally selling major points to the Crockett organization from the Carolinas in the late 1970s. Always a staunch NWA member, Tunney was like Sam in keeping good relations with everyone; and he was never averse to using NWA, WWWF, or AWA champions.

For Sam, wrestling's various closed-door political battles were "just business." (How often during my ten years with WWF did I hear Vincent McMahon Jr. use that very phrase?) In truth, Muchnick felt it was the ambitious Mondt, a longtime player in the wrestling business, who pushed Vince Sr. into controversial positions in the early 1960s. "Mondt was the manipulator," Sam told me, explaining how the legendary power-player would limit other NWA promoters' access to Rogers, and that he was convinced Toots was behind McMahon's move to form the WWWF.

But was Muchnick angry with Mondt?

Consider this. When Mondt retired in the 1970s and moved to St. Louis, where his wife Alma was from, he often visited Sam's office. They would laugh about old confrontations. It was both nostalgic and, for me, a tremendous learning experience. Whoever first said "don't burn bridges" could have been talking about the business of wrestling.

To top it off, and perhaps shine a further light on Sam's philosophy, when Gagne bought into the St. Louis Wrestling Club, the other person Muchnick seriously considered for the stock purchase was Vince McMahon Sr. The one thing Sam made clear was that he would never allow more stock to be sold to Kansas City operators Bob Geigel, Harley Race, and Pat O'Connor, because they were far too narrow in their view of the business.

By the late 1970s, when time had taken its toll, Muchnick was moving away from his position as the head of wrestling. Two NWA presidents tried to follow in his footsteps — Fritz Von Erich (Jack Adkisson) of Dallas and Eddie Graham of Florida, both Muchnick supporters over the years, and in Fritz's case, a dear friend. But Sam was bitterly disappointed: Von Erich and Graham both put their own territories ahead of what was right for wrestling in general. The constant barrage of what they considered minor headaches may have turned the two of them away in aggravation from the duties of the president. Where Sam would spend endless hours on the telephone mediating, Fritz and Graham clearly did not have the patience for arbitration.

The upshot was that James E. Barnett consolidated even more power as executive secretary, treasurer, and booker of the champion. Jim Barnett was another brilliant manipulator, one who knew the business and its characters almost as well as Muchnick. In locations as varied as Detroit, Australia, and Atlanta, Barnett had run slick operations that produced superb profits. His goals with the NWA, however, were as unlike Sam's as night and day. Likewise his relationships with those who comprised the alliance. When Bob Geigel was named president, the role was nothing more than a figurehead: someone who did little more than a few TV interviews. The deathwatch began.

Vince McMahon Jr. saw all this happening, and better than most understood the significance. Maybe he wasn't privy to every detail, and maybe he didn't understand each nuance as events occurred, but the ambitious young fellow clearly recognized that the wrestling's time-tested business model had ruptured. He also was likely the first to grasp how changing technology might affect wrestling. And McMahon clearly sensed that others, Gagne and Von Erich (with his red-hot "World Class Championship Wrestling" program) for example, might share in his aspiration for a national promotion. It was certainly the business justification for his most controversial moves.

But here's a little-known fact, something that could have changed the course of wrestling history had the stars aligned correctly. In the late 1970s, after Sam had relinquished the NWA presidency, he was approached by a gentleman named Haskell Cohen. Cohen was no stranger to wrestling: he'd been involved with broadcasting the sport nationally on the Dumont network. At one point, he was also the PR chief for the National Basketball Association. When he approached Sam, however, Cohen represented a company that had just launched a communications satellite. Talk about newfangled! Imagine, being able to distribute a show to many different TV stations, across the country, at precisely the same time.

From his office at 770 Lexington Avenue in New York City, Cohen worked with Muchnick to put together what they hoped would be a series of wrestling programs to be telecast around the nation. In other words, someone in Memphis or Portland or Charlotte might see a wrestling show produced by someone other than the local promoter. Many in the business were up in arms, especially when the show was slated for Kansas City, using then NWA champion Harley Race against Sam's good friend Dick the Bruiser in the main event, and also displaying talent from Gagne's AWA. Everyone involved, save for Bruiser, was part of the St. Louis business with Muchnick.

I was selected to be the play-by-play commentator and, because I was part of Muchnick's office, I heard plenty of what went on between Cohen and Sam. I also listened to those tense talks between Muchnick and other promoters. Muchnick promised everyone that the new program would use talent from all the different territories over time, and that they would move the show to different locations. It would be good for business, Sam vowed. "Wary" and "worried" would be polite ways to describe how the rest of the wrestling business felt about this venture. Muchnick might have been older, but he was still a crafty fox, and the natural distrust of promoters led many to think some sort of hostile revolution was afoot.

My flight was booked, publicity had begun, and Cohen was lining up stations to broadcast the show. If it clicked, it was likely that more stations would jump on the bandwagon in the finest tradition of TV. Some clearly shuddered in fear: was *Sam Muchnick*, of all people, going to engineer some national operation that would compromise their earnings, their kingdoms?

One week before the show was to take place, the satellite disappeared. Literally. Gone. Poof!

Cohen assured everyone involved that these things happened. And yes, in those days, satellites did indeed occasionally detonate or vanish. Considering the furor that had been stirred in the wrestling world, and the long delay before another satellite could be launched, the idea was dropped, and I didn't go to Kansas City.

In hindsight, likely only a small number of stations had actually signed on for the broadcast. And for all anyone in wrestling ever knew, Cohen's people may have simply got cold feet and pulled the plug. Maybe the missing satellite story was just that — a story. Whatever the truth was, there were always certain things working against the venture. Cable TV was not even in its infancy; it was still little more than a concept, yet to be developed. Most meaningful markets only had five or six stations — three that were network oriented, an independent or perhaps two, plus a PBS station that wasn't about to touch that dastardly wrestling thing. It was nothing like today's entertainment landscape, where a couple hundred stations beg for product. Back then, there was a limit to how many stations might want the show because there simply wasn't as much TV time available as there is now.

Perhaps even more significantly, Muchnick was long past his prime. This wasn't 1955 or 1964. It wasn't even 1972 — when every promoter would still fall in line (a few, of course, reluctantly) with whatever the kindly but powerful old gent wanted. Muchnick had already stepped away from his baby, the NWA. His influence was waning every day. Wrestling as a business was quietly starting to fragment, even if it wasn't quite about to implode the way Harley Race sadly predicted to me it would. When Sam stepped down, a brick here and a brick there began to crumble. Harley understood what was about to happen. He just wasn't right about the timing.

During the 1970s, Muchnick often spoke of promoters wanting to build empires and have big booking offices. "I don't want to work that hard," Sam would say. "I take too many phone calls. I'm satisfied." Clearly, Muchnick wasn't hungry enough to shove a national show down wrestling's throat.

The Cohen-Muchnick plan might have been right, but the time and the players were wrong. Such a grandiose project needed refinement and patience, but the people to do that refining were not in place . . . at least not yet. Even those greedy enough to annex a town, as Verne Gagne had tried and failed to do in both San Francisco and Los Angeles, did not have the necessary expertise, contacts, resources, or just plain balls to get it done.

Naturally, Vince Sr. knew about Haskell Cohen. And so Vince Jr. probably did, too. Like me, the younger McMahon was an announcer, a staple on numerous Northeastern outlets. We might have been the two youngest announcers in the country in the mid-1970s. Vince Jr. also ran towns, did various promotions, and was obviously headed for bigger things as his dad phased himself out.

But it would be rash to argue that Cohen's idea of a national show influenced McMahon. I have no idea whatsoever if it's true. After all, Vince was ambitious and imaginative enough to pop the concept on his own. But the fact that what Cohen dreamed almost became a reality demonstrated that the idea of a national promotion was drifting within the collective unconscious of the wrestling world, unnerving more than a few comfortable local promoters.

In cable's infancy, Madison Square Garden programs began appearing in different markets around the country. Hindsight tells us that when WTBS, the superstation from Atlanta, began to grow significantly, the future was already upon the business. Jim Barnett was the boss in Atlanta then, but he barely fiddled with the idea of expanding. Vince had the vision, and he did everything he felt he had to do for his business.

What would Sam Muchnick think about his old friend's son if he were alive today? No doubt Sam would be disgruntled, to say the least, about some of the WWE's content, especially when it came to material of questionable taste. He would hate the run-ins, the ref bumps, the outlandish gimmicks (not all of them, though), the carny thinking, the sexual exploitation, the freakshow elements of the programming, the ever-dwindling time spent on wrestling and athletics, the concentration on high spots. . . . This list could go on and on.

Nonetheless, Sam Muchnick was first and foremost a business-man. He loved to play the stock market, and he was quite good at it. Sam would take one look at WWE's annual corporate report and salute Vince as an excellent businessman who did exactly what he had to do, not only to thrive in today's market, but to actually bend it in the direction he wanted. Muchnick certainly would have approached things differently, but he wouldn't begrudge Vince his success.

Vince (who reportedly prefers VKM, for Vincent Kennedy McMahon, or simply Vince) was the person who took wrestling to the next level as entertainment, the media landscape, and TV itself changed. He had the guts, the courage, the smarts, the energy, the hunger, and the sheer drive that, in all honesty, no one else had. When he was knocked down — it wasn't often, but it happened — he got back up, swinging.

There remain misconceptions about what the business was like when McMahon started campaigning for wrestling dominance. It's important to remember that TV had *not yet* changed. When the WWF started buying up talent and TV station contracts, syndicated programming was still the key. When McMahon began taping at the Khorassan Room of the Chase Hotel in January 1984 (the WWF also taped cards from Kiel Auditorium), part of his deal with KPLR was that the station would produce and distribute his new syndi-cated show, *Superstars of Wrestling*, to markets that had once belonged to Gagne, Graham, and others.

His raid on the in-ring talent and office staff of existing pro-motions had nothing to do with cable or other changes on the horizon. Vince ruthlessly and efficiently moved in on existing deals between promoters and stations and, by offering better terms, usually stole away prime time slots and outlets in impor-tant towns. He had the bucks, and he wasn't afraid to spend them where it mattered — on TV.

Some promoters were promised buyouts that never material-ized. Others laughed at McMahon and predicted he'd never succeed at the very same time as the foundations of their business were being washed away. Territorial wrestling promoters didn't fare nearly as well as TV stations in the wrestling revolution. Many never saw a dime promised to them, or were simply forced out of business. Stu Hart, and Calgary's Stampede promotion, provides just one example. Vince promised the father of Bret and Owen Hart 100 grand a year for ten years for the rights to his towns. But just a year into the deal, the checks stopped coming. (Hart did receive a percentage of the receipts for shows in Calgary and Edmonton.) According to Vince, another Hart son, Bruce, had started a rival promotion, violating the terms of the agreement's non-compete clause. Vince had Stu's best talent, and his television at this point; he told Hart he was free to resume business, because he wasn't going to pay another dime.

One possible reason Vince might be forgiven is simply this: wrestling had a long, shady history, and this history in turn maybe justified eschewing ethics as the war raged. Except in rare cases, usually involving Muchnick, integrity was never in large supply in wrestling's circles. Those in the game knew what the ground rules had always been, and so, from Vince's point of view, "whatever means necessary" was acceptable. Ethics be damned.

Most wrestlers made more money after they joined the WWF simply because they worked before bigger audiences and more often. McMahon once told me, "I don't like contracts. They never work." Of course, the deals he inked with TV stations were stable. Wrestlers, fortunately enough for him, were used to living on promises. Only a very few — Hulk Hogan being the big one — hired a lawyer and signed a real contract.

What McMahon realized was that as syndicated programming began having less and less impact, and as nationwide cable became stronger, it was time to move in a new direction — and to his credit, he did. He had clearly grasped the importance of a national presence when he struck his historic deal with NBC, plus he was already running a weekly program on the USA Network.

All the while, he was sucking up big names, seasoned talent for the World Wrestling Federation, as well as providing a colorful, generally wide-open product featuring all-star matches between *all* the stars from the now-gasping territories. It was the perfect business model for a fast-expanding operation.

I began working for the WWF myself in January 1984, two years after Muchnick retired. I had split with the collapsing St. Louis Wrestling Club the year before, and for a while ran my own independent promotion with TV on KDNL in St. Louis before joining Vince under stressful circumstances. Part of my deal with Vince had me helping supervise as KPLR churned out programs for the rapidly expanding syndication network every week for over a year. It was a monstrous job, building in original interviews for almost every outlet and then shipping to, at one point, over 70 different stations on a weekly basis. The ordeal was made harder because, in those early days, the fellow from Vince's staff who gave me the run-time for each station had trouble figuring out total minutes. Each market seemed to need a different program length (one had 45:30 for content, one had 46:30, another wanted 44:00, and so on) because each station had different amounts of commercial time allocated for their hour. Jim Winkle and John Baker of the KPLR production staff joined me in making many quick decisions on trimming or adding time on individual matches.

Every program needed a separate group of interviews with wrestlers, feud-building spots that had to be inserted for a specific town's upcoming event. The best part (or is it worst)? We had a one-day turnaround — one day for post-production to shape a program that left just the right holes for the local interviews. Eventually, the raw bout footage wasn't even always from St. Louis, further complicating both our planning and the content. It quickly became much more than an eight-hour day. Additionally, for quite some time I did voice-over commentary for the WWF programs that were broadcast in St. Louis. It was all-consuming.

When Vince rolled the dice in 1985 with the first *WrestleMania*, it was clear that KPLR just could not keep up, since the number of stations featuring WWF content was growing almost weekly. Additionally, the WWF owed KPLR serious bucks. Vince was reeling financially because of the very expansion that was bringing him close to his fortune. Once, unknown to the WWF office, I silently listened in on an extension as Jim Barnett, who represented Vince at that point, talked to station general manager Barry Baker about the WWF's plans for the future. Barnett also asked for more time to pay the bills.

As everyone knows, *WrestleMania* was ultimately a home run, a massive closed-circuit event. Keep in mind, cable was barely a toddler and pay-per-view just a late-night dream. As fast as Vince had been moving and gobbling up outlets for the WWF, the pace accelerated. After the resounding success of *WrestleMania*, the money began to flow. Even then, Vince was quick to recognize and exploit potential new streams of revenue, primarily in the realm of merchandising. KPLR was eventually paid, but Vince built his own production facility — an inevitability as the company rapidly grew. Almost no one at KPLR was upset to see the WWF handle its own production and distribution.

The rest is by now an old story. Vince dodged a bullet in a federal trial about steroid distribution and won a momentous battle against Turner's World Championship Wrestling — possibly the most dysfunctional operation in wrestling history considering the amount of money with which they had to play. As Vince once told me, the WWF had become the big elephant and the big elephant sits any damn place it pleases. McMahon had revolutionized the business — in the ring with flash and sizzle, and in the boardroom with creative new ways to make even more money. No guilt, no remorse, no second thoughts.

So who is this man, this modern Barnum, who today makes professional wrestling tick, who draws in everyone from Donald Trump to Floyd Mayweather, who is the pulse of a controversial and incredibly profitable enterprise?

Vince McMahon knows wrestling. He learned well at the feet of his father and the other clever operators of New York. Vince's dad may have employed a different methodology than Sam Muchnick, but both made money and sent countless fans home happy. Nothing else matters, or ever did, at least to the outside world.

Yes, VKM failed at football (the mercifully quickly defunct XFL), and his weightlifting venture went belly-up. WWE feature films have been nothing to brag about. Nonetheless, his company has actually adapted much of Vince's own polished but pugnacious attitude that says stomp 'em, sock 'em, and sack 'em. Like Vince, WWE representatives have an aura of invincibility as they deal with the outside world. As for wrestling itself, and in the marketing of this strange discipline? Nobody has ever been better.

He has twisted and turned wrestling, making it into a TV and money-making tool. So much so that his respect for wrestling itself, on its own terms, as entertainment, might be legitimately suspect, even as he himself is clearly a fan of certain types of performers and the mystery of the action. He has no problem telling the media and government agencies that wrestling is not a sport, especially when those statements fit his agenda, and then turning right around to profess, "but this — now this part is real!" Vince does what he feels he must do to keep his product in the spotlight, drawing heat whenever it helps his cause.

What a fascinating way to exploit what has always been manipulated for the benefit of the business. That debate — real, not real — has always been part of the allure, the magic. Once upon a time, wrestling told its customers: "It's all real!" (Wink, wink . . . pretty much.) Now WWE says, "It's *not* real!" (Wink, wink . . . well, okay, except that little part there.) It's a brilliant hook, playing on whatever fans want to believe or disbelieve. Sure, the psychology is reversed, but it's really the same. Vince put it all out there, flipped it around, and left everyone wondering whatever they wanted to wonder. Confused? Welcome to the club.

Writing in *Esquire* magazine about culture, celebrity, and pornography, Stephen Marche said, "The art is to hide the art." That used to be true about wrestling — and isn't it apt to compare those subjects to McMahon's vision of wrestling? — until Vince altered the concept to: the art is to *expose* the art, and use that to hook an audience.

And still there's the enigmatic man who made it all happen. How much of the authentic VKM is ever on display? What is work and what is shoot?

This much is true: Vince is comfortable with power; he's always had it. Even when he was learning the ropes, there was an aura about him. "The boys," the wrestlers, knew he was special. He never shows it, but he knows that he's always being watched, scrutinized, judged. There's a reason behind every word he utters and every move he makes in public, the dressing room, or his office. He's comfortable being the center of attention and familiar with the sense that he is special. Vanity is a vital part of his character: he knows we can't help but look. People react to *him*! McMahon is never the one reacting.

More importantly, Vince McMahon understands how to elicit a response. He can sense — can probably *smell* — the tiniest weakness. He almost certainly enjoys being intellectually challenged by other people's ideas, personalities, intentions, and tactics.

No matter how valuable, how rich, and how tough a wrestler thinks he is, sitting down with Vince McMahon one-on-one is nothing short of a life-altering moment of truth. Almost everyone is over-matched. Some maintain that meeting him behind closed doors is best, believing he keeps his ego in check in these circumstances. Supposedly, without an audience, he does not feel the need to indulge in alpha male shenanigans. And this may well be true for those with whom Vince feels the highest degree of trust and intimacy.

McMahon should never be underestimated. Like any smart man, he does not always have to be driving a bulldozer — although it often seems that way. When the situation demands, he can be subtle, clever, and sly. Concentrating, he assesses a companion as expertly as a psychologist does a patient, though for quite different reasons. If there is a way to convince Vince of something, it is certainly not by confrontation.

The self-belief that he has an edge, that he is the ruler and everyone else is a supplicant, is always there to some degree. For a Hulk Hogan or a Dwayne Johnson, it might not be quite that extreme, but here is a solid bet: even *they* feel Vince's sovereignty and, unconsciously, they blink too — or at least they have, at one time or another. McMahon knew exactly what message he was sending inside the industry when he made the Million Dollar Man's catch phrase, "Every man has his price." On a daily basis, behind the scenes, Vince proves exactly that.

Plenty of wrestling people — "off the record," of course — will speak negatively or critically of Vince McMahon. When it comes to the public record, suddenly everything is positive or, at worst, neutral. People understand his power. They are working in hopes of getting a job, another payday. But do they really believe he doesn't know? This behavior, which is actually like kneeling before the throne, must amuse him.

Yes, Bret Hart punched him once — a decade ago. Big deal. Who is the still the boss? Today, the fallout from the Montreal screwjob is part of *Vince's* legacy, part of *his* legend.

What is Vince like when he sits down with Dick Ebersol of NBC or Bonnie Hammer of NBC Universal? Does he submerge his sense of divine right, instead substituting the kind of supreme self-confidence that executives love? By virtue of both attitude and accomplishment, McMahon can deal with all of them as equals. Even Donald Trump raves about Vince.

Captains of industry share a mindset with Vince. Assembly line workers (in this case, wrestlers and other performers) are resources to be utilized, discarded, and replaced. Wrestling today operates no differently than General Motors, Exxon, or Wal-Mart. But who is to say how Sam Muchnick might have managed things, in a similar position? He, too, was a shrewd, tough businessman.

Sometimes doing the "right thing" is not always best for business. There is no room for sentimentality, unless it has a value to the company. Running a business leaves no place for guilt or second-guessing. Vince understands this better than most, thanks to the world in which he was raised. Just because wrestling lacks social acceptance amongst upper-class society does not mean it functions any differently under Vince than other conglomerates do under their executives. Argue about the social implications, but it's the way of this world.

Vince recently blasted the "elitists" who dislike wrestling and its followers, saying snobs aren't welcome in his audience — one he argues is actually representative of America. But who has been responsible for most of the angles, the worst storylines, that have made today's media lambaste the sport of kings? Wasn't McMahon responsible for making Trish Stratus crawl and bark like a dog; wasn't he the one who okayed a necrophilia storyline? Lately, he's been better at restraining himself, but his tune could change with the snap of his finger if he once again decides "attitude" or something controversial is better for his bottom line.

It's clear that even truth, whether it reflects positively or negatively upon WWE, has become a commodity, something for Vince to spin, market, or use to draw heat. This is not about what's wrong or right, but rather the reality of the wrestling mentality. But hey, wait, politicians do it, too. Vince McMahon? Wrestling's master politician takes it to a whole new level.

Up close, McMahon's a truly engaging personality, a man with the ability to laugh or sympathize — at least superficially, and depending upon who he's talking with. He can charm if he so desires, and he can be brash as well. He can be generous. WWE, which really is Vince, has done laudable, important charitable work.

Yet so much, if not all, of Vince McMahon's life is defined by the business of wrestling. His work ethic is unrivaled, his imagination always lively and eager. The energy and drive are still there even after all his success. Vince is notoriously hands-on, and often becomes submerged in the smallest of details, tasks other executives usually leave to the employees.

No one who goes to work for McMahon should be surprised by a 2 a.m. call from the boss: when he wants to know something about the website, a T-shirt design, a licensing deal — even the tires on the truck that moves his rings — he wants to know *now*. He likes to be involved in everything and has been known to go ballistic when his instructions aren't followed. Obsessed with every element of his business, he can be a micro-manager, even as his focus is divided by a promotion that has grown both so monolithic and diverse. Approaching him about business matters is best done tactfully, cautiously, and respectfully — even by those he likes.

All Vince does is work — and work out. No hobbies. No golf. No tennis. No vacations. There's wwe, and going to the gym; that's it. The day his fingerprints aren't on every aspect of wwe will be the day the dirt is thrown on his coffin.

Like most executives, though, Vince often delegates the chore of delivering bad news, whether it's the dismissal of a marketing or storyline idea — or an employee. Early on, Jim Barnett was the hatchet man. Ed Cohen was also often cast in the role. Currently, the task seems to frequently fall to talent coordinator John Laurinaitis. Just because Vince roars "You're fired!" on *Raw* does not mean he wants to be perceived as the "bad guy" in reality.

In fact, many who have felt the wrestling axe fall maintain a fondness for Vince, even when it was Vince's decision to cut them off. Tough, but fair; a stand-up guy; willing to battle, but loyal. This is the image Vince appears to covet. And there's truth here, but there's also loads of grey — very dark grey — amongst the black and white.

Remember, Vince is the business mogul who derided Congress for its steroid investigation because he thought it made good tv. Around talent, he's boasted about thumbing his nose at politicians. But privately, he made sure his company complied with every request for records or documentation. Often, it appears he turns business challenges into personal affronts, as if they were an attempt to get *him*. Maybe it's the way he motivates himself.

McMahon does, in fact, have enemies, loves to invent even more, and can personalize most any challenge to his empire. Perhaps painting such a large target on himself is a cunning way of deflecting criticism from his performers and the sport. Then again, maybe it's an equally clever method of making himself the star of every wrestling drama.

After all these years, can anyone really be sure about Vince? Have longtime employees — like Howard Finkel, for instance — ever seen him vulnerable or legitimately wounded? Is Kevin Dunn, his tv director from day one, in any way intimidated by him, or are they equals? What about Joe Perkins, who helped teach McMahon the tv ropes and was vital in syndicating wwf programs around the country? What did Ed Cohen, who carried a massive load, booking arenas and tour dates for years, actually *know* about his boss?

Vince loves being king, the dictator. He likely needs that sense of entitlement by now. In the 1980s, he crafted a persona that at various times focused on everything from his sexual prowess to his mercurial nature to his business acumen. Was it another marketing tool? On-screen character development? Or is it a case of what you see is what you get?

The "real" father of Shane and Stephanie McMahon, who have become fictional characters in their own right, surely has a life none of us can access. How many little league games or dance recitals did *he* attend? But is that even part of the equation? Wrestling is the McMahon family business. The family has "worked" together — in both the wrestling and every other sense of the word. Was what happened to them on screen their playtime?

What does his wife Linda see when the lights are out and the doors are locked? How deep do the emotions run? When the crowd and the entourage are gone, in the dark of the night, does he have doubts or feel guilty? Has he sensed his own mortality?

Is he happy? Really?

Anyone reading this book has a right to know how much the author's feelings affect his view on the subject, and certainly about one so prominent as Vince. On a personal level, generally, I have always liked Vince. I like him as someone who has a certain shared background with me, someone who is bright and inquisitive, someone with whom I could spend time and enjoy the minutes.

He was a gracious host when I first came to New York for a Madison Square Garden show and to watch the WWF tapings in Allentown, Pennsylvania. When the St. Louis promotion left by Muchnick was failing, Vince was a sympathetic sounding board for my frustrations. He once asked me what I really wanted for myself and St. Louis. He was generous with advice and strategy without pushing his own view on me. And, at times, we could laugh at the absurdity of it all.

When the turmoil had subsided, and I was working for the WWF, I recall sitting with Vince at Kiel Auditorium before a show as he told me about wanting wrestlers and wrestling itself to get the media credit it deserved for being a rare art form that was tough and athletic. That clicked for me. I felt the same way.

Early in my time with the WWF, I would travel to Vince's office and pitch my thoughts on booking. I did not get my way very often, but his imaginative interaction was honestly always invigorating.

Yet everyone knows a person who was enjoyable and who became an acquaintance, or more, and quietly left the impression that he was a rung above and beyond. Vince was that guy. He always gave the sense that he was chosen one, the special person. A part of him was always withheld from me, and I am sure from most. Vince was a step removed from that instance when two people bond and become friends. That did not happen regardless of how many talks we had, and whether I liked him or he liked me.

That said, after what happened in 1983, I hated Vince. Because I worked for him and made money, I buried the animosity below the surface. Surely, in some ways, that hostility colored my feelings and thoughts. Actually, wrestling was going to change whether Vince was there or not. The way I learned the business from Sam Muchnick was going to change; thus, my dreams of following in those footsteps at least in some small form were doomed anyhow. For all the backstabbing and maneuvering that happened in St. Louis, though, I blamed Vince, and still believe I am correct.

I got caught in the middle, like many others, but at one of the very first, critical junctures. It hurt like hell, and I was angry. Still am to some extent, even though I realize that Vince just altered when and how the changes to come happened. Yet I accept that Vince was meaner, tougher, and smarter (oh, it hurts to admit that). Rest assured, many others hated him too, and at one point or another, they all worked for him.

Do I hate Vince today? With the benefit of time, hindsight, and experience, I understand much more and accept some things I did not accept before. I work diligently to be balanced and fair as I try to comprehend and explain Vince.

I would never trust him, nor believe him at face value. Funny, because I would almost surely have a great time telling stories with him and enjoy every moment. I'd like him — with limits. Does it matter in the end? Well, perhaps it matters to the extent of how Vince relates to people, to employees and to the business on which his imprint is most prominent.

Yes, Vince McMahon is just as human as everyone else. But how much of what anyone knows about him is real? What's a work and what's a shoot? The danger for anyone involved in wrestling has always been that those elements sometimes become far too easy to confuse, and Vince is no more immune than anyone else. The border between fact and fiction blurs far too easily.

Wrestling's true king can afford to be benevolent. Anyone who witnessed Ric Flair's remarkable retirement ceremony on the March 30, 2008 episode of *Raw* has seen it first hand. Triple H, the father of Vince's grandchildren, played host. Familial ties aside, Paul Levesque (Triple H) is known as a student of the game and a longtime admirer of Flair — he was an appropriate choice as MC. As Flair battled his emotions, and tears flowed, Triple H introduced many of the central characters from Flair's past, from those involved with the Four Horsemen, like Arn Anderson, Tully Blanchard, Barry Windham, and J.J. Dillon, to partners and opponents like Greg Valentine, Ricky Steamboat, and Chris Jericho.

The "Nature Boy" sobbed as his wife and children came to the squared circle. And Ric was obviously humbled when every wrestler on the WWE payroll came to the ring apron to applaud the man who set the standard to which all contemporary wrestlers aspire. Babyface or heel, for once it didn't matter. The Big Show (Paul Wight) climbed up to hug his childhood hero. Randy Orton, whose father Bob ran with Flair in the glory days of the Carolinas, wiped away tears. Edge (Adam Copeland), unable to stop beaming, led the wrestlers' applause and a "Thank you, Ric" chant.

Kayfabe — that word for wrestling's exotic and complicated carny-derived practice of keeping its inner workings and secrets private — was pretty much forgotten. (Only The Undertaker remained in character, paying his respects to Flair once the cameras had stopped rolling.) For once, refreshingly, it didn't matter. Many a football player has retired and been hugged by the players who were his fiercest opponents. Baseball, basketball, and hockey players have their fraternity too. Wrestling humanized itself in this rare public display of honesty and true emotion.

WWE's state-of-the-art production was flawless and the "beauty shot" (McMahon's term for a camera angle from high up in a packed arena) was nothing short of stunning.

Yet even this shining moment of mat history needs to be scrutinized. Yes, it's a little sad, but given McMahon's history, it would be foolish to simply become caught up in the positives. If nothing else, the surprisingly touching, expansive TV segment demonstrates how pragmatic the man can be if he wishes. When wrestling's great war raged through the '80s and '90s, McMahon could not pile enough garbage on the credentials of wrestlers affiliated with the NWA or AWA. Naturally, Vince was attempting to prove that his brand of wrestling was superior to what wrestling fans had been getting from other promoters. He wanted his company to look bigger and better, and if that meant beating or burying the wrestlers local fans had always considered stars, so be it.

Dory Funk Jr., for example, was a highly respected and effective NWA champion, even if his style was methodical and relatively unspectacular when compared with the WWF's standards. When Dory finally moved to the WWF, Vince buried him under the ridiculous gimmick of "Hoss" Funk and what looked like a ninety-gallon cowboy hat. Even Dan Blocker of *Bonanza* fame would have rebelled! With absolutely no mention of his storied history, Dory was relegated to prelims after years of headlining the world over. Dusty Rhodes suffered a similar fate. The American Dream had always had weight issues — and unbelievable NWA success. When Dusty joined Vince — as almost all of the biggest NWA stars eventually did — he was forced to wear . . . polka dots. A former NWA champion, Rhodes looked like a fool, a gigantic cartoon bumblebee, in the WWF ring.

That was the norm for the time. A few got better breaks, depending upon their past ties to McMahon and his family (Jack and Jerry Brisco are good examples; they sold their stock in the old Atlanta promotion to Vince), or if McMahon himself repackaged them successfully (Ted DiBiase, as the Million Dollar Man, is perhaps the best example). But generally, unless Vince himself came up with the gimmick, or the performer had a history with the WWF, high expectations were inadvisable.

Over time, as the glories of other promotions faded in the collective memories of fans, things relaxed a little. Still, when none other than Ric Flair first came to the WWF to battle the "immortal" Hulk Hogan (a potential box office champion versus champion goldmine), Vince watered down the confrontation by demeaning the value of Flair's NWA success. In fact, what could have been one of the greatest programs of all time amounted to little. It was all about ego and pride — Vince's — not business.

Time, however, changes almost everything. As the new century dawned, the WWF was without meaningful competition. McMahon had won the Monday Night War and controlled the wrestling assets of WCW, but many longtime fans had begun drifting away. In creating WWE's 24/7 channel, Vince clearly hoped to resurrect the history of wrestling — on *his* terms. He used his vast wealth and power to buy up tape libraries and resurrect old names that resonated with fans in their 40s, 50s, and even 60s. (Perhaps they'd buy pay-per-views, too . . .) Of course, old WWF shows got the spotlight, while other promotions were relegated to 2 a.m. slots. Some documentary DVDs were made about promotions like the AWA and World Class Championship Wrestling, and they were laudable, even if viewers left them feeling the WWE spin, that what happened in New York was the *real* big time.

McMahon has even created a wrestling Hall of Fame, supposedly to recognize the history of the business. It's a superb idea, although cynics, after observing how it actually functions, have rechristened the HoF with the initials H.O.P.E., for the Hall of Politics and Employees. Plenty of deserving figures, people like Flair, are in there, but a boatload of those who *must* be recognized are not. As for some of WWE's inductees, well . . . Put it this way: Vince Sr.'s limo driver is a bona fide Hall of Famer. So is Mr. Fuji, a good guy, but essentially a prelim performer that achieved "legendary" status simply by working for Vince and his dad for years. They're joined by the likes of Baron Scicluna and Johnny Rodz (how many jobs did he do, more than a thousand?): good workers and loyal WWE employees, but hardly Hall of Fame material. As for Pete Rose and William "Refrigerator" Perry . . .

McMahon's putative Hall of Fame does *not* include Sam Muchnick or Lou Thesz, for that matter, but it does feature Black Jack Lanza, once a main-event performer but not a superstar, who became a longtime WWF agent (and, some claim, "stooge," someone who'd leak the negative stuff said back to the boss). Maybe if a *WrestleMania* were held in St. Louis, some of the most glaring omissions would be remedied; after all, the induction ceremony is mainly a marketing ploy geared toward generating buzz in the metropolis where the event is held. Recent *WrestleMania*s saw the induction of Eddie Graham and the Brisco brothers in Florida, and Verne Gagne in Chicago. The 2009 event in Texas ushered in the Funks, the Von Erichs, and "Cowboy" Bill Watts. Oh, and from WWF prelims, Koko B. Ware.

And then there's one of World Wrestling Entertainment's most influential stars from the recent past: Randy Savage. How can the "Macho Man" not be honored? Well, there's the little matter of his often outrageous, bullheaded battles with Vince. How about the most glaring omission of all: Bruno Sammartino, the wrestler who put the WWF on the map. The fact is, Bruno, who once announced TV with Vince, is on the outs with his former partner. If they ever make up, Bruno will get the nod, guaranteed.

The WWE Hall of Fame is no Cooperstown, though most of those enshrined there sing its praises to anyone who'll listen. While who should be inducted every year is openly discussed, it's Vince who makes the decision. No votes are counted to reveal the "winners." And when asked when and where the "Hall" might be built, he's actually said it already exists — "in my head."

Not surprisingly, as a marketing tool, the HoF is a masterpiece for WWE. Younger fans, unfortunately, without hindsight or the context of wrestling's rich history, rarely question its validity. But it, too, is a work. Survivors get to write, or rewrite, history. Vince most assuredly is a survivor, one with the bucks to do just about whatever he pleases.

None of this changes the fact that Vince McMahon gave Ric Flair the kind of send-off he richly deserved. It was the perfect tribute to one of the sport's greatest performers. Ultimately, the right thing happened, whatever the reasons.

So, what does the ceremony say about Vince? What were his motives and what did he have to gain? Maybe that's not quite fair, and maybe it should be judged for just what it was, but still, McMahon called the tune. He had to have an angle, right?

Would Flair have been celebrated if McMahon had not believed the ceremony would help boost ratings? wwe's vested interest in those weekly numbers cannot be underestimated. Actually, the tribute to the Nature Boy was a ratings success, even though the numbers weren't impressive enough to keep some within the wwe power structure from privately expressing disappointment.

What other reasons could McMahon have had for memorializing Flair's career? Giving the pageant main-event status probably helped shore up relations with the talent, the many wrestlers who grew up idolizing Flair, the countless men who salivated at the idea of working just one match with him. Letting all of them demonstrate honest, unscripted emotion boosted Vince's stock with his employees, an often-insecure group. Smart move.

Honoring Flair was also a way of reaching out to a number of the ambivalent TV viewers and pay-per-view buyers who had soured on wrestling since the Chris Benoit tragedy. Did it erase what had happened to men like Benoit, Eddie Guerrero, or Owen Hart? No, clearly not, but to those who had become disenchanted, who were offended by Vince calling their beloved wrestling "sports entertainment," who were bored by the soap opera booking, saluting Flair may have been a way of saying to them, "Please come back." Nature Boy was the last bridge across the gap between what those fans knew and loved and what wrestling has become today.

Or maybe it was McMahon's way of symbolically saying good riddance, finally, to all the "old stuff" — the style and the history — Flair represented.

Whatever the case, Flair was the perfect person for that spotlight. Wrestling has always meant the world to Ric, and he is completely uninhibited in the ring — there was no doubt his emotions would bubble over and carry everyone away. He would cry, of course, but he would deserve every plaudit. What great reality TV and what a fine way to maximize Flair's value for the last time.

The latter theory certainly looked flawed not even five months later as Flair left the company to book himself independently. Yet, as the 25th *WrestleMania* rolled around in 2009, look who was back! None other than Ric Flair — not wrestling but allowing himself to be mugged and bloodied in a nasty little angle. When the issue is making a buck, Vince is generally — though definitely not always — quite flexible. Ric Flair is, too. (Walking away from the ring, the public spotlight, and all the financial rewards has proven nearly impossible for the Nature Boy.)

At any rate, today, WWE is again marketing itself to six-to-ten-year-olds — a formula with which it has had great success in the past. This ploy makes all the sense in the world. The kids of today are blank slates, blissfully unaware of the legacy of a Flair or Hulk, and certainly ignorant of Sam Muchnick or Bruno Sammartino. John Cena, Batista, and Jeff Hardy, to them, *are* Sports Entertainment, though here is a bet that the kids still call it wrestling. Flair's retirement ceremony, therefore, became a way to reconcile what Vince wanted recalled from the past with chapters of WWE history in the process of being written. It also happens to be smart business: phasing out past glories while replenishing the fan base with youth and enthusiasm.

By the way, did anyone else wonder what Hulk Hogan was thinking as *he* watched Vince canonize *Flair* before more than five million viewers? Was McMahon throwing another not-so-little dagger?

Hey Hulkster, how did you like that, brother?

Hulk may have won the matches, but Flair won the war. In the end it was Ric who toed the company line, and it was Vince who put in the finish. Therefore, upon Flair is bestowed the hallowed mantle that by rights should have been Hogan's. They all said it, on WWE TV, for everyone to hear: Ric Flair was the greatest, ever.

Now, if the contractual problems he was having with McMahon just a year earlier had not been resolved, would Ric Flair even have made into the Hall of Politics and Employees? Isn't the answer obvious? Another question to consider: why wasn't Vince himself a part of the televised ceremony? After all, he's never been shy about taking a place in the ring. Was it kayfabe? Or is that just a convenient cover for Vince not wanting to diminish himself? After all, in WWE's world, unless something happens on TV, it hasn't really happened. The Undertaker and McMahon offering Flair their congratulations only when the cameras stopped rolling, meant they were, for the official, historic record, "absent." Perhaps kayfabe is not as dead as some maintain.

Okay, that could be too cynical. Maybe, deep down, Vince McMahon simply loves this messy thing called wrestling. (Oh hell, of course he does!) Even as he renames it "sports entertainment" or just plain old vanilla "entertainment" for reasons few but him seem to understand, he probably does truly respect what Flair has contributed to wrestling. Vince has been around too long not to have great affection for a sport and lifestyle that essentially raised him. Maybe we just need to accept the charming moment for what it was. So what if we were manipulated? Audiences flock to plays, movies, concerts, and sporting events to be manipulated, and entertained, each and every day.

Vince and wrestling were made for each other, a perfect fit. They are pretty much identical, each as chock-full of contradiction and controversy and mystery as the other. Like wrestling, he throws out a lot of smoke; his motives, like the facts, are almost always hidden. A certain amount of speculation, inference and deduction needs to be indulged if you're going to make sense of it all. But does it really matter which parts of Vince McMahon are illusion or which are real?

Think about it. It goes a long way in explaining why Vince McMahon is professional wrestling today.

CHAPTER THREE

LOCKING UP WITH THE DREAM

Dreams must be chased. It's as simple as that. Damn the torpedoes, full speed ahead.

But then reality sets in. And the first thing a young dreamer needs to understand is that almost no one makes it far enough to earn a living as a professional wrestler.

Kids who want to play pro baseball, football, or basketball face seemingly insurmountable odds. For example, with only 30 MLB teams, and only 25 players per team, that means just 750 places in the big show. Yet that's at least 600 *more* spots than what's available in wrestling today. What are the odds of a career in the squared circle? The chances of making it in Hollywood are better . . . by a hair . . . maybe.

Knowing this rarely stops the men and women who scratch, claw, beg, lie, cheat, steal, and pray to make it in the glamorous world of pro wrestling. At the lowest local level, where almost everyone has to start, there is at least a 50-50 chance that an ambitious rookie will cross paths with one or more of the following: con artist trainers who do not, themselves, have a clue about how to perform; unscrupulous promoters; rip offs; miserable, risky rings; long trips; crowds that could fit in a living room; and opponents who, because they simply don't know how to work, are dangerous and likely to cause serious injuries.

For every straightforward promoter or capable trainer, there are a dozen tricksters preying on the hopes and dreams of others. Even in the best circumstances, learning how to wrestle comes with a price. Those who teach golf or tennis, or even piano lessons, are remunerated for sharing their time and expertise. And so it is with wrestling, whether or not the instructor truly does know something about what he is teaching.

In wrestling, the things that are absolutely vital tend to be intangible. A unique drive is as necessary as the right look, physique, and raw ability. The required determination often verges on, or surpasses, obsession. Often it comes with its own personal price. In his colorful way, Rocky Johnson called it: "having the eye of the tiger." It's the thing that "separates the ones who at least might have a chance from the weekend warriors," he said, "the guys who suck beer, eat too much, work out once in awhile, and then pretend to be wrestlers on weekends." Rocky knows because he had the passion himself. He saw it in his son Dwayne, too: it was there for football, then wrestling, and finally acting. It's what made the man better known as The Rock a success in everything he's tried.

Many on the independent wrestling scene convince themselves they have a chance because they've mastered a few big bumps. An amazing percentage of these performers actually believe that it's only a lack of opportunity holding them back — that they could outwork and outperform those on the big stage given the opportunity. It looks so simple on TV, exactly the way it does when Albert Pujols hits a screaming line drive or when Tiger Woods blasts a shot down the middle of the fairway. Were it only so easy. Tom Hanks said it best in *A League of Their Own:* "If it wasn't hard, everyone would do it. It's the hard that makes it great." Becoming a major league wrestler is hard — very, very hard. Only a limited number have what it takes, and even then luck, politics, and timing can play a major role in making or breaking a career.

The right appearance and athletic ability is just where things start. There has to be training — constant, arduous training — and real mental discipline for someone to become special. Most wrestlers eventually discover where they belong; there is a definite place for independents, and an audience, though small, that enjoys their matches. But it's a million miles away from stepping into the WWE ring.

Who decides to become a wrestler? What is their background?

Do they have college educations? What part is exhibitionist, what part is entertainer, and what part is athlete? Is becoming a wrestler their first choice, or did it suddenly become a dream when other career options soured and, thanks to TV, wrestling seemed an easier and fancier path to financial security? Over the years, many off-the-wall people have come to the business. How many truly love the sport *and* have the tools to make it? How much confidence do they actually have in themselves? How much are they willing to sacrifice?

When the passion is strong, and the work ethic is unmatched, and the willingness to sacrifice is unparalleled, and the heart is large enough. . . . Mix those qualities with real physical gifts and a remote possibility exists that a wrestler might stumble into an opportunity, and just *maybe* get near the stage that sparkles so brightly on national TV.

Truly, it is amazing that anyone gets through the muck and — almost a miracle — finds himself or herself on the roster of a company like WWE or even TNA. A select few are recruited because they possess the look and size that tickles the fancy of the powers-that-be. But even of the tiny crew invited in by WWE, most will wash out; chased away by the difficult lifestyle, or because they simply can't cut it physically, mentally, or emotionally.

Only a microscopic group survives the constant weeding-out process, and then they learn the *toughest* lesson: staying in the swirling mix at the top is even more difficult, and the chore can grind a person into dust. Getting onto the roster means serious, throat-cutting competition. And there's still much, much more to learn, to assimilate both in and out of the ring. Getting to the big time is one thing. *Staying* there is something else entirely.

In a recent newspaper interview, Triple H, arguably one of the most established superstars of today, complained about some of the young guys he's watched come into the business recently. Himself a student of Killer Kowalski, Triple H pointed out the experience available for newcomers to WWE with agents like Ricky Steamboat, Arn Anderson, and others around. HHH never wanted to leave the ring when he was breaking in, he said, while the new guys seem more interested in iPods or video games. A true student of the game, Triple H found it disappointing to see younger performers doing the same things — the same moves, spots, and promos — over and over again, without growth, change or improvement.

Once they make it into the spotlight, rookie wrestlers soon learn what it is they have gotten into. There is constant pressure. Directed to maintain a certain look, some are provided with the excuse they need to use artificial "enhancement," although drug testing makes this a dicey game. Because the need to impress both bosses and peers with both your look and action never disappears, without real progress in performance, a wrestler's stay in the spotlight can be short, indeed.

Another reality? Pain is a constant companion. Work or not, the hurt is real. Physical risk is a reality in both training and wrestling at the highest level. Wrestling's unwritten but omnipresent code says there is a difference between pain and injury — so suck it up and get out in that ring. And if you don't? There's no paycheck. Or worse, no more job. Public scrutiny and the reality of keeping company assets healthy have nudged WWE into being more generous and helpful in recent years, but the lack of health insurance or long-term disability for damage caused by wrestling is still a problem. So learning to deal with physical discomfort and its monetary burden is a necessary evil.

And then there's travel. A wrestler must travel, travel, travel — and it gets old fast. Changing time zones, riding to and from airports, and opening the door on another anonymous hotel room, again and again, will send almost anyone to the bar, or worse. Find a place to work out, and actually do it. Get adequate rest. Try to eat healthy, or some semblance thereof, and watch the expenses (the road can devour money). Every personal weakness gets exposed. Bruiser Brody always maintained that the road would break any man, an opinion with which most wrestlers would agree. For long-term success, the performer had best have a strong nomadic streak.

Surprisingly perhaps, as exhausting as the travel is for modern WWE stars, it actually pales in comparison to the way it was "back in the day." An analysis of the number of matches worked during 2007 put the average around 130, while main-event stars like Batista, Jeff Hardy, Randy Orton, and John Cena worked closer to 170.

On the other hand, legends like Ric Flair, the Funks, Gene Kiniski, Harley Race, and so many more must shake their heads when recalling that they usually worked a minimum of 325 shots per year in the 1960s, '70s, and '80s. In some cases — Flair and Race were probably the most notable, though they were not the only ones — the actual count would probably exceed more than the 365 annually, because they often did two shows per weekend day between TV outings and arena bills. In an interview with the *Sun* Randy Orton recently noted how much better today's schedule is than when his father was away for two months at a time, pointing out that he's almost always home two days a week.

While some modern gladiators would claim that the old school headliners did not take as much physical punishment in their time, those folks forget that the bouts themselves were not only more numerous, but also each duel went longer. Therefore, an impressive number of bumps were simply spaced out over more time while executing a slower but stiffer, less acrobatic but more psychological, style. Granted, some of the bumps back then might not have been as extreme, nor have come at as fast a pace. All bumps hurt, however, and all bumps add up. To be rolling and bouncing around the ring 365 times a year is surely somewhat comparable to doing wilder bumps 170 times during the same period.

It was around 1980 when Fritz Von Erich (Jack Adkisson), a key power broker in the National Wrestling Alliance, approached Nick Bockwinkel with the idea of replacing Race with Bockwinkel as the NWA champion. At the time, Bockwinkel was working for Verne Gagne's American Wrestling Association, a promotion many stars enjoyed for its favorable schedule. Since the AWA controlled a number of good-sized Midwestern markets, where houses and payoffs were good, it was unlike most territories that ran every night, seven days a week, in towns big and small. Gagne could make a tidy profit and afford to take a couple days off each week, which was unusual for that era.

Bockwinkel examined Race's dates — about 360 in the previous year. He considered his calendar, approximately 200 bouts over the same span. Nick turned Fritz down, saying he made almost as much money working "part time." Working "part time," that is, at what is currently considered a full-time slate! Is it any wonder that so few legends have sympathy for today's workers? Remember, too, this was true for *everyone* on the card, including the consistent and dependable journeymen. Imagine doing more than 300 matches, annually, for ten, or even *twenty* years!

During the 1980s and well into the '90s, the then-World Wrestling Federation ran an incredible number of auditorium cards. Almost every night there were two or three different shows around the country. Working two cards in different cities on Saturdays and particularly on Sundays was the norm. Pay-per-view had not supplanted house shows as the primary revenue source yet, plus the promotional war with wcw was raging. The seeds were sewn for much personal destruction during this time. Workers were lucky to have one or two days off per *month*; there was wide-ranging drug abuse, including a heavy reliance on steroids and pain-killers, and injuries were seldom properly attended to, never mind the damage caused by *mental fatigue.*

It was the all-time peak of insanity-producing wrestling travel, with wrestlers flying and changing time zones every couple days. Of course, just because someone working a smaller territory might be able to drive home a few nights each week did not make having a sore back or battered knee feel any better when jammed into a car with three or four 260-pounders for a four-hour trip . . . followed by another five-hour journey the next day with a few nights in different hotels tacked on after.

Cowboy Bob Orton, the father of wwe ace Randy Orton, was one of those who headlined during both periods. "If you were in a territory like Atlanta, you worked Atlanta tv Saturday morning, Columbus tv Saturday afternoon, and then a house show Saturday night plus a double shot on Sunday — for five matches in one weekend," Bob explains. "There were a few territories which had a couple or three tv shows to do in one weekend, plus the house shows. Then you had a show every weeknight, so you could work ten matches in a week pretty often. You would be able to drive home most nights, though, even if it was a two or three hundred mile trip."

Somehow that demanding schedule paled compared to Orton's WWF slate. "I was with Roddy Piper a lot in those days," he notes. "Piper and I often were gone from home 80 or 90 straight days, wrestling every night, all over the map. It got to the point that once in awhile I'd fly home at my own expense early in the morning, spend a few hours with my wife and kids, and then fly out in the late afternoon to a different town to wrestle the same night. Once, thanks to the different time zones, Piper and I worked a main event early on the show in Detroit, flew a Lear jet to Chicago, and then worked the main event there at the end of that card the same evening!"

Why did the performers accept such an exhausting schedule? "It's just the way it was," Bob says. "I tell people today about how often we worked and how long we were on the road. . . . They don't believe me! Nobody can even conceive of doing all that."

But these wrestlers did, and more than a few paid the price in injury or addiction. Bob Orton was one of the strong, lucky ones. He survived.

Economics, naturally, is wrestling's driving force, Stone Cold Steve Austin's "bottom line." Now, thanks to the small fortune brought in by PPVs and merchandise, wrestlers top to bottom (but especially at the top), can make more money than in the recent past of relentless travel. But being on the road is still being on the road: demanding and difficult. Being away from home, working half the year or more, is a frightful grind for anyone. As the WWE expands its global reach, frequent overseas tours add to the stress. While the wrestler's lot has improved in some ways, the strain and insecurity might be even greater today, because there are simply so very few options. Beyond TNA, there's no other "territory" for someone no longer welcome on WWE's roster.

Ready for the big time? Well, be ready for the barrage of implausible stories, rumors, gossip, and just plain old lies. The industry has a long history of insiders who stir the pot. Jim Barnett is one of the most prominent examples; he'd leak information or plant stories to manipulate business and ultimately affect the career trajectory of individual wrestlers. A few stories are even based in truth, but some become so exaggerated they're eventually unrecognizable. Gary Hart used to call it "wrestling lore." With the advent of the Internet and the proliferation of books about wrestling, much of this lore, whether truth or fabrication, from sources of varied reliability, has greater reach. A thick hide and the ability to ignore the chatter are more than helpful.

Want to have a life? Get married? What about kids? How many wrestlers have wound up divorced? The percentage is daunting. Wrestlers, believe it or not, are real people. Wrestling is a business that makes relationships difficult to maintain. Acknowledging that fact hardly makes the turmoil any less painful.

Get to WWE and financial security is assured, right? Well, hold on a moment. Want to know what to do with all that money? Save some. It's a balancing act: keep a home and family functioning financially while paying bills on the road for lodging, food, gym time, and more. That's right, professional wrestlers must cover their own expenses, except for transportation. A guaranteed payday that looks impressive can dwindle quickly when all those expenses are tallied. When all is said and done, except for the legitimate stars, most wrestlers do no better overall financially than electricians, teachers, or even policemen.

As the cynical Brody used to preach, in wrestling there are ups and downs. A guy better save when he is on the top, because it is guaranteed the time is coming when he will be on the bottom. Save a lot. There are no benefits in wrestling, no retirement plans, and definitely no pensions. When the wrestler's value to the company is gone, he is gone. Save more money. Save as much as you can.

Speaking of money, not everyone makes those *really* big bucks. In fact, only a few are paid that well. Getting rich is naturally part of the goal of every wrestler who ever pulled on tights, but the reality is its uncommon and, sometimes, a source of friction between the haves and have-nots who must work together. Anyone who claims there is

no competition in wrestling . . . Well, they clearly have no understanding of the struggle to climb those last few, very slippery rungs.

To insulate themselves, many wrestlers create and protect a
macho ego. At times the simplest response to the stress of the business is blaming someone else for not getting headline billing. "I
deserved a shot on top; I'm as good as or better than any other performer; it was all politics," is the mantra many chant. And there is
a degree of truth here. It was as true in 1935, 1975, and 1995 as it is
today. Politics, personality, connections, manipulation, and mind
games all play a huge part in who gets the big money of main
events, or even the tenuous security of a long-term role higher up
in the roster.

Here, though, is the hardest truth: Most wrestlers were — and are
— not good enough to be the champion. Most of them were and are
not good enough to be in main events. It's exactly as it is in other
sports, entertainments, or businesses. Only a handful can survive at
the pinnacle. This is not a criticism, just a realistic description of a
competitive world. Honestly, deep down, most professional wrestlers
realize this and are satisfied with the superb achievement they can
claim in simply having made a living in the profession.

This is not to belittle the talent or effort of wrestlers. Promoters,
from Paul Bowser to Sam Muchnick to Vince McMahon, are in this
business to make money. They simply cannot succeed if they have
the wrong wrestlers on top of the bill. The choice of who to push to
that lofty position is based on a thoughtful (hopefully) decision
about who can get the job done. Naturally, personal preference
plays a part. But there isn't a single promoter who picked his main
event without believing that this was the best way to make money.

And finding main-event talent is tough enough under the best
of circumstances. The theater and music worlds work this way, too.
Life works this way. There are politics to everything, so finding
sympathy from the general public may be difficult.

Nonetheless, the decision must always be made: who gets featured and who gets preliminaries? Who is the star, and who is the
supporting cast? Maturing talent should be able to accept this. A
few remain bitter — loudly so, saying politics cost them their time

in the sun. Occasionally this may even be true, but there's always been a big difference between having a great preliminary match and being in the main event of a stadium sellout. Headlining a Broadway production is miles away from being a stock player at a community theater. Get used to it.

"Star" is a word thrown around far too loosely in today's wrestling world. According to Vince McMahon, everyone's a "superstar." Just appearing on a national TV show does bring recognition. A few minutes of TV time, however, doesn't create a real star, someone who makes a difference — especially at the box office. With hundreds of channels and an almost infinite number of programs available, the light emanating from most of today's wrestlers is obliterated by the sheer volume of so many others. While calling a supporting performer a "superstar" may be good for his or her ego (even when it isn't accurate), the *real* star of any wrestling show is in the headline position, driving the storyline, drawing money, and bringing in the audience.

The sport's casual followers only get hooked on real stars; they make a difference in the bottom line only when customers make an emotional connection or investment in them.

To reach the main event requires — in fact *demands* — that the wrestler become more than obsessive in his hunger for success. But no matter how hard a guy works, there is yet another level, more effort to give. Again, it's not just about wrestling. How much drive do the likes of Tiger Woods or Tom Brady, Brad Pitt or Bill Gates, bring to the table? Talent alone is simply never enough.

In wrestling, however, luck and timing may play an even bigger role, especially today, when there's such a small window of opportunity for those locking up with the dream. A star has to become something of a political mastermind, or at very least become both mentally and emotionally tough enough to earn and keep his spot in the pecking order. Since there is always pressure for a wrestling promotion to create new stars or reinvigorate established ones and keep the product fresh, the intensity really never lets up.

The true superstar has time-tested, lasting power — developing a body of work with dramatic matches, drawing big live houses, and attracting larger-than-average PPV buy rates, again and again, to cement his status. The brand names attached by companies to PPV extravaganzas only go so far in luring buys without real stars.

At times, it is easy to forget that role players, too, are vital. Lou Thesz once told me that wrestling's talent pool forms a pyramid. At the top are the stars — and their number is few. Preliminary workers, the vast majority of wrestlers, are at the bottom or base. In between are the mid-level role players. The stars have always been paramount, of course, but without the support of the men in the supporting cast, the entire pyramid will collapse. That's why Thesz rightly believed that even the guys who will never be headliners still deserve respect.

What a wrestler needed to do to climb to the top of this pyramid may have been different in Lou's era. An athlete's ability to take care of himself on the mat meant so much more back then. Being known as a "shooter" (a legitimate tough guy who could hurt someone) or "hooker" (one of the very few even tougher than a shooter) played a part in determining how high someone ranked among his peers. It also clearly influenced how someone was regarded by the fans.

The pyramid's base is by far the largest part of the industry, and it's composed of solid, reliable, dedicated hands. The majority are now likely younger and less experienced than in Thesz's day. Every step up has room for fewer performers, and naturally enough, they make more money than the ones below. The peak is a rarefied atmosphere all of its own, with air enough for only a select few.

The soldiers at the foot of the pyramid win a fair amount, lose some, and help make the stars become stars. They accept they are professionals in a dynamic business and are proud of their accomplishments. It's still a well-paying job; these performers, realistically, are earning more than they ever envisioned when they were first stepping through the ropes.

As in all sports, a wrestler's career is limited. Particularly today. At a certain point, maybe two or three years into a run, there may be nothing left to do with a character. Chewed up and spit out, wrestling says goodbye with nothing more than a pat on the back.

Wise, mature hands, men who teach just by having a solid outing with a newcomer, are in short supply, and there is a reason.

Here is where the territorial system served wrestlers well. Today, when the creative powers say that they have nothing left to do with a performer, it's thanks, but no thanks, and best wishes. Once upon a time, when the booker said they had nothing for a wrestler, a call could be made to Tampa, Portland, Dallas, or New York to see if there was another spot open. The desire to keep things fresh for audiences across the country usually meant that there was a job to be had somewhere, which in turn meant many solid professionals had lengthy careers.

After struggling just to get a foot in the door, is it any wonder that today's wrestler is most concerned with "*my* spot on the card, *my* billing, *my* booking, *my* finish, *my* money"? And whether its WWE or TNA, a certain insecurity is encouraged among the troops to keep them from getting too relaxed, too satisfied. Almost every performer, down deep, realizes he can be replaced. No one is indispensable in the world of pro wrestling, where someone else always decides who wins, who loses, and who gets paid the most. The company has all the leverage.

It's not all just showbiz. Even Ultimate Fighting Championship (UFC), the leading promotion in mixed martial arts, is the same when it comes to money. Realists who do what they can because they can, they are running businesses that need to turn a profit. This is why wrestlers, especially, who are almost cultivated to be naïve about these specific realities, need accountants and lawyers. They're no different than baseball players, but they do not share the luxury of a powerful union.

So, are wrestling promoters evil schemers who plot to destroy careers and steal money out of the mouths of their performers' children? Do not confuse the cartoon characters they sometimes portray on TV with the reality. In fact, they are businessmen who ask a simple question: who gets more, me or him? Isn't that just how the world works? They're not all paranoid, serial crooks (well, maybe a few have been); they simply follow the time-honored American tradition of getting ahead by taking care of number one.

And here's another great American tradition: promoters and wrestlers, like management and labor, work together to develop an appealing product, but they are almost always at odds about how the profit should be split when the work succeeds.

Obviously, today's wrestler — except, perhaps, for the biggest, established stars — cannot expect the equivalent of a thirty-year career with AT&T. Of course, that is also a reflection of the modern workplace as a whole. Going back to the independent scene can be a bitter pill to swallow after tasting the big time, and it's perhaps even more painful when early retirement, so to speak, has been forced. Walking away is damn hard. For all the headaches and problems, the wrestling business is a drug. A highly addictive drug.

A refuge from the myriad pressures and madness is hopefully the dressing room. Baron Von Raschke said, "We used to have fun in the dressing room, as well as on the long car trips. It was also a chance for young guys to learn from being with and talking to the more experienced hands. I don't know if it is that way anymore."

Some believe the cold and corporate atmosphere of modern wrestling has infiltrated the locker room. Before a TV shoot or a pay-per-view, the backstage area can become tense, jammed with people — make-up artists, for example — who are not a true part of the guts of wrestling.

But on the road, especially, the locker room can still be a sanctuary, a place to interact with others who share the passion. Part of the craziness, a wrestler truly realizes what it is to live a dream that once seemed so unattainable. Despite the politics, the juvenile pranks, jealousy, and competition, a rare camaraderie grows. Perhaps the only place even more uncorrupted is the ring itself.

Wrestling *is* fun. Making the crowd roar, no matter what its size may be, is fulfilling. The adrenaline rush cannot be duplicated. Actors, singers, and dancers will understand this, too. For an athlete, the opportunity to still be a kid, to be inside the illusion and feel a part of a sport, is almost impossible to ignore. At very least, those who have glimpsed the prize at the loftiest level can share the truth with those who still dream.

The mentally draining parts of the job disappear in the spotlight, in the satisfaction of being in the moment, the purity of the excitement that the wrestler discovers in the ring. While this might sound like New Age mumbo jumbo, it's actually an expression of the sport's simplest truth. When a wrestler finally cracks the upper echelon, whether in a main event or preliminary position, he is wise to seek out this balance between his role in public and his *life* in private to maximize what he gets from the experience.

The most important thing a wrestler may ever learn is to never believe his own hype. The image a wrestler creates in the ring seldom resembles who he really is, even when a part of his personality is amplified to draw attention. It's terribly difficult for many performers: even "The Immortal" Hulk Hogan eventually became confused about the difference between the Hulkster and Terry Bollea. Bruiser Brody related many times he had to work at remembering that he was really Frank Goodish.

Mainstream media provided one example of the performer forgetting who he was in the movie *The Wrestler*. If ever a grappler lost touch with reality and his own soul, that character had to be Mickey Rourke's Randy "the Ram" Robinson. A movie is only a movie, but Randy "the Ram" pretty accurately portrayed what happens to someone who forgets that what happens in the ring is only a few fleeting moments, loses his family and his money, gets trapped in the drug and steroid culture, has developed no useful work or people skills for when the ring lights dim, and falls victim to his own "con." All he has left is wrestling.

Former WWE champ and current UFC kingpin Brock Lesnar perhaps explained it best in a recent interview with *Maxim:* "You get so brainwashed . . . It's not real. But some guys who are still in the business think it is. You look at Mickey Rourke in *The Wrestler* — he just couldn't let it go. You live a double life. I was tired of being who I was in the ring and then coming home for two days to become normal. They didn't allow you to be."

Not every wrestler ends up this way, not even close. Nor is wrestling completely at fault. Wrestling is what those who are in power make it to be, although the addiction to the thrill of performing is tough to keep in perspective regardless of what the prevailing reasoning is or has been. Additionally, plenty of humans are capable of messing up their lives, whether they are wrestlers or computer programmers, doctors or firemen. Wrestling does seem, however, to find many who are vulnerable. The struggle to protect the true self is ongoing, for the day of reckoning with the real world comes to all. Rourke's character represents those who could not deal with that truth, who were failures waiting to happen.

Outlandish personalities and behavior have almost always been encouraged in the world of wrestling. Performers are actually competing for both positions and money with the very people who hold their safety in their hands. Each entrant into this cold, cruel, and colorful world is buffeted by constant pressure. Staying grounded is more than difficult, but also absolutely necessary, for the good of every performer.

A certain percentage of wrestlers — the number may not be all that large, but it's still notable — no longer appreciate their profession; they hide their lack of self-esteem with bluster and bravado. Somewhere, somehow, they look down on themselves and the value of what they do. Sadly, they do not respect the fans who support them and have the attitude that these followers have been tricked into believing. Equally as discouraging, they do not respect themselves.

Most wrestlers begin their career full of fire and passion. Over time, as in any profession, physical and mental duress can take their toll. It seems even more poignantly true of the current generation of performers. Cynicism and disappointment sets in early for many, who perhaps never really grasp the way things work or learn how to find personal satisfaction in what they do on a daily basis.

Terry Funk once explained he believed wrestling uses up 98% of those who participate, despite the excitement of the money and the glamour. In the end, Funk said only 2% came out right, happy and financially secure. While I would like to believe that Terry is being too pessimistic, I must acknowledge that even a 50-50 success-to-failure ratio is nothing to brag about.

With all of this being said, once a wrestler finally gets a break, learns to center himself, realizes he has to watch his money, and accepts that the mechanics and politics of the business are seldom fair or democratic, he can concentrate on the *fun* part — telling the great stories and making the thrilling matches that excite fans.

When it comes to performing, a wrestler has to know how to project his intensity, his personality, and his passion. He has to sell himself. This might seem odd, but Bruiser Brody used to compare wrestling to religious TV programming. The whole point has always been getting a personality over, making viewers buy into the message. Somehow, it's not so ironic that several ex-wrestlers have found their way into evangelical ministries. Their success on the pulpit is in no small part based on what they learned about projecting their personality as wrestlers.

Ted DiBiase, who has worked as a minister since retiring from the ring, once unintentionally addressed the issue in talking with Sam Muchnick and me before an important St. Louis TV outing. A red-hot babyface and leading contender for the NWA crown at the time, Ted said he knew he was over with the customers when they cheered him on without being prompted; he further admitted that he was never comfortable "asking" the fans to react with stereotypical hand gestures or that kind of thing. He wanted to inspire a response, not mug or beg for it.

In WWE rings today, most babyfaces are their own cheerleader. There's nothing wrong with that — there is a long history of subtle signals being employed to build the crowd to a fever pitch. The point DiBiase was making was that when a crowd was truly *with* a performer, when they responded to his jeopardy and his comeback, he was going to draw money without needing to play pied piper.

Ultimately, this goes a long way in explaining how crucial it is for a wrestler to be accepted as something more dynamic than just a performer of moves. Getting over with the audience requires much more than a series of gymnastic patterns, stunt fights, or big bumps simply for the sake of taking bumps. Mastering how to *work*, in both the athletic *and* the psychological sense, is vitally important. When the bell rings, being believable matters. Just another lesson to learn — one upon which almost everything else hinges. As any novice should see, wrestling is a character-driven business, now more than ever. DiBiase once got over as a clean-cut competitor, then again later as the haughty Million Dollar Man. Is there a better historical example of being able to embrace the subtleties of character and translate it for the crowd?

Many neophyte wresters try to become characters when they are working ground-level, independent shows. They imitate what they've seen on TV and become a cartoon creature, relying on entrance music or costume to get over. As far as catching the attention of the big boys goes, those tactics probably won't work.

A young, aspiring grappler once complained to me how difficult it was to talk on the microphone and do interviews. Thanks to the huge emphasis on talking during TV wrestling shows, the cart is sadly placed well ahead of the horse for people wanting to become wrestlers. First, rookies need to learn how to bounce off the ropes correctly . . . among other fundamentals! A messed-up interview is done over. A messed-up bump ends with a broken neck. Promos are at the end of the chain. Navigating comfortably and safely around the squared circle is first and foremost, the essential lesson that must be learned.

Next, being natural, looking sharp and professional, plus casting aside inhibitions to allow real emotion to appear, are more likely to catch the eye of anyone who is looking for potential high level performers. It's not easy to find, especially when so many are fixated on being something they are not. If lightning strikes, and a wrestler gets an opportunity with WWE, rest assured that Vince and his creative team will be choosing the role they're going to play, the words they're going to say, and how they're going to say them.

Of course, there's no guarantee that creative control is going to work better than when a true performer is allowed to expose the most dynamic parts of his own personality. When did Stone Cold Steve Austin click? It certainly wasn't as The Ringmaster or, worse, as Chilly McFreeze. Could anyone other than Frank Goodish have created Bruiser Brody? A star has to infuse his spirit into the role he is playing, and it is easier when that role incorporates a real, fundamental part of who he is.

Vince has always maintained he can make a star out of anyone with his TV programs and clever booking. And he has, on a few occasions, but there have also been many notable flops. Not even McMahon can alter the basic law of thermodynamics. Energy cannot be created, nor can it be destroyed. In other words, either you got it or you don't!

A great example is The Undertaker, a Vince gimmick that Mark Calaway was smart enough to make his own. Calaway fit the role, in no small part because of the overall caliber of his in-the-ring work. He also added a visual and emotional edge to The Undertaker that made the Dead Man more than just another gimmick. Someone else, given the exact same spot, might have lacked the natural energy, skill, and wisdom to get over. The 'Taker franchise could have easily joined the long list of wrestling's failures.

When the right kind of young talent clicks with fans, whether they worked in Texas in 1980 or for today's WWE, the entire product can be energized. As they try to incorporate their ability with what they have seen for years on TV, wrestlers put little twists on familiar moves, and that adds both value and excitement for fans.

From the beginning of the grunting and groaning game, wrestlers have copied moves from one another. Wrestlers, especially those who are just getting started, want to emulate the big stars. Young grapplers, especially, tend to try to be what they think the promoters who will make or break them really want. Buddy Rogers and Gorgeous George, for example, begot a zillion bleached-blond bad guys. After hundreds of failures, the world was finally given Ric Flair. The vast majority of the imitators simply did not have the requisite talent and charisma to pull it off.

What works in the squared circle evolves. An example? How about the suplex? Most would credit Harley Race for turning what became known as the vertical suplex into a killer finisher guaranteed to make spectators holler. Harley probably picked up the idea from somewhere else, but nonetheless he was the one who developed it into a "big move." After lifting and rotating a rival 180 degrees, head pointed down toward the mat, Harley was strong enough to "pose" the bump, to let anticipation build before slamming his hapless foe backward. All the success of the finisher was in the wait, the expectation.

Quickly, everyone seemed to have a version of Race's suplex. Some were low, some were high, some were fast. Unfortunately, every successive suplex diminished the impact of the original until the move itself became just another high spot.

A clever announcer could assist Race, or anyone else who performed the move nearly as well, and make fans believe his type of suplex would inevitably lead to a pin, by explaining the subtleties of the Race method were more deadly. Opponents could help by selling Race's version in more dramatic fashion, rather than just bouncing up for the next move. Booking could always play a part, scripting the deadly suplex as the end of the story. Today, however? The move is often little more than a run-of-the-mill headlock or a punch.

Compare that to John Cena's dangerous and devastating "FU" finisher that's also now known as "The Throwback" or the "Attitude Adjustment." The reality is, it's merely a tall version of the old fireman's carry, a tactic used by amateur matmen, as well as pros, for decades. The only difference is that Cena, like Race before him, stands and "poses" the move, with the victim on his shoulders, before dumping him onto the mat for what almost always is a pin. Wrestlers sell for Cena, lying prone and groggy for long seconds. The announcer "gets it over" with an increase in volume and wisely chosen words of praise. Finally, the booking supports it: nearly 100% of the time a Cena FU is a match's climactic moment.

What about the "Go 2 Sleep" finisher of C.M. Punk? Once again, it begins as a simple fireman's carry. The difference, in this case, is that Punk eventually sets his rival back down, onto his feet, as he throws a vicious knee toward the gentleman's face. (It's essentially an updated version of the Mr. Wrestling II or Bobby Managoff knee lift of yesteryear.) Hopefully, the opponent is not too tall — the move looks a wee bit soft if Punk's knee doesn't quite connect with the target's exposed jaw. Regardless, down goes the bad guy, knocked unconscious as booking and selling bolster the effect for spectators.

The FU is no more, and probably less, dangerous than the vertical suplex; same with the Go 2 Sleep. Whether and why they work at all is in the context, and this is something every aspiring grappler would be wise to understand. It's precisely this kind of perspective that protects the wrestler from falling for his own hype.

Let's also consider the figure-four leglock. The aforementioned Buddy Rogers was likely the first to make the old "grapevine" notable. (Why did promotions ever stop calling it a "grapevine," a much more colorful term than, blah, "leglock"?) No matter what it was named, Rogers had mastered what appeared to be a difficult-to-apply maneuver that left rivals writhing in agony — and often with injured knees. In the early 1960s, when Cowboy Bob Ellis was reputed to have developed a reversal for the figure-four grapevine, fans were engrossed, fascinated with the idea of seeing him manage the feat. Politics, however, got in the way before Rogers and Ellis could carry their passion play around the country, and Buddy was booted off the National Wrestling Alliance throne before the feud got wide play.

In wrestling, though, good ideas never die. Ten years later, Jack Brisco was utilizing the figure four while his arch-rival, Dory Funk Jr., was devastating opponents with the spinning toehold. Apparently, Brisco cultivated a counter to Funk's move that ended with Dory trapped in the figure four. Both finishing moves had been sold to fans as a devastating finisher, something that could force any star, no matter how prominent, to submit.

It wasn't long before Dory's brother Terry had developed a method to counter Brisco's counter. He was able to catch Jack in an inside cradle, and dethrone Brisco to become the new NWA king.

Somewhere in all of this, the reversal of the figure four became an incredible, high-emotion spot. Ellis and Rogers must have been jealous. Another decade later, when the figure four became Ric Flair's bread-and-butter, it seemed like every single credible foe managed a reversal. The sequence almost always resulted in screaming, standing audiences.

But why?

Again, it was because announcers explained it, the wrestlers working the move sold it, and the bookers endorsed it as they laid out matches. Bret Hart came up with the figure four's distant cousin, called it a sharpshooter, and got plenty of mileage out of it as well. When the figure four became a rushed and common spot in Flair's duels during his late WWE tenure, its impact was lessened, demoted to just another moment in a match.

The Undertaker recently came up with a gogoplata submission grip that struggled to catch fans' imagination because all the elements did not fall into place. With all the creative minds employed by WWE, couldn't someone think of a more catchy name for the hold than the "choke?" The actual insider term for the move was "gogoplata," which came from the world of MMA and Brazilian Jiu Jitsu. Needless to say, WWE was not about to use that. Probably a year passed before a legitimately descriptive name, "The Devil's Triangle," was devised, which was then changed to "Hell's Gate" apparently . . . at least for a week or two. Actually, Devil's Triangle sounded better, but — what the heck — something is better than nothing.

Why doesn't the sleeper hold mean squat anymore? At one point, several WWE stalwarts worked sleeper attempts into their bouts and crowds reacted with yawns. How could everyone in power miss the obvious?

What the sleeper hold needed was one meaningful, big name using it to, first, leave "enhancement" foes out cold, before finally making another star snooze at the end of an important struggle. The sleeper had to bring victory for a wrestler in main events. The sleeper had to defeat major opponents. Once the context was correct, with announcer, workers, and bookers all on board, the sleeper's story could have been told, and fans would have responded with something other than dozing off themselves.

Why does Triple H's Pedigree bring spectators to their feet? As a move, it's no more hazardous than the suplex, the FU, or even the figure four. All an opponent has to do is bend over, face downward, while his noggin rests between H's knees, wait until Triple H is ready, and then fall onto his belly. It's certainly not one of those terrifying bumps that might leave someone crippled for real.

Still, the crowd buys it, because Triple H, built from the same mold as Race or Rogers, teases the anticipation before the impact. And then, of course, the announcers yell, workers sell, and bookers tell.

These aspects always make a big move big. If not supported by all aspects of the promotion, the finest finishing move in history will mean absolutely nothing to the audience.

Some newer followers of wrestling scoff, saying this kind of emphasis on psychology is old school and declaring that it's no longer applicable today. Yet those same critics will watch the NFL and became totally entranced with an explanation about why a team's passing game isn't working because they cannot execute their ground game.

There are lessons here for fans, wrestlers, and promoters at every level. One surely is that doing the same move other stars do waters down the effectiveness of that maneuver. Everyone wants to dunk like Michael Jordon, swing like A-Rod, or Pedigree like Triple H. But guess what? Not everybody can pull it off. Each performer must learn both what fits his style, and why, if he truly wants to discover how wrestling works.

When wrestling puts the package together efficiently, whether it's old or new school, the web it weaves gets thicker, stronger, and stickier. Sure, glitz and glamour, fireworks and music can prove attractive to a new visitor or a casual customer. Then, as soon as they spend a little time with the product, a well-woven trap of context will create a reliable fan.

And that kid who had a dream, who struggled against all odds, who outlasted heartache and paranoia and physical discomfort, who gloried in the moment he did battle, who finally became a *wrestler* . . . He is the key to making it all happen.

CHAPTER FOUR

DISMAY

When Chris Benoit killed himself, his wife, and his young son in June 2007, everyone in the world of professional wrestling was simultaneously shocked and horrified.

Many found ways to cope with the tragedy in rationalization. Those who were close to Benoit obviously felt a pain beyond imagination. Outsiders investigated, analyzed, and tried to make sense out of something that will never make sense. A few were trying to cash in, but many were sincere.

World Wrestling Entertainment surely, from a purely financial perspective, must have felt pressured to somehow "spin" the catastrophe to protect its assets. The majority of their manipulations seemed to backfire, though in the end the company pulled through without much of a dent to its bottom line. Considering all of that, it's important to stress that people at WWE felt intense pain, too. No one ever imagined anything like this could happen.

Those of us who claim no personal relationship with Benoit? We just felt pain — because we have been or are part of professional wrestling. Our connection, our passion, was with this perplexing business, and thus linked to Benoit. It wasn't just the situation, but the appalling details that drilled away at the gut of anyone who has experienced the rollercoaster from the inside.

Wrestling has the capacity to create both great joy and satisfaction, while at the same time it can inflict personal pain, upheaval, and instability that's almost unimaginable. But try to let the cursed thing go. Maybe we idealize wrestling, yet it's also sometimes a disease, an addiction. The good hopefully overcomes the bad, or at least seems to, until something like the Benoit tragedy happens.

To make myself feel better, I wrote. I wrote out of despair for what I believed Benoit's calamity said to the world about professional wrestling. Writing was my way of trying to heal the ache, whether or not anyone ever saw what I wrote.

A few half-hearted efforts convinced me that the mainstream media was not interested in a serious consideration of what had happened, although when my friend Bob Costas read the essay he called to say that he understood and completely agreed with the feelings I had expressed. Dave Meltzer, who has an intense connection to wrestling, whether or not the powers-that-be want to admit it, felt strongly enough that what I said made sense that he posted it on wrestlingobserver.com.

Wrestling isn't a pop culture phenomenon that just suddenly appeared in 1984, but a business with a long, rich, and controversial history. That's part of the reason why, even if it is "just a work," it matters so much to so many. Its appeal bridges time as well as class. And as time passes, perspectives change. Here is what I wrote in the summer of 2007:

> Pro wrestling was once fun, a mesmerizing illusion of athletics and drama. Although generally unacknowledged, its audience always was huge and cut across age, social, and financial boundaries. Who cared if the so-called elite scoffed at the colorful spectacle, but then enjoyed it in secret?
>
> From Thesz to Rogers, from Sammartino to Brisco, from Gagne to Flair, pro wrestling was a chance to have a great time and relieve the stress of daily life. What did it matter how "real" it was?
>
> During the late 1960s and 1970s, I learned about this crazy business from legendary promoter Sam Muchnick in St. Louis, where wrestling had more respect as a sport than anywhere else. Getting the opportunity to know the performers and promoters, to do commentary on the famous television show *Wrestling at the Chase*, and eventually to help book matches was a dream come true for somebody whose father had seen Strangler Lewis and Jimmy Londos.
>
> Any dreams about this version of wrestling have become nightmares

today. The horrible murder-suicide of Chris Benoit made that fact perfectly clear. The sport is less real, but it's also *too* real. Young people die. I never had to announce, or worse, "spin," death.

While the media and regulatory agencies laughed that "it's just 'rassling," real human beings with hopes and fears, parents and children, wives and siblings have had their lives destroyed. The seeds of this catastrophe were planted when Vince McMahon and the World Wrestling Federation (now World Wrestling Entertainment) took over the business in the mid-1980s, when steroids and phony physiques became a key part of making money. Essentially the pro wrestling business today is WWE.

Wrestling was always a dicey deal behind closed doors, as now-extinct regional promoters battled each other while trying to cheat and control their own in-ring talent.

For the past two decades, it has been much worse. As the business hooked itself on artificial enhancements, the influence and abuse of those chemically engineered muscles spread to other sports and to the nation's youth, who have always followed wrestling in big numbers.

At least baseball and football try to hide the effect of such drugs. WWE glamorizes and merchandises the results on national TV each week. Forget the pious pronouncements of drug tests and wellness programs that are spurred by disasters and soon forgotten. Only a fool could fail a steroid test as given currently; the more potent concoctions are supposedly impossible to detect.

Wrestlers trying to earn a living today know that looking a certain way is the key to moving up the ladder. These performers give everything to their craft, wanting to excite fans and support their families. Sadly, though, this business has become a paranoid culture rife with steroids, painkillers, uppers, downers, so-called recreational drugs, and alcohol, along with a staggering number of nasty injuries.

Add in the cynical manipulation of eager athletes who are pawns, and even the strongest can be damaged. There is virtually no protection for the individual — no union, no pension, no defined healthcare, no independent support system, no meaningful bargaining power.

Freedom of speech is non-existent, for most are either afraid to talk or so brainwashed that they chirp the company tune. Health, sanity, and happiness are in short supply because "kayfabe" (not telling out-siders secrets about pro wrestling) is not gone, as some claim; it has merely changed. Kayfabe today means wrestlers, for whatever reason, follow a twisted version of the code to protect the company.

The wrestler believes he must do *whatever* it takes to keep the job and earn more money. The pressure can break the weak. Only a select few escape unscathed.

How many have died so young while the outside world ignored the grow-ing disaster? In 20 years, there are enough names (Eddie Guerrero, Owen Hart, Bam Bam Bigelow, Miss Elizabeth, Rick Rude, Curt Hennig, Sherri Martel, Davey Boy Smith, Big Bossman, Road Warrior Hawk, John Studd, etc.) to fill most of this commentary. Does this happen with such terrifying frequency to mailmen, accountants, or soccer players?

Did it happen to wrestlers 30 years back?

Is pro wrestling itself responsible for these deaths? The answer is a definite *no*. Benoit is responsible for what he did, just as everyone is responsible for what they do.

The sport is, at its simplest, harmless entertainment. What it has grown into now through WWE, however, must share the blame for these deaths. Performers and even fans have been coerced into a mindset that has led to this situation where the outcomes are as pre-dictable as the winners of bouts are predetermined. This result was obviously not intended, but it is the result nonetheless.

Simplistic answers, politically correct excuses, or outright deception just do not cut it anymore.

I love this goofy thing called pro wrestling, but not what it is today. For all its faults, wrestling can be exciting and entertaining. It can be escapism at its most enjoyable, both to watch and to promote.

But now *I* want to escape from wrestling itself. Wrestling has become dangerous, disgusting, and degrading. There is only so much exploita-tion to be tolerated. Death might finally make everyone (or please, perhaps, someone!) take a critical look at an industry and company that is its own worst enemy.

Oh, for the days when pro wrestling was fun and the big debate was whether or not the promoter decided who would win instead of arguing who the next casualty might be.

Unfortunately, the clock cannot be turned back. Nobody can heal the wounds of those hurt so badly or bring back those whose lives were sacrificed.

But must there be more?

Do I still feel this way today? Well no, I don't want to escape any more. I've invested too much time, too much emotion. I know I am hooked, and I still love the damn thing, warts and all. I am still here, still trying to make sense of wrestling, and still wanting it to be better and more fun.

Is wrestling itself — wrestling, the pseudo sport — to blame for what happened to Chris Benoit and his family? Does the fault instead belong to the greedy and uncaring power brokers along with the short-sighted performers who infected the simplistic canvas of wrestling with their own psychoses? Why should poor ole wrestling be guilty because of the perversions of the people who run it, or because some of those participants did what they did during a particular time period?

How much responsibility belongs to the fans, intentionally blind and unquestioning as the crisis grew? What about baseball and its followers, equally ignoring what was obvious? (Though in that case, at least nobody died.) Or is all that just the rationalization I needed to go back when the bell rang?

To their everlasting credit, and regardless of their motivation, wwe has apparently strengthened its policies and testing. From a distance, it looks like the situation has improved — although the physiques of some wrestlers still raise eyebrows. Maybe, though — and that's a big *maybe* — the dark clouds have lightened a little.

At the same time, the sordid history of the business means it's impossible to talk about wrestling today without considering the impact of steroids. Aren't we, though, really just talking about all forms of artificial physical enhancement, one of the earth's many contemporary plagues? And, bluntly, does anybody give a shit? For all the furor in the aftermath of Benoit's crimes, with so much prominent public attention focused on wrestling, how much has changed?

Sure, the business took a small hit. Television ratings slumped briefly, only to rebound. In less than a year, however, a lot seemed to be the same as before. In my own case, I went from thinking I never wanted to watch wrestling again to probably peeking at a show within a week, and then I kept peeking until I was right back where I started. And I too began to rationalize, telling myself that it was also *my* business.

Calls for a Congressional hearing all but disappeared when the Mitchell Report cast the spotlight onto Major League Baseball. Clearly, there was more publicity to be mined from discussions with Roger Clemens, Barry Bonds, and Bud Selig about whether the home-run records or strikeout totals were influenced by drugs than a truckload of dead wrestlers. Wrestling, after all, is only a work. It isn't *real*, right? So does that mean the corpses no longer count?

Mitchell referred to his investigation of steroid use in baseball as a "boondoggle." If baseball was a "boondoggle" to the esteemed former senator, what would he have said about wrestling, where there were *real* broken bodies and souls, and not just broken records?

Eventually, the politicos did conduct informational hearings late in 2007, during which nobody was under oath, which meant that no threat of perjury was involved should the truth not be told. Media coverage was at best minimal. The McMahon entourage, including Vince himself, wife Linda, daughter Stephanie, several wwe medical figures, and ever-present attorney Jerry McDevitt testified before Congressman Henry Waxman's panel, as did tna chief executive Dixie Carter Salinas.

All in all, Vince delivered a remarkable performance, ducking responsibility and finessing — or outright bullying when required — the situation. The end result was that Waxman pointed to "systemic deficiencies in the testing policies and practices of professional wrestling" before tossing the fascinating data to the Office of National Drug Control, where the report is likely never to be seen again until the next disaster in the wrestling industry.

Granted, the attention made wwe buckle down and tighten up on certain aspects of the business that had created the atmosphere in which a culture of drugs grew to devastating proportions.

Cleaning up, though, is taxing. Maybe the public just doesn't care. For all the letters and phone calls, how many people refused to buy a pay-per-view because they thought the headlining wrestler was "on the juice"? The message to the promotion was, and for the most part still is: the fans don't mind. Fans are, in fact, on one level, enablers. But straightening out the mess should not be their responsibility alone.

Wrestling has always had a beauty contest undertone. Mostly naked guys, and occasionally girls (talk about artificial enhancements, the cost of which is also sadly ignored), are right there, up close, in the viewer's face. They had better look good — or at least different. Appearance is a big part of the business, now more than ever before.

Let's not forget that all sports, no matter how "legitimate" they may appear, are also entertainment. What happens in a football or baseball game will not create a cure for cancer any more quickly than will a wrestling match. To those on the outside, it is about escape and entertainment. To those within the sports, however, it can be a kind of life-or-death situation.

That magic "it" quality promoters and producers talk about makes a difference, as much on the gridiron or diamond as in the ring or on the silver screen. "It" sells tickets. In the modern world, "it" definitely boosts marketing revenue. The physical appearance or style of Tom Brady or Tom Cruise, of LeBron James or Denzel Washington, of Alex Rodriguez or Jennifer Lopez, sometimes fires the imagination more quickly than their actual talent. It's not that they are not talented — their gifts are just more quickly recognized because of how they look.

Attorney Mel Hutnick points out that "sex appeal is always part of marketing. Every business does it, from pretty models at car shows to the cheerleaders for National Football League games. What about the sleek swimsuits on Olympic athletes?"

Why would wrestling be any different? Jim Londos earned a spot in the sport's dusty annals because he drew money as the striking "Golden Greek" of the 1930s. Lou Thesz was a handsome, articulate, super athlete who meant box office riches well into the

'60s. Some claim that the fascination with physique and looks was born in the early '80s, but consider stars like Londos, Thesz, Buddy Rogers, Cowboy Bob Ellis, or Jack Brisco. Obviously, how they were built — trim, athletic, visually appealing — was parlayed into fan appeal. Even "old school" bodies and faces mattered.

Throw out any major name, from Johnny Valentine to Bruno Sammartino to Ric Flair, from Randy Savage to The Rock to John Cena. Something distinctive, in their appearance or about their charisma, sets them apart.

Here is a more down-to-earth assessment of what "it" is. At our local health club, my daughter Kelly, who played volleyball in college, often trained in the summer with a woman named Cheryl Venorsky, a female police officer who had been a college softball standout. The officer is an extremely intelligent woman, and she's also earning her Master's degree in management. As a child, her family regularly watched *Wrestling at the Chase*, and she has fond memories of rushing home from church on Sunday mornings to enjoy the show with her dad.

Who were her favorites? "Definitely the Von Erichs. They were soooooo hot!" she once told me.

Sex appeal, plain and simple. Maybe that's what "it" is.

From the male perspective, perhaps "it" is slightly different. I remember a grizzled fellow who had seen decades' worth of wrestling once telling me: "When I'd see some stud like Gene Kiniski or Dick the Bruiser come down that aisle, I knew they were the real deal. Those guys could fight a chainsaw, and you could tell it looking at them!"

Bleached hair, gaudy robes, sexy valets, crazy gimmicks. It actually fits into the same category to some extent, especially for those without the natural charisma of a Rogers or a Flair or a Thesz. The goal is to be more than the sum of all the parts, bigger than life, to project a marketable image. For some, the accoutrements help. More often than not, however, they fail. The results can be almost sadly amusing.

Consider Angelo Poffo, the father of both Randy Savage and "the Genius" Lanny Poffo, who once decided to bleach his jet-black hair a golden blond. That amateur dye job left Angelo with a gorgeous head of *orange* hair for an appearance on *Wrestling at the Chase* in the mid-'60s. At least it was easy for the crowd to know who the heel was.

Black Jack Lanza also needed to keep up his image in the late-1970s and apparently doctored his greying hair before a Kiel Auditorium match. The problem was that whatever Lanza used on his hair ended up creating big, black splotches on the white ring mat. And the turnbuckle. And, once Lanza got caught in a side headlock, on his opponent's ribs and arms. Getting heat is difficult when the first ten rows of fans are laughing at the nasty bad guy with black shoe polish in his hair!

What do spectators think today when they see a Shawn Michaels or a Mr. Kennedy begin to melt before their very eyes? Spray-on tanning products don't stand up well to hot ring and television lights. High-def makes the results even more noticeable. And so today, spray-on tans are being phased out, toned down, or applied better.

With so much riding on the beauty contest, with appearance being so important, what else should we expect? It's even more ironic given that someone like Michaels hardly needs artificial extras to get over. He's proven he has "it," in the middle of the ring, many times over.

The pressure to get ahead, to be noticed, to climb the ladder, to keep a lucrative spot, is so intense that some wrestlers take risks much more dangerous than orange-tinged dyes. Even when a wrestler might seem to have "it," he thinks, or has been conditioned to believe, that "it" is not good enough. And fearing for his position in the pecking order, he might be tempted to reach for artificial assistance. Insecurity secretly runs rampant in wrestling dressing rooms.

Somewhere along the way, wrestlers discovered that steroids, or their distant relatives, could enhance "it." Consider this: if Terry Bollea had not used steroids to slab his tall and lean frame with camera-friendly muscles, would he have become Hulk Hogan? Would he have been cast as Thunderlips in *Rocky III*? Would he have been lured away from Verne Gagne's AWA by Vince McMahon to herald the start of the wrestling war that changed the business?

Bollea had charisma. But without the extra "ripped" bulk, would he have been just another Ron Fuller who, at 6'9" and a mere 225 pounds, was slim and skilled but not being chased down by movie producers and wrestling promoters alike?

Does that make Hulk Hogan a bad guy? For that matter, does it make Vince McMahon bad? How many businesses other than wrestling stress that it's *winning* that counts, not *how* you win? The end justifies the means. The name of the game is making a profit, as big as possible. Why should Hogan or McMahon be any different than other ambitious people, wanting to make their mark in the world?

Who had any idea that artificial enhancements could lead to all these modern horrors?

The wrestler said, "It made me bigger. It made me stronger. It set me apart from the herd. It brought me to the attention of promoters who could help me reach my dream."

The promoter said, "He looks special. He looks like a dynamo. He can make me money. The fans will love him."

Does anyone really think that a wrestler and a promoter in 1930 or 1960 would have reacted any differently if they'd had similar options to consider?

Many of those who cherish the history of wrestling put Sam Muchnick, my mentor and former boss, on a pedestal. No doubt, he deserves to be honored. But would Muchnick have refused to book a major star who used steroids? Would he have even realized they were on the juice?

Truthfully, the question is unfair, even if considering it is interesting. To most of the world, steroids were not an issue during the vast majority of Muchnick's tenure. For those not involved in making their own bodies bigger, prettier, or stronger, talk of steroids or whatever they were called back then was like spinning a yarn about magic potions. Or Popeye eating his spinach!

At the time, medical knowledge was relatively limited, or at least unknown to the general public. The potency of the ingredients was certainly lower, if getting stronger on a regular basis. Damages and injuries were not yet linked to steroid usage, if that would have even been to blame. Legal issues were just beginning to emerge.

Though there were a few eye-catching builds around, the decisions back then were based on whether a wrestler could work well enough to get himself over and draw money — muscles or not, no matter how they were developed. Bluntly, Muchnick and his fellow promoters did not care, nor was there any reason for them to care.

Nobody had died. But the seeds were quietly, unknowingly, being sewn, even during Sam's time.

A perfect example is Dick the Bruiser, who was a star for Muchnick for two decades. Before entering the mat universe, Dick Afflis was a professional football player in the 1950s. Afflis had the kind of face that commanded attention. He was also an avid weight lifter. When Bruiser began wrestling, he had huge muscles concreted across his shoulders and chest. In the mid-'60s, his body could be favorably compared to Triple H's at his biggest. Add a turbulent personality, in a time when wrestlers were not expected to fill a role as they are now, and Dick the Bruiser was a remarkable box office attraction.

By the 1970s, Dick had settled into a spot as owner of a promotion in Indianapolis and a top star for Muchnick, along with a few other Midwest operators. Mike Huber, a young Indianapolis athlete bitten with the wrestling bug, was beginning the long, arduous, and ultimately depressing climb to get somewhere in the business. He was also married to Dick's daughter.

It was frustrating for Mike, who came to be nicknamed Spike. Huber was short — too short, according to some promoters, for the standards of the day. In addition, he struggled to bulk up and gain muscle mass, no matter how hard he worked. Finally, Dick took Mike aside (he was fond of the boy obviously) and gave him some pills. "This will help you get bigger, be able to work out more and harder. Look what it did for me," Dick said.

Before he even realized what was happening, "Spike" gained thirty pounds of impressive muscle. Unfortunately, the pills his father-in-law gave him could not make Huber taller. Still, Spike

Huber carved out a nice spot on shows in the heartland until the business itself aggravated him so badly that he had to walk away no matter how much he loved wrestling itself.

Bruiser (and he most surely was not the only one) had provided what was likely some early version of today's human growth hormone. Added to Dick the Bruiser's genetics, it helped create a unique look.

Barry Biehl, a retired police chief who was active in the weight lifting/body building scene around 1960, said he remembered others taking Dianabol and Winstrol at that time. "It wasn't in the quantities or the strength that came later," explained Biehl, "but it sure made guys bigger, even then."

When Dick gave those pills to Huber, he believed he was helping a youngster chasing his dream. Nobody understood the ramifications. All the territorial promoters understood was that Dick the Bruiser was a monster, in both looks and performance. And, of course, he could draw a house.

What about Superstar Billy Graham? In the '70s, how many promoters recognized what Graham had done to enhance his body? Muchnick booked Graham regularly — at least until Superstar failed to show up for a date. Point is, he didn't stop using Graham because the man took steroids. Did Muchnick even know? Even if he had, would it have mattered?

Ken Patera was a superstar grappler and a world-famous weight lifter. He competed for the United States in the Olympic games. When he lifted, Patera was well over 300 pounds. When he was in main events around North America, he tipped the scales at a hard and eye-catching 265. Patera was a tremendous worker and lured many huge gates.

When he talked about his Olympic experience, Patera made no bones about the fact that he had taken steroids — and more than tacitly implied that it was expected. Even though there was superficial testing, everyone used the stuff — the Russians, the East Germans, everyone. To compete at that level, it's what an athlete had to do. Natural athletic gifts were important, to be sure, but to reach that next rung on the ladder, to compete with others just as talented, something extra was needed.

Did Patera, who had good genetics and superior training methods, continue to use steroids throughout his wrestling career? If so, what he was taking was likely nowhere near as refined as what's available today, which perhaps minimized the dangers. With his "legitimate" sports background, excellent in-ring talent, and superb look, Patera was a fixture at the top of St. Louis programs and respected by Muchnick, who understood that Patera had paid a price, whatever it might be, to become a world-class athlete.

Isn't it a sad commentary that any past star with an imposing physique is now questioned? Yet that is what the modern controversy has wrought. In the earlier era, what was the difference between taking pills that were considered more potent vitamins or drinking protein shakes?

Kerry Von Erich was a Muchnick favorite, primarily because of Sam's friendship with his father, Fritz. When stories about the Von Erich boys' recreational drug use leaked back to him, Sam would ask around. It was something he did not want to believe or accept.

In Kerry's case, the drugs likely included steroids, at first to help what his dad hoped would be a track career, and then to build up his body for wrestling. He had little body fat and shared the genetics of brothers David and Kevin. Combining steroids and more weight lifting gave Kerry a fabulous look.

After one Kiel Auditorium show, however, he collapsed in the dressing room and began urinating blood. The combination of symptoms made it look like more than just a bump had gone bad. Sam called Fritz immediately and wanted to rush Kerry to the hospital. Fritz said no, just get him settled down and send him home on a plane first thing in the morning. Sam did as his friend asked.

Kerry Von Erich eventually committed suicide. Steroids alone cannot be blamed.

Kerry had many other demons to deal with, other drugs, including painkillers, among them. When Sam checked in about Kerry a couple days after after his locker room collapse, his father said he was okay. Sam continued to book Kerry in main events.

What would McMahon have done? There is no easy answer.

This is not a knock at Muchnick; it's reality. How many promoters used Bruiser, Graham, Patera, Kerry Von Erich or, for that matter, "Mr. Universe" Earl Maynard or Gene Stanlee in an earlier era? Bluntly, what was wrong with booking them? No one realized there was a downside to steroid use at the time: no one really grasped what excessive amounts of enhancement drugs could do to an athlete's health.

Nonetheless, somewhere in the background of all this, there had always been an inkling that something wasn't quite as it should be. How do some of the guys look like *that*? It can't all be genetics and training, right?

The growing winds began to howl as the business changed in 1984. When the WWF and McMahon conquered the mat world, it became clear Vince liked big muscles, overblown cartoon characters, supermen in tights. Make no mistake, the audience did too. Vince made his vision the industry standard. And because of his television exposure, most fans willingly bought in.

Here, though, is a key point to make about Vince McMahon. While the legalities were changing, and some medical questions might have been raised, the bottom line is that, at the time, nobody had a clue what the future held. Would Vince have altered his philosophy at least to some degree had he realized what catastrophes lay ahead for so many performers? Would Vince have changed his thinking if he had understood how other dangerous drugs would infiltrate along with steroids? Can anyone really know the future?

McMahon loved the look of Graham, and was likewise surely smitten with Superstar's personality and interviews. He was a colorful character, especially after the more traditional likes of Bruno Sammartino, Pedro Morales, and Bob Backlund. The extra attraction for McMahon may have been his own fascination with conditioning and lifting.

On October 23, 1983, Vince was in St. Louis to see me, Charlie Mancuso (manager of The Checkerdome and my partner in a new, opposition promotion after Sam Muchnick's retirement), and Ted Koplar (owner of KPLR-TV, the home of St. Louis wrestling) at the Chase Park Plaza Hotel.

It was a tough meeting. The negotiation culminated with Mancuso and me folding our promotion and Vince promising to compensate Mancuso for any and all financial losses Charlie's backers had incurred. Not unexpectedly, some would say, that did not happen. What *did* happen, after plenty of backstage maneuvering, was that McMahon, with me working for his WWF, took over the prestigious KPLR time slot to launch his bid to dominate the business.

After the tense and difficult discussion, I drove McMahon to his hotel and Mancuso to The Checkerdome parking lot. As we rode, we talked; it was the kind of moment where people try to relax and accept everything that's happened, to set business aside and get a feel for someone they've just butted heads with.

Maybe it was the fact that McMahon was going to Minneapolis the next day to sign Hulk Hogan away from Verne Gagne's AWA that led us to talk about muscles, conditioning, and working out.

Noting the fact that he looked much bigger under his suit than when I'd first met him a few years back, I said, "You look like you've really been working out."

Charlie added, "You're starting to look as good as one of the wrestlers, Vince."

The barometric pressure changed suddenly. We could literally feel Vince just sucking in all the air in my car, the simple comments puffing him up and making him beam. Vince acknowledged that he had indeed been working out hard and was pleased with the results.

Seeing him in tights and cut-off shirts over the years, it's clear that Vince shares the same hunger for a beautiful physique as those who perform for him. Is there any question he likely considered doing the same things wrestlers did to make himself look like a powerhouse? How many sixty-year-olds have biceps like that?

This is not a knock, either, just another fact. Vince was into a certain physical image and he transferred that interest into his business, which in turn made buckets of money featuring his ideal. Wanting to train, be in shape, and look great is no sin. Furthermore, steroids are not simply a black-and-white issue. Yes, there are certain legalities that have to be observed. Much has been learned about the potential dangers, and some real benefits, of the wide range of drugs known as steroids. Consider two very different situations . . .

First, take the young baseball player with a lot of talent — but not quite enough to bust out and make the majors. So close, yet so far. If he could only throw 94 miles-per-hour or add another 20 feet to the towering fly balls he hits near fences. How tempting it must be to go for that extra edge, to see whether steroids might put him over the hump.

He is young; this is his dream. He can always stop later. Besides, at 24, he still feels immortal. The idea that he might pass away at 60 instead of 75 has little meaning in his world. Another thing, he thinks: What about Lasik eye surgery? The few thousand dollars guys spend on improving their vision, to pick up the spin on the ball an instant quicker. Isn't that an enhancement as well? Shouldn't it be classed with steroids, at least as a distant cousin? And what about sleeping in high altitude chambers, blood doping? Where is the line and when is it crossed, and for which athletes?

Now consider my own circumstance. I have spinal stenosis, a narrowing of the spinal canal that leads to extra bone forming over the years, which in turn pinches nerves. Having ignored the symptoms for so long and blaming my limp leg and gimpy knee on basketball and running steps to stay in shape, I suffered nerve damage before I finally saw a doctor, learned about stenosis, and had surgery to open my spinal canal. But nerve damage cannot be reversed, so I limp and struggle for balance. It may get worse.

If someone I trusted said to me, "Take this steroid and it will reverse the nerve problem. You will walk easily, maybe be able to jog. But you will die four years sooner."

Is that a clear-cut choice? Neither of us has an easy decision to make. Not that my examples apply directly to wrestling, but they're still relevant. Gain versus loss. Risk versus status quo. Different pressures.

From the beginning, being huge was a prerequisite for getting a push in Vince's WWF. Any wrestler with half a brain could understand what he had to do in order to get the boss to take notice. If steroids were the answer, and that was a wrestler's goal, a decision had to be made. Natural 230-pounders felt they needed that cut look to succeed. Bigger wrestlers wanted to be monsters.

My battered brain recalls a chat Vince had with "Big John" Studd. The three of us were sitting on the stage in the empty hall at Kiel Auditorium before a 1984 television taping. Studd, whose real name was John Minton, was a surprisingly easygoing fellow who likely had 325 pounds on his 6'9" frame. Vince was telling him that if he were bigger, there was surely a great run for a feud between "Big John" and Andre the Giant.

Vince fondly punched John's arm and said, "If you just were a little bigger . . ."

Studd listened and not long afterward he began to weigh in at over 375 pounds. Big John and Andre went on to draw great money around the circuit. Vince never offered up specifics about how to get bigger; he just delivered the message that John and Andre would continue to battle if . . .

In the early 1990s, after I had left the WWF and Studd had retired, John came to St. Louis for a golf tournament and to promo the sports court business with which he was involved. I was saddened to see how he struggled to get around. I recognized subtle changes in his body, even in the shape of his skull, particularly his forehead.

John and I had always had great rapport and also shared a friendship with the late Bruiser Brody. He told me he had taken steroids and various exotic concoctions. Some of it he'd taken before his WWF run, as he struggled to fill out his college basketball player body. He began taking a lot more with the WWF. It was about business, and this was the price one paid for success, he explained.

On March 20, 1995, "Big John" Studd died. He was not yet 50. While his family maintained their privacy, stories leaked that steroid use played a role in creating the cancers that killed him so young.

Vince had his own headaches, especially in 1991, with the Zahorian trial. According to Dave Meltzer, one of the charges the federal government made was that McMahon conspired with Dr. George Zahorian to distribute steroids to wrestlers. Dave claimed that Vince knew Zahorian was a steroid dealer since Vince got stuff for himself from the guy. Meltzer said that if Vince had in fact hired Zahorian as a company doctor, McMahon would have been convicted.

Somehow, though, word leaked back through Vince's wife Linda that the government was investigating Zahorian. The wwf cancelled Zahorian's contract before he completed his first day on the wwf payroll. In his prior contact with Vince and the wrestlers, Zahorian had been invited into dressing rooms as a guest — as the athletic commission doctor.

End result? Vince and the wwf had never employed Zahorian; there was no evidence that Vince told Zahorian to sell steroids to his wrestlers. "Why would Vince need to tell him, since he [Zahorian] had been doing it for twelve years already?" Meltzer points out.

Another charge Vince faced was that he, personally, distributed steroids to Hulk Hogan. That was tossed out of court, as Meltzer documents, because McMahon's Connecticut office, where the transfer allegedly took place, was outside the trial's Eastern District of New York jurisdiction. An attempt was made to demonstrate that McMahon sent steroids via limo driver Jim Stuart to Hulk at the Nassau County Coliseum. But Stuart never showed up to testify, and the prosecution made various errors in the way it presented evidence.

One positive that came out of the proceedings: the wwf began testing for steroid use. It wasn't long before some wrestlers began to shrink, and then business went into the dumper by pre-investigation standards. McMahon spent a small fortune defending himself and the business against the charges. Financially, the company was hurting.

McMahon apparently blamed the lean economic days on how the guys now looked, especially in comparison to Hogan and Ultimate Warrior in their heyday. The noticeable change in wrestler physiques was only part of it, though. The fact that truly talented workers were not being featured was for the most part ignored.

It is not difficult to understand how McMahon may have come to see everything that had happened as persecution, by both the government and the many enemies he'd made within the wrestling world. There may well have been some truth to it. The list of wrestling's dead had not yet begun to grow; drugs of all kinds, not just steroids, were rampant throughout society. Why the wwf? Why him?

Everything he'd been accused of was apparently equally true for what was left of the old school promotions, which had essentially become Ted Turner's wcw. At the time it was clear that Vince felt Turner had gotten off easy. After all, wcw had the Road Warriors — walking advertisements for steroids.

As time passed, little changed. Recreational drugs were as accepted as drinking beer had been in the 1960s and 1970s. Painkillers and speed were required, at least according to many, in order to survive the intense schedule of performing every night. That shadowy, destructive culture of drugs had become part of the everyday lives of wrestlers.

Testing became less and less exacting, and once again, wrestlers became cartoon-muscled giants. Business rebounded, though most serious observers would claim that had more to do with the suddenly hot cable battle between wcw and the wwf. New stars emerged. With the mysterious "it" factor (and likely a good dose of physique-enhancement as well), they clicked with the public.

Did steroids help Stone Cold Steve Austin and The Rock become superstars? Make no mistake: both were unique and magnetic performers, with or without. Seriously, does anyone really doubt that well-trained, attractive athletes, with their ability on the mic, and benefitting from a promoter's super push would become anything but serious money-makers, steroids or not?

Steroids, as far as I am aware, have never had anything to do with how well a performer communicates or, for that matter, the quality of their work inside the squared circle. In fact, beautiful physiques were never the lone reason for wrestling's so-called rebirth in the second half of the '90s any more than they were in the '80s. Pretty muscles were just one ingredient in the total package of slick production, sophisticated marketing, wide-open booking, and especially red-hot characters.

But wrestlers were starting to die at younger ages and in greater numbers as the 1990s closed. Little scandals popped up more regularly, and controversy spiked with the accidental death of Owen Hart. Still, the mainstream media ignored almost everything. The trend, however, was becoming frighteningly clear.

What was going on in the heads of wrestlers? Stories about guys "getting off the juice" so their wives could become pregnant became common. Unusual injuries like torn biceps, triceps, pecs, and quadriceps attributed to muscular and joint imbalances caused by steroids were reported with alarming regularity. (Vince McMahon himself blew out both quads for what it's worth.) A number of "anger management issues" popped up. In the late '70s, an ill Bruiser Brody told me he just knew something was going wrong with his body, something caused by the drugs he'd taken to both enhance his massive frame and maintain it through injuries. Brody quit cold turkey. Now, though, a whole new generation of wrestlers began to feel something amiss in their systems.

Still, nobody spoke out. Kayfabe. Us and them. Keep the secrets; protect the business. Who wanted to risk being fired when the job pool was shrinking and the money guys were making was bigger than anyone ever imagined possible?

Then Eddie Guerrero died, suddenly, on November 13, 2005. Prolonged steroid and narcotic use was listed as the cause of the heart attack that killed him. Enough attention and sober reflection emerged that WWE instituted a "wellness" program, and testing once more became important. The program had obvious flaws, gaping holes through which anyone who wanted to stay big with artificial assistance could easily jump. And they did. Critics argued the loopholes were deliberate.

There it is: the broad strokes of how a culture of drug-enhanced physiques, when mixed with street drugs and painkillers, eventually brought wrestling to the precipice of Chris Benoit's unfathomable acts. It's a mixture that shattered one life after another, that broke hard, tough men. Chris Benoit broke worse, harder than anyone before or since.

This doesn't even factor in the damage a wrestler like Benoit sustained from concussions, or repetitive, pain-producing injuries.

Eric Bischoff, who was the boss of WCW both when it soared high and also when it crashed into collapse, had another take, putting more blame on the wrestlers for all the tragedies. During an interview with Michael Landsberg on *Off the Record*, Bischoff claimed that performers abused painkillers like Vicodin and Somas. He alleged — likely correctly — that some guys used them recreationally to numb the brain and get a buzz. Furthermore, Bischoff maintained that more wrestlers than not can handle the travel schedule without drugs, which hopefully is correct. Despite Landsberg's prodding, Bischoff — perhaps not unexpectedly — downplayed the role that the modern wrestling environment played.

Former WWE champion Bret Hart, who obviously knew Benoit and the entire situation far too well after spending his entire life in wrestling, said during an interview with Canada's *National Post* that the schedule was not the reason wrestlers were dying. While he agreed the travel and the wrestling schedule was demanding, Bret called it "just an excuse."

Hart pointed out that a lot of wrestlers don't own up to the fact of their drug problems. He zeroed in on prescription painkillers as creating a sad epidemic that the public does not care enough about since wrestling often lands in the gray area between entertainment and sport.

Wrestling and its demons aside, there's also the possibility that something simply went haywire; the circuits may have become dysfunctional in Benoit's brain. Suicide is one thing — murdering one's own family is on another level of horror entirely. Maybe the drugs and the wrestling lifestyle made him more likely to crack, maybe not. Like it or not, however, the wrestling business and what Benoit did will always be, perversely, intertwined.

Even giving wrestling the benefit of the doubt, the public responses of performers like Mr. Kennedy and Chavo Guerrero were disturbing. Clearly they did not understand the implications of what had happened or what might happen in the future. Analyzing what they actually said in public interviews is simply disturbing. Kennedy, for example, claimed he'd never done steroids — then later clarified his statement by saying he had never done steroids since WWE adopted its Wellness Policy. The next chapter of his story is by now embarrassing history: government raids soon revealed that he'd been receiving steroids and growth hormone at his home the entire time. Why did he lie when it seems so obvious that the truth would inevitably come out?

Similarly, Chavo maintained he was clean, although his name was on the same lists as Kennedy. Sadder still, he told the media that it was a different generation, the guys from the '70s, who had drug problems which led to early deaths. His peers, he said, were fine — despite what had happened to his Uncle Eddie and his best friend Benoit.

It was worse than depressing, and the cycle seemed unbreakable. Congress got stirred up, the media followed the hot story of the week, and then everything petered out. Wrestling, after all, as pundits pointed out, is just entertainment. It's just a work. The young corpses were merely casualties of doing business. Dying was now one of the risks of being in wrestling.

Even more irritating is the claim that fair competition is what makes Olympic track events or baseball more important. Wrestling is not a sport, goes the excuse, so there is no competition. What a joke. The competition in wrestling to get on top, to be the best performer, to earn the giant payday at *WrestleMania*, is every bit as real to the athlete as hitting a baseball or clearing a hurdle in record time.

But it doesn't matter, because that is what general opinion is always going to be.

Wrestling has to clean up its own filthy backyard, to accept accountability. Arguing about every detail, or whether the scrutiny is fair, is just a way of diverting attention from the bigger issue. Even worse and more hypocritical was WWE teasing a drug overdose by Jeff Hardy, who has a history of problems, the night before *Survivor Series* in late 2008. Planting that story on the Internet about a supposed incident to either trick the media into coverage or a few fans into buying a pay-per-view, WWE made a mockery of its own genuine attempts to never face such a dreadful situation again.

The hard reality is that, despite the fact that the business has hooked millions of fans for generations, wrestling's problems are not going to get serious media attention unless something else terrible happens. Wrestling will always exist on the fringe, despite huge profitability and tremendous worldwide interest. The responsibility to protect workers resides with wrestling; it must happen from the inside.

No matter what any Internet geek writes on his blog, Vince McMahon does care. Argue his beliefs, argue his tactics, argue his tastes: that's all fair game. He hurts, though, like any other human being. To assume otherwise is ridiculous. Vince McMahon and WWE do not want wrestlers to die. But the existing philosophies of the industry, and whatever part Vince played in establishing them, did create the atmosphere in which these tragedies happen.

Logically, simple business sense says that an asset needs to be protected, kept valuable and profitable. Once more, performers — though not everyone — have appeared to shrink to more reasonable physiques. Vince deserves praise for offering rehabilitation programs at company expense to wrestlers, including those no longer with WWE, who admit to having drug problems. Research is being done, both by WWE and independently by other concerned parties, about the affects of injuries like concussions.

Of course, in a seemingly contradictory move typical of Vince, during the informational Congressional discussion the fact came out that active talent sent to rehab paid half the cost themselves, which was deducted regularly from their pay upon return to action. Vince described the policy as a reminder that the performers involved should not relapse, a practice that actually makes sense.

When the issue arose about offering rehab for wrestlers who at one time were under contract but were no longer, Vince was reported to answer, "Two words. Public relations. That's it. I do not feel any sense of responsibility for anyone . . . it is a magnanimous gesture."

Still, the question remains: if an athlete can perform and talk, does he get a chance on the big stage? If those in power continue to push the fellow with the ripped body, no matter how much more athletic or engaging a smaller worker may be, then intentionally or not the message will remain clear to those desperately trying for a slot: get big . . . or get out.

The beauty contest elements of wrestling are not going away. They're not leaving our culture, in general, any time soon. Wrestling has always, always, been drawn to big, powerful guys. A more realistic approach to what is expected of an athlete's body, notably in terms of appearance, could lessen the pressures that lead to steroid use.

For those rare cases who are genetically gifted, more power to them.

Because wrestling *is* a business, if fans learn to react to less mind-blowing physiques, if they erupt with excitement about moves, skill, and personality, then wrestling will learn to accept different ways of making money. Unfortunately, if the business of wrestling believes fans are not willing to hand over their dollars because muscles are deflating, there is going to be a problem. By the same token, wrestling has to present performers with real opportunities, not with a wink but a sincere effort, for change to occur. Perhaps most importantly, fans have to buy in as well.

So many imponderables are at work here that wrestling may well just take the easy road, hide from responsibility and explain that wrestlers are individual or independent contractors who make their own decisions. Wrestling will maintain that it has tried to "counsel" them as best it can. But isn't that what's been happening for years — unsuccessfully?

Without question, training techniques have improved tremendously. A targeted diet can increase strength and enhance muscular appearance. And there are those small few with terrific genetics and supreme discipline. A small, small quantity of men and women will look great without artificial assistance, but there's always a qualification, isn't there?

In today's world, with what is at stake financially, everyone always looks for an edge. In wrestling, precedent makes what works obvious. No matter how vigilant a company's drug screening is, offenders will sneak through. Plus, and this is crucial, fans will always react to certain body types. It's human nature.

Does that mean wrestling is such an awful thing? Baseball knew what was going on with Mark McGwire, Sammy Sosa, and many more, but looked the other way. Football has a vaunted testing program — but it also has vast numbers of 300-pound offensive linemen who tipped the scales at 265 in college. Consider the Olympic track competitors who have been caught. Suspicion is appropriate, and not just in wrestling.

Wrestling receives extra attention because today's version is marketed directly to youngsters, especially impressionable teens and pre-teens. If young people identify with a colorful musclehead on a flamboyant TV show, looking like him can become a priority. If there is only one way to do *that*, kids are lured to substances that have the potential to create serious problems down the road.

The bottom line is that steroids, except where medically prescribed, are illegal. Their effects should not be glamorized, especially when the human toll has been so incredibly high. Yet some undoubtedly believe that steroids, *used correctly*, however that might be, are not destructive. The response is: name one good thing that steroids have done for the entertainment fields that include sports and wrestling. Helping Sylvester Stallone, Arnold Schwarznegger, Barry Bonds, and Hulk Hogan make money does *not* count.

What a miserable predicament wrestling devised for itself by sliding into the abyss of steroids and drugs. Rationalizing does not change the fact that the business willingly opened the door that led to the tragedies that have wounded it. Nobody can be absolved of blame for his part in the disasters that have scarred wrestling. Like so much else in wrestling, though, its failings mirror those of the culture of which it is a part.

No, wrestling is not innocent. But neither is baseball, nor football, nor track, nor bodybuilding, nor the media . . . nor society itself. So we soldier on, promise never to forget, and hope for brighter days.

CHAPTER FIVE

HOW INDEPENDENT IS INDEPENDENT?

One of wrestling's most enduring fables involves the "independent" or free-spirited nature of professional wrestlers. Getting anywhere in the business has always meant marching to the beat of a different drummer — it takes a strong personality, someone willing to make his own decisions, follow his own path. The legal term for the situation of an individual wrestler, a term that the business has employed and exploited for years, is "independent contractor." However, due to some of those same characteristics a wrestler must possess, a profound change may be coming to the industry.

Back in the day, wrestling's rugged individualists handled their own travel arrangements (promoters reimbursed flights, but driving expenses came right out of the performer's wallet), washed their own tights in hotel rooms (for which they paid), found their own way around strange towns, bought themselves every meal on the road, and maintained a home they were seldom at. They approached different promotions in areas they thought would be a good fit for them, had at least some control about where and for whom they worked, battled over finishes and payoffs, managed their own finances with widely varying degrees of success, and took pride in what they did. They were independent — at least as independent as they could be.

But were they really independent contractors? And are they today? Certainly, it's the independent mindset that helps explain why no wrestling union ever came legitimately close to evolving. Something about wrestlers was always unlike baseball or football players. At the same time, from a legal (and tax) standpoint, to whose benefit is it — promoter or wrestler, management or labor — if professional wrestlers are classified as independent contractors?

For decades, wrestlers were seen as performers who hired out their services to individual promoters for specific shows. This allowed the promoters to avoid having to pay Social Security tax on their employees. Nothing was withheld or taken from their pay. It also meant that no insurance was purchased to cover the potential injuries or long-term damage performers might suffer.

Since there were numerous individual and autonomous promotions active into the 1980s, until that time wrestlers arguably had a good measure of control over who they worked for, where they worked, and what they agreed to do. (How much control, however, may be legitimately debated; the question even triggered the government investigation that led to a consent decree with the National Wrestling Alliance in the 1950s.) Many promotions were audited by the Internal Revenue Service over the years, so the idea of a wrestler being an independent contractor, at least as far as U.S. tax law was concerned, had an air of legitimacy.

When the grappling landscape changed and WWE finally dominated, the concept of the wrestler being an independent contractor became an important factor in the economic picture of McMahon's operation, despite the fact that many performers signed contracts that bound them to WWE. (Or WCW while it was alive, or TNA today.) Of course, the wrestling world was drastically different. The number of companies with which a wrestler could earn a full-time wage could be counted on one hand with fingers left over. It is that way now.

Today, wrestlers still pay for their own hotel rooms, local transportation, and food. They still argue about finishes and ideas for their characters, manage their own finances with widely varying results, keep a home running, and buy their own insurance. But there's nowhere else to go, no other territory or employer, if things aren't working out.

As far as WWE or TNA are concerned, wrestlers are independent contractors because that's what best fits their business model. It's a business reality that's been part of wrestling forever. And despite claims to the contrary, sports entertainment is wrestling. It is also a hard, serious business venture that regularly hides behind controversy and fantasy. So, this issue is always about money and how it is distributed — and maybe one other thing, something called *control.*

Sam Muchnick is often spoken of in glowing terms for clearly and honestly setting aside 32% of net gate receipts after taxes to pay his talent. Due to the economics of the time, that figure represented most, if not all, of the promotion's revenue, because there was almost nothing else — merchandising, licensing fees, or video sales — generating income. The formula allowed everyone to make money — particularly and understandably the promoter, who was shouldering the financial risk. It was a simpler time: the bigger the house, the bigger the profit — for everyone. From the lowest hand on the card to the most established star, everyone involved in wrestling had a stake in drawing a crowd.

Actually, most promoters used the 32% figure as the base from which to compensate wrestlers, although more than a few took more than just taxes from the gross before arriving at the total from which to subtract the performers' cut. Some, for example, would subtract the cost of producing televised wrestling programs, or perhaps a portion of advertising, before cutting the wrestlers in.

Enough promoters skimmed for themselves before they ever started their calculations to leave a feeling of distrust among the performers, some of whom were pretty adept at counting a house and estimating the receipts. Of course, how many modern headliners have even an inkling of, or the ability to obtain, the exact amount of revenue produced by a pay-per-view event, much less what percentage is due each performer?

At any rate, back then, this kind of manipulation of box office income gave promoters a tidy sum above their normal profit because expenses and talent were deducted from what was actually an altered gross thanks to their sleight-of-hand. In fact, calculating the 32% after expenses then is comparable to how many entertainment businesses today juggle what is and what isn't profit or net when it comes down to how and how much performers should be paid.

One reason Muchnick gets praise is the totally transparent manner in which he informed and remunerated the boys. Because Sam usually included a copy of the box office statement along with what he was paying main-event stars, wrestlers could easily see whether the 32% figure was being reached fairly. The bottom line is that 32% was acceptable to both promoter and wrestler in that era.

However . . . If today the owners of Major League Baseball or the NFL went to their players and offered to pay them from 32% of net revenue, they would be met with a strike of biblical proportion. The reality is that more than 55% of total revenue goes to the athletes who perform in major league sports today — men who have powerful unions along with smart legal and financial advisers. Even actors have a union, along with their own personal representatives.

While true that wrestlers today can earn more money than anyone ever anticipated, what percentage is it of all the money taken in by World Wrestling Entertainment? Even with the royalties from DVDs and toys, it is safe to say that the portion the wrestlers receive is much closer to their traditional 32% than it is to the 55%-plus other, similar performers earn.

Does that mean Vince McMahon is doing something wrong, unethical, or illegal? No, of course not. It's not bad; it's just business.

He and his company are simply operating in a manner that the laborers appear to be content to with — they've certainly never protested in any meaningful way. Attempting to maximize profits for both himself and his stockholders, Vince is doing good business — exactly what the execs of General Electric, Wal-Mart, or Google would do if their situation allowed them to. Vince works the same way his father did. The same way Sam Muchnick did.

Likewise, pro wrestling is often compared to the Ultimate Fighting Championship (UFC) organization in the way both do business. Though it is a shoot inside the cage, UFC is not without its own internal politics, manipulation, questions about how revenue is spent, and power plays as to booking and contracts with its performers. They, too, are a major company that, in addition to regarding its fighters as independent contractors, naturally operates in its own best interests, exactly like WWE. Some fighters may not always agree with the end result of that philosophy.

A student of UFC and mixed martial arts from the beginning, Dave Meltzer of *Wrestling Observer Newsletter* explains: "UFC has some merchandising rights in its contracts, but they consider guys independent contractors, which they really are to some degree. They can turn down fights, work when they want, take vacations on their own, train when they want. But they can't work for other companies, although they can do appearances on their own without clearing them (with UFC) and get their own sponsors, which Vince's guys can't do."

In the summer of 2008, however, a potential bombshell was lobbed into the WWE's Stamford, Connecticut offices when three wrestlers filed a lawsuit against WWE and challenged the conventional notion of wrestlers being independent contractors. Scott Levy (best known as Raven), Christopher Klucsarits (known as Chris Canyon), and Michael Sanders — all former WWE employees — claimed that they, and all other performers, were not at all independent. Further, the trio maintained that WWE had been "unjustly enriched to plaintiffs' detriment" by defining its wrestlers as independent contractors.

Legal experts not aligned with either side felt that there was a legitimate issue in dispute, and that the plaintiffs had at least as good a chance of winning as losing in court. Who has what degree of control is a major issue. The attorneys for Levy, Klucsarits, and Sanders obviously understood that and listed several points of contention.

The WWE, always at the top of its game when it comes to legal skirmishes, landed a big blow early in 2009 when it got a dismissal on various technical issues. No arguments were made on the numerous points brought up in the suit, and the complainants went back into the struggle after apparently strengthening those weak areas in their argument. Still, the odds are against success for these particular accusers at this point in time.

Win or lose, however, that might not be the end of it. In baseball, a single player's failed lawsuit nonetheless led to all players eventually gaining free agency, a stronger union, and better personal protections. Wrestlers have a long, long way to go in that regard. The true key to the issue is whether or not current wrestlers have the sense, the smarts, and the courage to do what is actually right for them in the long run. Ask any older wrestler if the emergence of a union, which could be a spin-off result of the Levy lawsuit, would be meaningful and helpful for former participants. The answer is almost always a resounding "Yes!"

Big Bill Miller was a main-eventer in the '50s and '60s who also had a degree in veterinary medicine from Ohio State. Many within the business were surprised when he cut back on his schedule at the dawn of the '70s. He was still on top when he began working as a state veterinarian. He actually began to wind down his in-ring career because he realized there was zero chance of wrestlers unionizing. Miller clearly recognized the problem — 40 years ago.

Nothing is wrong with cornering the market, as WWE and Vince have done, but if wrestlers became sophisticated enough to protect their own interests, WWE could end up the victim of its own success. The lawsuit might be a first step in that direction. Because of WWE's power, the inquiry is about control of individuals and possibly even restraint of trade. For instance, in this particular action, the plaintiffs claimed that WWE "exercised total control over all aspects of the wrestlers' employment." Their filing then alleged that WWE determined the training regimen, the skill-training regimen, the locations where the wrestlers performed, whom the wrestlers competed with and against, the duration and outcome of each match. Additionally, the trio asserted that WWE as promoter determined the costumes and hairstyles that wrestlers wear, the wrestlers' stage persona and specific traits of that persona, the mannerisms used while performing, the signature moves and props used and when wrestlers may use them, plus required wrestlers to adhere to certain storylines, including specific dialogue.

Even more to the crux of the matter may have been that Levy, Klucsarits, and Sanders asserted that WWE reserved the right to use a wrestlers' likeness or image in perpetuity (yes, that means *forever*), to negotiate and enter into any agreements for the exploitation of intellectual property based on the wrestlers' personae for merchandising, commercial tie-ins, publishing, personal appearances, performances in non-wrestling events, and endorsements, to require that wrestlers submit to drug screening, and, finally, to determine, unilaterally, how wrestlers were compensated.

Now that's heavy, heavy stuff. Some of what they were arguing was clearly true — and it had been for decades. Some of it reflects the realities of doing business in the 21st century. Either way, the issue strikes at the heart of how the wrestling business operates.

Once upon a time, wrestlers developed their own personalities, characters they carried from territory to territory. Obviously, that's no longer the case. If Vince's company generated the character, he has a vested and justifiable interest in protecting that image and profiting from it. That's legitimate. And should today's performer happen to come up with his own idea for a character, it is still ownership and the creative/booking team that has the final say. All told, everything the suit outlined would appear to be a significant challenge to the notion of wrestler as an independent contractor.

Carried further, that potentially leads to tax issues — and real, fiscal consequences for WWE and the industry itself. Naturally, WWE made a spirited and astute defense of its position. Vince's legal team is intelligent, shrewd, even ruthless.

When the suit was filed, it appeared to leave the door open to a class-action process should other wrestlers wish to join in. An important question is, what was the real goal for Levy and partners? A quick payday after a quiet settlement or an overhaul of the industry? How long would they fight? As the legal bills piled up, how deep were their pockets? How smart were their lawyers? Rest assured, McMahon's pockets are very deep for something like this — and his lawyers are very, very smart.

But again, the outcome of this individual suit may not matter in the end. When Curt Flood refused to accept a trade from the St. Louis Cardinals to the Philadelphia Phillies in 1969, he sued Major League Baseball over its reserve clause. Flood was unwilling to accept the fact that he could be moved without his consent from one team to another — the reserve clause declared he had no choice. Even though he was well-compensated for the time ($90,000 per year), Flood said, "A well-paid slave is nonetheless a slave."

After a nasty, angry battle that wound up in the Supreme Court, Flood lost and his career was ruined. Regardless, the idea behind his principled stand was valid, potent, and timely. The baseball players' union grew stronger, the brilliant Marvin Miller led that organization into negotiations that changed the situation of the game's players, and Andy Messersmith and Catfish Hunter eventually became free agents and signed amazing contracts.

Baseball's financial landscape was forever altered. Ownership had less control. Yet today baseball is as popular as ever. Both players and owners are richer than they ever were. Fans pay higher prices to see the action, of course, but there are more spectators now than ever before. Baseball, like most other sports or entertainments, learned, and continues to learn, how to utilize television and technology to pay the bills and turn a profit. And thanks, in part, to Curt Flood, players are protected and compensated better than anyone ever expected.

Could the independent contractor lawsuit lead to similar things for wrestling as time marches on? The odds on that won't be clear for years to come. When Flood made his stand, ball players at least *had* a union — even if it wasn't as powerful as it would become. Like those in other sports or entertainment, the performers recognized that they shared concerns, and everyone, both stars and supporting cast, could benefit if they fought for their ideas and principles.

Wrestling has nothing even approaching a union. The outspoken, opinionated, and influential Jesse Ventura made some noises in the 1980s while he was working for Vince, but the idea was pretty handily dismissed. At the time, Bruiser Brody joked that three wrestlers could not even decide where to go for breakfast. At once realistic and cynical, Brody figured it was highly unlikely that an important group of wrestlers would band together with the guts to buck the establishment and form a hard-nosed union to improve working conditions and compensation for anyone else but themselves.

The stars were then (as they are now) too afraid of losing their lucrative deals in a union containing lesser attractions. Worse yet, wrestling's entire stable of performers is, down deep, insecure, each one knowing that his position, whatever he may be, is totally reliant on decisions the owner makes, and not necessarily on what he can do in the ring. There are no batting averages in wrestling . . . although who is responsible for drawing a big house might be in question.

Consider this. If wrestlers are not independent contractors, but rather employees, then a wrestling promotion would be obligated to pay Social Security taxes and even perhaps purchase some type of health insurance. This would cost WWE more money. A *lot* more.

There is something else to consider, however. If wrestlers were to become employees, they would be assets — just as baseball players are to their teams, racehorses are to their owners, and trucks are to moving companies. Baseball and other sports not only depreciate the value of the contracts of their players, but they can also write off what the teams pay in benefits. Business depreciates equipment.

Would the tax advantages of having wrestlers considered employees actually balance out the financial edge of having wrestlers as independent contractors? Could it be, to some extent, a wash, when it comes to dollars and cents? If so, why would WWE fight so tenaciously?

Surely the boss wants to take care of his people, to protect his assets.

Again, the real issue is about control. If in fact wrestlers are employees, the obvious next step is a collective bargaining agreement and some sort of union. Times and conditions have changed. The independence of yesterday is not the independence of today, where options for earning a living are so severely limited.

Once the camel has his nose inside the tent, the tail is sure to follow. Employees lead to unions, collective bargaining agreements, and negotiated benefits like per diems for food and lodging on the road, health insurance, and retirement packages. The method of compensation and percentage given for royalties would become bargaining points. Curt Flood's battle did not obliterate the reserve clause, but it changed both that proviso and the entire playing field to the benefit of the performers as the union and players became powerful. Likewise, the control WWE enjoys now would be lessened.

Furthermore, Vince would logically not want to be responsible for the long-term care of employees who were only working for a few years. Yet the injuries from performing in the ring or using whatever enhancements a performer believed to be necessary for his employment (another potential minefield) could continue to plague the wrestler long after his boots were packed away. What about pre-existing conditions if a labor pact were forged five years from now? Who would be responsible?

The control and financial issues are a hornet's nest, but one with which the parties must cope for the health of everyone.

The time for wrestlers to truly take care of themselves may not yet have come. Unfortunately, far too many are as hooked as the fans on the illusion of who they are. How much education and experience do those who enter wrestling today really have? What other marketable skills can they fall back on if injuries — or for that matter politics or lack of charisma — end their careers abruptly? Do they really understand that for all the hoopla, wrestling is a business and, for them, a way to earn a living?

Forgetting that wrestlers are human beings is way too easy, what with all the glitter and grandeur. But every wrestler has to go home sometime. He has to buy food at the grocery store, stop at the pharmacy, get gas in the car, and pay the electric bill. A wrestler worries about his children's grades and the fading health of his parents. A wrestler is just like your next-door neighbor — a neighbor who happens to be involved in a spectacular profession. He's a person, not a robot. Health, retirement, home, and — yes — happiness matter to him and those he loves. After a moment in the sun, life continues.

Would a wrestling union protect the sport's working man, its bread and butter, as well as the headliners? Would such an entity benefit the business as well? A sports union like this, unlike those representing other professions, does not specify how much each worker is paid. An organization of this type recognizes where its field is unique and seeks to define basic safeties and guarantees while leaving room for individual negotiation as well.

A change in the relation between wrestler and employer will require strong, smart, and motivated people providing extra effort, organization, and courage for all the pieces to fit together. It requires something like the Levy lawsuit, or a similar effort — or maybe a few brave souls who recognize the value in fighting to protect their futures may light the fuse. It all depends on the motivation and sophistication of those who earn their living in the squared circle.

Some fans probably worry, wondering whether a union would change wrestling as we know it.

Honestly? Wrestling has *already* changed in the ring. The business of wrestling has also transformed from many smaller wrestling promotions to a mammoth marketing conglomerate that admits to promoting wrestling only when it serves company purposes. The next logical step in the evolution deals with the talent, whether employees or independent contractors. Luckily, enough basics of performing have somehow survived so that the spectacle itself, in whatever form, continues to entertain.

Vince McMahon, like other captains of industry, did not reach his position by accident. He is intelligent enough to adjust and prosper if he understands the challenges and the changes he faces. The strength of labor in professional sports and entertainment hardly ended those businesses. To the contrary, the popularity and the revenue generated for both owner and performer are now bigger than they ever were. Wrestling today wishes that were true for it, too.

Did superstars get hurt in the transition? Well, check the incomes for Alex Rodriguez, Peyton Manning, LeBron James, George Clooney, and Julia Roberts. The Triple Hs, Cenas, Batistas, Hogans, Austins, and Flairs of the world can sleep safely at night no matter what happens. Of course, Triple H, being the son-in-law of the owner, likely sleeps well anyway . . .

Wrestling lore has always colorfully related the legends, tales, gossip, and even the professional reality of a controversial marriage of business, sport, and athletics. Fact or fiction, accurate assessment or exaggeration — what's the percentage in each account?

The era of the fiercely independent wrestler and businessman, while a bit romanticized and painted perhaps with a touch of fantasy over time, has essentially faded away. Once, though, the lore was pretty much true.

That was then. This is now.

Today, the realities of a changing business have rudely interrupted. How independent is independent? The question remains.

CHAPTER SIX

EVERYONE WORKS

To be successful in professional wrestling, it is absolutely necessary to *work*. This work is not the kind of toil that the general public does to earn a living, though there is plenty of that, too. When it comes to the uncommon reality of wrestling, the word *work* has a different connotation.

Working, here, means getting people to believe or to do something, by hook or by crook. The *work* is supposed to be invisible, at least to the public. (Come to think of it, that's probably true in advertising and politics as well.) In wrestling, promoters work the talent. The talent works the promoters, or tries to. The television shows work the viewers. The company works the facts. Everyone works the fans. Wrestlers work other wrestlers. Sadly, wrestlers even work themselves. So do promoters, believe it or not. What happens inside and around the squared circle is, ultimately, a work, although perhaps of a different nature.

Obscure the truth. Utilize facts imaginatively. Disguise motives. Shade the discussion. Tell someone what he wants to hear until he does what you want him to do. Tell yourself what you want to hear until you actually believe it. When the stakes are high enough, lie. Convince and persuade, divide and conquer.

Steve Winwood might as well have been describing wrestling in "While You See a Chance Take It." Listen to it sometime. He talks about how the "road" and a "sad old dream" exact a price. Even more to the point, he explains that there's a time when you no longer even believe yourself, and therefore, finally, cannot be fooled.

Doesn't that sound like wrestling? The constant tension of

dealing with *work* can do that to anyone. Broken promises. False hopes. Failed dreams. Looking for a favor and saying what it takes to get that favor. The guarantees are timeless, and usually worthless. Over the years, what did they sound like?

"The big money is right around the corner." "Hey, kid, you got what it takes. I like your look. We're gonna put our eggs in your basket after this other program ends." "Do this favor tonight, and we'll give you a really big push starting next month."

How about: "This house wasn't as good as we expected, but business is picking up. You'll do better next show." "Live with this guarantee now, because the big money is coming soon." "I got the old man's ear in St. Louis. I'll get you booked there." "Gagne's known me for years. I'll talk to him for you." "You got the stuff for Madison Square Garden. New York listens to me; I'll get you a shot."

And the real favorite, told to easily more than half of the wrestlers who ever laced up the boots: "I've got pull with the Board of Directors. I'll put your name up to be the champion. You'd be a perfect champion!"

That was and is only the tip of the iceberg when promoters and bookers work their own talent, whether simply to motivate, or to get someone to work cheaper than he wanted, or to do a job when he hesitated. No wonder cynicism sets in if the talent pays attention, because in most cases a realistic assessment should warn them that the championship run or the main event at MSG are not in the cards.

Ego, though, is a hungry impulse that most manipulators learn to feed early. The fantasies of which guys convince themselves can be even more hurtful in the long run. More often than not, the wrestlers believe or, perhaps worse, even persuade themselves of their own greatness. Winwood got it right when he cautioned against believing your own fictions.

And today? Well, the words may be different, but the content is the same. New twists for an old game. For instance, substitute *WrestleMania* for Madison Square Garden. Replace the old man in St. Louis with Vince . . . or Stephanie. Insert HHH for Gagne. Instead of "You got what it takes, I like your look," the line now is "We have a perfect character for you to express yourself."

The financial and booking rationalizations are likely very similar. Championships of various sorts get handed around like attendance prizes. "You've got a spot with us forever. We're family." (I actually was told that by Vince himself in 1984; "forever" ended in 1993. I later discovered that more than a few others had heard the same pitch — with the same result.)

Of course, here is the modern pitch. "We're a gigantic entertainment machine. You have the qualities to be an actor, to be a *movie star*, not just a wrestler! You're an entertainer!" Somehow ignored in all this propaganda is the hard fact that becoming Brad Pitt or George Clooney is about as likely as becoming Bruno Sammartino or Ric Flair. Does John Cena actually fit into either classification?

Why is everyone working everyone else? To make money, to deal with the politics, to look good, to have influence, to get a reputation, to get what they want.

Why is everyone working himself? Simple — because each person wants it so damn bad; he wants to believe so much. It takes a toll on anyone with even a modicum of intelligence and sensitivity.

Pretty soon, distinguishing between work and shoot, fact and fiction, can become perplexing, because every little word or gesture comes with a motive. The work becomes reality in order for any individual to have success.

Yet there is a special time within the work, a different and unique category of working that moves into the potentially magical area of performance.

The most pure moment of working is what happens in front of the fans when the bell sounds and the performers begin their intricate dance of combat, squaring off for a rapt audience. The key is that all involved have the same goal. Nobody is trying to get something from someone else. The wrestlers want to create an exciting reality for the fans to enjoy, just as the fans want the wrestlers to provide escapism with a special thrill not available elsewhere.

If this work fails, everything else disintegrates. Even the distortions, exaggerations, or flat-out lies mean nothing if the work of the performers fails to capture the imagination and hearts of an

audience, exactly the way a movie or play flops if a group of spectators cannot be drawn into a story.

Most wrestlers would probably define a great worker in the ring
as one who is capable of executing many things athletically, is ver-
satile, can make the customers believe in the match taking place,
and — importantly — will not injure his rival. Unfortunately, that
type of performer does not always prove to be the guy who can put
asses in seats and make money for everyone involved in the business. However, all those characteristics are a critical part of the
formula for success and add to the credibility of the product. If the
terrific worker, the truly talented hand, can also draw bucks — all
the better.

Trying not to harm an opponent while making a battle look real
is not nearly as easy it sounds. It is one thing to be stiff, laying in
blows that actually do hurt because they look more real, quite
another to be dangerous. Those who aren't trusted don't last. Some
performers work light as a feather, or loose, where the most horrific
blow is nothing but a gentle breeze a hair away from the recipient.
A few wrestlers, yes, do work stiff, believing that a certain amount
of punishment is necessary for the good of the performance. And
then there are "crowbars," men with all the flexibility and dexterity
of a steel girder.

Most good workers fall somewhere between the light and the
stiff. Once upon a time, unlike today, top hands also had to know
how to take care of themselves. Along the line, the moment was
bound to come when a wrestler would be tested inside the ring,
when he had to be tough and stand up for himself.

Supremely talented performers, like Dick Murdoch, move back
and forth with ease. They can work with a broomstick, as the old
wrestling saying goes, and make it entertaining. (Lou Thesz
claimed that all working took was the willingness of one combatant to make his adversary look better than he was.) Murdoch's
punches were renowned for looking absolutely real, and that's
because they often were. When ABC Television produced an
"exposé" in the mid-1980s, it filmed a tag bout pitting Murdoch and
Adrian Adonis against Jack and Jerry Brisco. At one point, produc-

ers slowed down the action to demonstrate how "fake" one of Murdoch's punches was. The problem for ABC was that Murdoch really nailed Jack with the shot. To the day he died, Murdoch bragged about "potatoing" Jack Brisco on national TV.

An example of someone who fell in a category somewhere between stiff and crowbar, and yet who was warily trusted, is Big John Studd. A decent, amiable, but limited in-ring performer, he had a reputation for being difficult to work with. Ted DiBiase explained, "John never realized how strong he was. He hurt you when he just touched you."

Studd was at his best with certain types of opponents. A huge, natural heel, "Big John" was a perfect foe for the likes of Hulk Hogan, Andre the Giant, and Fritz Von Erich on one hand, or against someone like DiBiase or Pat O'Connor on the other. Against men of similar statures, his matches would be narrow in scope, but they would snare audiences as two bulls butted heads. Against a DiBiase, however, his opponent's in-ring skills made for a different kind of bout. The work was seldom smooth, but usually quite believable.

The bottom line remains, however, in the right *context*, could Studd draw? Yes he could, to an extent. Was he a good worker by strict definition of the term? Well, with all the respect in the world for an old friend, no.

By the same token, Hulk Hogan was not a great worker either, using the standards set by men like Buddy Rogers, Lou Thesz, Terry Funk, Nick Bockwinkel, or dozens, if not hundreds, of lesser-known prelim guys. Hogan did, however, know exactly what worked *for him*. He never hurt anyone, he could be trusted, and superb workers, like Curt Hennig, became human bump machines for him. His genius lay in the way he would make a crowd react. Plus, Hulk drew money — gigantic, unbelievable money. Workers lined up, either to be his opponent, or to be on a card headlined by him. Everybody made bigger deposits at the bank because of him — and that makes him one of the greatest, period.

At the highest levels, being a good worker encompasses more

than safely executing a lot of solid wrestling and brawling, believable spots, or neat maneuvers. Working successfully means emotionally connecting with the fans, which is much more than just having big muscles, colorful attire, and taking inventive bumps while the crowd watches appreciatively but without serious empathy.

Working has to include getting the character over with as many people as possible. The sad fact is that, in the history of wrestling, there are numerous excellent workers, athletically and intelligently gifted performers, who could not draw flies. Respected and appreciated by their peers and most promoters, they are the spectacle's glue. Solid workers fill out cards and provide good entertainment. On their own, unfortunately, they do not sell tickets. Further, if a promotion does not make enough money, a lot of good workers will be looking for jobs at the convenience mart. Today, if this type of performer cannot fit into a low-level gimmick, he gets squeezed out of the business.

The complete package, naturally, is the performer who can do lots of moves in an exciting fashion, make the audience believe in him and his struggle, and be gold at the box office. *Smooth*, however, is not always the best answer. Rough edges, mixed with personality and spirit, can be more believable and exciting. The likes of Cowboy Bill Watts and Dick the Bruiser were not slick, but they had an innate ability to get over with the crowd, to incite passion. And they drew big money.

Accomplished workers come in different packages, and when a hand becomes special, he has accomplished something exceptional. He can convince even the most cynical onlooker to buy into the fantasy.

Obviously, that great worker has mastered an encyclopedia's worth of skill and psychology. In the annals of the squared circle, that fact has never changed, whether the name is Strangler Lewis or C.M. Punk (not to say that Punk or anyone else on the WWE roster is a worker in Lewis' category). Even today, it takes a lot more than a monumental bump, or a series of high spots, to establish fan loyalty across broad segments of society.

Gymnastics exhibitions do not make for greatness, nor does

stunt fighting, not even close.

Why release a hold that has someone trapped, screaming in pain, and maybe ready to concede? After smashing an opponent with a tremendous move, why are both participants up and at each other with barely a breath? Hooking a leg and putting weight onto a foe's hips, while leaving his shoulders uncovered, doesn't do much for the credibility or the reality of the action: even the greenest neophyte sees that a pin isn't possible. How embarrassingly sloppy.

The old school still has something of value for today's wrestler because the goal hasn't changed a bit. Whether it's called professional wrestling or "sports entertainment," the dang thing looks pretty much the same. (Save for the pyrotechnics, which still cannot disguise a crummy worker.) Two guys in colorful tights with a lot of muscle lock horns in a ballet of direct conflict inside a squared circle surrounded by three ropes or cables wrapped in rubber.

Today the workers often fly through the air before their bodies go "splat!" Sometimes they land on ladders. Sometimes they fly off ladders. Or they crash into tables and steel steps. This generation's grapplers take lots of big bumps. Even so, the pendulum swings — the bump-bump-bigger bump era peaked a few years back, when hardcore wrestling was more in fashion. A growing catalog of nasty injuries, however, led to some things being dialed back, at least insofar as WWE is concerned. More than enough physical jeopardy, however, remains. Though a work, wrestling has always been dangerous.

Crusty "old school" guru Gene Kiniski, who held the National Wrestling Alliance crown when "titles meant something" (ahem), growled his advice to rapt youngsters for years: "The body can only take so many bumps before it wears out." A cardiac wonder who at age 50 still looked like he could run through a brick wall, Nasty Gene would take a bump, willingly, but it doggone well better lead to or be a penultimate part of a big-money main event. He understood that merely working meant taking plenty of lesser bumps (is a hard body slam really a lesser bump?), and that the realities of the work took a cumulative toll — even before you figured in those occasionally horrifying spills big matches demanded.

Esteemed sportswriter Kit Bauman once joined his friend Lou Thesz at a luncheon honoring many of the legends in the early 1990s. Suddenly Lou leaned over and told Kit, "There's probably half a million dollars' worth of artificial hips and knees in this room." Bauman was amazed at the price all of those bumps and beatings had extracted from performers from two decades earlier. Think what a comparable gathering of workers from today might be like 30 years from now?

Without question, pro wrestling was and is just as dangerous, and produces every bit as many injuries, as mixed martial arts or so-called shoot-fighting. Factors adding to the hurt in wrestling are the huge number of bouts, and the general lack of treatment and little time for recovery and rest. In addition, many a football player who also wrestled claimed that the action in the ring did just as much damage, if not more, to the body as did the action on the gridiron. The bumps of all kinds add up.

What is a bump? It really can be as simple as a basic back body drop or as spectacular as a dive onto a foe (or an empty space if he moves) from the top rope. A bump can be a leap from the top turnbuckle onto the hard floor (hopefully with an opponent there to break the fall), or crashing onto and through a table. Up into the air, down onto a surface. Body slam. Power slam. Smash into the turnbuckles. Miss a giant splash. Every landing is potentially dangerous and career threatening.

Tragically, Japanese superstar Mitsuhara Misawa became a graphic example of how perilous basic bumps can be in June 2009. A fabulous worker, Misawa died in the ring after receiving a Greco-Roman back body drop, originally made famous by Lou Thesz but now used in various forms by many performers. The Japanese style in which Misawa excelled, though, has always been very stiff. In this case, the bump damaged Misawa's spinal cord, and he died just minutes after being dropped.

Even after something like this, some smart guys will smirk and say, "Well, they know how to fall." Yes, that would be a wise skill to acquire in a profession where one is knocked down on a regular basis. But the old school masters and today's wrestlers alike would agree: *Learn how to fall? What a joke.* Don't see what's funny? Okay, stand up in the middle of the living room. Jump up and fall, backwards, flat onto the floor. Now, repeat that six times. Every day. For years.

Are you laughing yet? No?

Run into walls, full speed, shoulder-first. Give clotheslines to trees. For good measure, jump up on the coffee table and dive, head first, onto the floor.

Knowing how to fall may help, but the impact still hurts. Like the devil! As wrestler Jerry Lynn once said: "You can't fake gravity."

Go ahead, learn how to fall. Try it at home and see how much the knowledge helps with that aching spine, hip, and elbow.

And that's not even taking into account a metal chair shot to the back or — thud! — to the top of the skull.

No, not all bumps are created equal. The more mind-boggling the bump, the more likely that highly sought-after casual fan can be hooked into buying the event, at least so one theory goes. To the rookie trying to make his name, that gravity-defying feat might be the ticket to the big time.

What some observers fail to realize is that the wrestler *getting* the bumps — the worker who breaks a fall by deflecting or catching an airborne 230-pounder — is more than earning his keep. When a move like Red Bastien's flying head scissors was in favor, somebody had to catch Bastien and then flip to take a bump. More typically, the opponent has to hoist the bump-taker up into the air, and even if he receives a reasonable amount of help, that's serious weight being lifted — which is no walk in the park. More than one old school grappler became fed up when a foe repeatedly called for bumps that needed assistance. The result? In aggravation, he might just drop his opponent on his head. Or move out of the way. "You called for it, now give me some help" was the name of the game.

"Save those goddamn bumps for when they matter, kid. Save 'em for when you can make the big money," Kiniski would say. Legends like Bruno Sammartino, Terry Funk, Verne Gagne, and even Vince's longtime consultant Pat Patterson, surely offered similar guidance to wide-eyed hopefuls.

Even the supposed wonders of steroids couldn't change the realities of human physiology or the laws of physics; in fact, with the tightening of joints and bloating of muscles, steroids probably increased the number of injuries and shortened careers. Working off a hold can be a rest break, or it can require real effort in order to be effectively sold. The bumps necessary to the story become much more meaningful — and perhaps less hazardous — when they're properly sold. Today's more ridiculous moves have turned some wrestlers into stunt men, and often the bumps are either pre-taped or gimmicked to provide the performer with extra protection.

Despite recent changes, WWE's product still leans toward the bump-bump-high spot style. What the wrestler/entertainer of today needs to ask himself is when, exactly, do those bumps matter?

Mick Foley by all reports was never a steroid guy. He was, however, seemingly addicted to over-the-top physical risk, willing, for example, to fall from the top of a cage as high as two basketball hoops. (Now that's a high spot!) Foley was also crippled into semi-retirement at an age when the likes of Kiniski or Ric Flair were starting to cash their biggest checks.

The fact is that Foley probably *had* to take those bumps because he was wrestling in the body-beautiful era, competing for the attention of Vince McMahon. He never would have gotten a second look if he hadn't. But not even McMahon and his advisors could ignore a deranged bump-taker who risked everything for the good of an exciting match.

Those bumps gave Foley the opportunity to cash in on his dream. Therein lies the dilemma for today's upcoming crew. Maybe John Cena can afford to be cautious about how often he throws his sharply defined physique into the air for a crash landing on a table. Perhaps Shawn Michaels can now afford to be stingy, as can Vince's son-in-law Triple H. The Undertaker is able to be pretty picky after the years he's put in. Gasp-inducing bumps, for this elite and tiny percentage of workers, can be targeted to pay-per-views and major television angles.

What about Shelton Benjamin, who has deserved a serious, legitimate push for some time? Unable to get over the mountain-like hump for higher billing no matter what role he's given, would a series of incredible bumps garner approval from the powerbrokers behind the scenes?

And then there's Mr. Kennedy, one golden "push" aborted by his uncannily ignorant public comments following the tragic death of Chris Benoit. Does he have that one gravity-defying bump in him, and would that put him back into favor? Or has WWE really lost confidence in his ability to perform safely?

Consider guys like Shawn Spears, who have been lost in developmental limbo. How much risk should they take, how far do they go to impress those who decide who gets the almighty push on the big stage? And that doesn't even recognize all of the anonymous hopefuls dreaming and taking scary chances.

The pressure, the possibility, the prize, and its price. That's working, too. And so, steroids and what they do to make the body beautiful become desirable. It's also why that breath-taking bump, perhaps watched by (oh my goodness) Vince McMahon himself, may have become what Kiniski called the moment that matters in a young wrestler's rite of passage.

For young unknowns who dream of glory, crazy bumps can be staged and filmed and sent to WWE talent coordinator John Laurinaitis. Really, though, is that enough to actually catch his eye? After all, he probably gets only 50 videos like this *every week*.

On independent cards around the nation, in front of crowds that often never top one hundred fans, more than a handful of hopefuls who have less-than-zero chance of ever stepping into a WWE ring perform spine-jolting, brain-rattling bumps to make someone — *anyone* — pay attention. If they only comprehended what "working" was, these dreamers would realize the art is not just taking bumps. Working is not high spot after high spot wrapped around swollen muscles. For that matter, high spots don't necessarily mean taking bumps; just as often they're created by unusually thrilling moments of ring psychology. Somehow, at some point, high spots and bumps became almost synonymous. It got so bad that the bumps became almost trivial, doing little but to shorten the careers of those getting whomped.

That's wrestling's reality: the bump and the high spot are part of the course curriculum. But all the bumps in the world won't amount to anything unless the worker can translate his personality into something the fans, and the promoter, care about. The best acrobat, high-flier, or bump-taker is not necessarily the best worker, despite how some newer fans have been educated, unknowing and never exposed to the many methods smart workers can use to get heat.

Edouard Carpentier had one of the finest nicknames of all time — the Fabulous Flying Frenchman. (Love that alliteration!) Yes, Carpentier could fly — and he could work. Harley Race described Carpentier as a "testy devil" who knew what clicked for him and exactly the moment he wanted to do those high spots.

When Edouard made his comeback after heat had been built, when he battered his shocked heel rival into a corner, and then scaled the top rope, he'd punch his enemy in the head then launch a picture-perfect back flip high into the air, stick the landing cold, nail his befuddled foe with a drop kick, and then gain the victory with a forward flip, "the steamroller," spinning his athletic body right into his victim's gut.

Now that is one long, long sentence, but it accurately describes the climax of many of Carpentier's best matches. It also explains why, when Edouard flew, it mattered: because he executed the moves at the *right* time, to achieve the right result. The back flip into the drop kick into the steamroller became a signature series of moves that electrified fans. And yes, give some credit to the recipients, who sold the steamroller as though they had been run over by a truck.

When, in the most important battles, against perhaps Buddy Rogers or Gene Kiniski or Dick the Bruiser, the heel escaped and Carpentier crashed flat onto his back, the stunning pin of the babyface made sense. Was it a "big" bump, like crashing off the top of a cage or through a gimmicked table? Maybe not. Regardless, it was executed so well that it was "big" enough to do the job. To the audience — and this is all that counts — it was a bump of earthquake-like proportions because of the match's psychology, because of the story being told.

There are always plenty of guys who can fly, who "go up and down" as some of the more cynical matmen often say. They don't, however, necessarily reach the top of a bill just because they fly. It is something in the spectacular high-flyer's demeanor (which Carpentier had), and perhaps more in how he uses his talent (which, again, Carpentier did so well). The Flying Frenchman picked his spots to make each aerial move meaningful. If the flying was all he did, it would matter little. Understanding this also probably prolonged his career, keeping his body from breaking down. Edouard could engage in mat wrestling, sold a heel's punishment well, had believable and noteworthy facial expressions, made some comebacks with no aerial moves whatsoever, and saved the climax for the climax.

Today, midcard guys who can fly can be important role players on a show, just as the power forward beside Kobe Bryant, or the number seven hitter in a baseball lineup, can be invaluable to a team's overall performance. The key, now as always, is keeping things under control so toes are not getting stepped on. Moves headliners rely on shouldn't be performed before main events. When they are, the danger is that the crowd loses some steam or becomes desensitized. A promoter never wants his audience grumbling, "Didn't we see that a couple matches ago?"

Working encompasses everything; working is what gets the fans into the match and makes them cheer, jeer, hoot, and holler. Every gesture and facial expression is important, as those visible emotions reflect the physical nature of what is going on. Experts like Terry and Dory Funk, Jack Brisco, Nick Bockwinkel, and Harley Race decry the simplistic idea that working is just a choreographed series of fast-paced bumps, performed sequentially no matter how the crowd reacts. High spot, high spot, high spot . . .

Their judgment can be harsh, for while they recognize that a quicker speed is fine, so few perform it well. Men like these are not alone in cringing when they see two wrestlers forget a spot and the entire match comes to an embarrassing standstill.

We missed a spot! What do we do?

(What gallops through the confused performers' minds, as they stand there like deer caught in the headlights?)

Well, whatever happened to improvisation? The ability to ad lib is crucial, because the best-laid plans, for finishes and for entire matches, can fall apart.

"Wild Bill" Longson, likely the first true heel to be recognized as the world champion, way back in the 1940s, explained working to this then-young writer long after Longson had retired from the ring. "Working is like sex, just like sex," he grinned, puffing on his cigar. "First, you get them comfortable. Then you take them up a little, but then take them down. Then you take them a little higher. And a little higher. And relax a little. Then take them a whole lot higher. And a little more. Then hesitate and wait a bit. Then take them really high and, if you feel it . . . *Bang!* You take them home . . . Now that's working, and that's sex, too."

Working is every little thing that draws a fan's attention, that gets them involved in the action. A facial expression. A wrestling move. A bump. Something unique. The workers' reaction to the audience, and the feedback the workers get from the audience — what a high spot! The intensity of the combatants. Getting heat. Slow it down, speed it up. Violence. A favorite fighting back from underneath. Timing. The comeback cut off. Brutality. More heat. More intensity. Telling the story. A heel gloating and a babyface grimacing. The fans' passions building — they want the comeback, bad. Tease it. Pace quickening to the comeback. Stopped again. This is it — the end! No, it's not. Fans stomping, clapping, *wanting.* Be patient. Babyface struggling, hurting, selling. The comeback for real. This is it! False finish. Another great bump. False finish. A sensational move backfires. Another false finish. They're screaming. And finally, finally, success or failure. Somebody wins, somebody loses. It doesn't really matter, because both have made lasting impressions.

And an audience is in the palms of the hands of the performers.

Make no mistake about it, being on top in WWE demands the same skills Vince Sr. or Sam Muchnick demanded: performers must be able to execute time-tested basics, and the best of the best — even if not as many as there once were — can do it in their sleep.

As always, this makes things tricky for those wrestling in supporting bouts. They want to shine, to earn their way to the top, but the show's structure does not allow them as much time and space to tell their tale. Some prelim guys respond by trying to "steal the show" with outlandish bumps. Occasionally, a booker actually urges undercard talent to try to outshine the stars, but ultimately this only hurts the show, even though the purpose may have been to motivate the stars on top to do more.

At the highest levels, it's a huge mistake. Those who have been around and understand the craft can almost always spot potential high-level material. Doing a bunch of acrobatic tricks will not change what the promoter or booker wants in a top guy. For the new and hungry, it's not necessarily a good idea to show off all of your moves in a five-minute segment. Being in the right place, communicating, demonstrating good timing, and responding energetically to the crowd and the situation will often do more to further a career than a spinning, upside down, backward plancha.

It cannot be stressed enough; the main event is what draws the money. The top guys need the space to do what they do best. Believe it or not, there are always opportunities for underneath talent to demonstrate the skills and charisma that lead to featured spots. There is not a promoter in the universe who is going to ignore someone he thinks can make him a serious profit.

Naturally, errors are made. Politics get played. But time, perseverance, and true talent more often than not shine through. A lot of overnight sensations have paid plenty of dues — look no farther than wwe's Jeff Hardy. The key is taking the time to learn and grow, and walking through the door when it's finally opened. No wonder certain personalities become single-minded, relentless, driven, often to the point of obsession, whether or not that is psychologically healthy.

A few years back, Bruiser Brody and I put together a couple matches for a show by a fledgling independent promoter in the St. Louis area. Brody was facing arch-rival Abdullah the Butcher —

clearly a different type of duel than Thesz versus O'Connor, Gagne versus Billy Robinson, or Dory Jr. versus Brisco. As a semi-final, we lined up Spike Huber against Steve Regal, knowing the two solid pros would provide a good, athletic, energetic up-and-down 20-minute wrestling match. It would be entertaining, and completely different from what Abdullah and Brody would do.

Unfortunately, the local promoter filled the undercard with well-meaning but mistakenly motivated troops who figured they would demonstrate to Brody just how hard-core and exciting they could be — hoping perhaps that Brody might recommend them to a Japanese promotion. With Brody beside me, I peeked out to see the curtain-raiser from the dressing room. We both were taken aback at the sight of the two young grapplers battling in the crowd, ramming each other into the ring post, and whacking each other with chairs. They weren't even managing to do it terribly well, it should be added.

If that wasn't bad enough, a minute or two after the opening bell of the second match, the heel launched a fireball and set the poor babyface's arm on fire!

Brody was irate. He told me to find the promoter while Brody brought Spike up to speed.

In no uncertain terms, Brody told the promoter, "Cut out this crazy bullshit or we're walking!" Shaken, the promoter said they were just putting on a show and asked what was wrong. Working, as only Brody could, he leaned into the promoter's face and snarled, "Because we're not going to let a bunch of goofs like that do shit using chairs and fireballs without Abby and me topping them. You won't like what we have to do! So get everybody on this goddamn card under control or we're gone."

Stunned, the promoter looked to me for support. He got none. I agreed completely with Brody.

Of course, the rookie promoter knew losing the only recognizable names on his lineup would lead to a mini-riot at best. He had his boys tone things down and stay in the ring, which sadly made them look even worse. They had tried shortcuts, using cheap methods for getting heat — chairs, fireballs. At least nobody crawled up a scaffold, crashed through a table, and wound up with a broken neck because he didn't know what he was doing. For the rest of the card, they had to actually work. Or try to. In most cases, it wasn't pretty.

From the audience's standpoint, though, everything came out fine. The thousand spectators jammed into the small gym recognized that Regal, Huber, Brody and Abdullah shouldn't be compared with the no-names. The undercard guys were appreciated for working hard and giving maximum effort. Spike and Steve put on a sharp, quick-paced battle, and the crowd was both happy and primed for the main event collision.

With their own match, Brody and Abby, naturally, made a point to the poor promoter, even though the opening bouts had been over for more than an hour and a half. They waged a knock-down, drag-out, back-alley war — blood flying everywhere — that went into the seats, up and down the bleachers, and onto a stage. There was no other performer on the lineup who could do what they did with such reality and intensity. The same was equally effective, in a different sense, for Huber and Regal. Everyone in attendance knew who the stars were, but little did they know what had happened behind the scenes to make the card more enjoyable.

Didn't the up-and-comers have the right to do whatever they could to catch a star's eye? No, actually, they did not. The show comes first. If they could not command attention by correctly executing the fundamentals, any dreams they had of making the big time were delusional.

Let's talk about blood. For years, wrestling people would say, "red means green," meaning blood draws bucks. And that's generally true — until it's done too often, or at the wrong time. Too many uneducated indie wrestlers can't wait to slash a razor blade across their foreheads to "get color." At times, major organizations overdid bleeding, most notably Jim Crockett Promotions during the Dusty Rhodes booking-era of the middle and late 1980s. When better than half the bouts on the lineup end up with wrestlers covered in blood, you actually run the risk of driving away a segment of the fan-base. When everyone is wearing a "crimson mask," what's left? Dismemberment? Machine-gun fire?

Blood, like bumps, can be overused, to the point where customers become immune or disgusted. While Vince has gone through periods where performers headed for a main-event showdown were opening each other up on a weekly basis, in the summer of 2008 he told investors that WWE would avoid using blood — except when necessary. Of course, things happen, and the hard way — a resounding punch to the head — can bring the red stuff. But Vince, apparently, has come around to the Muchnick way of thinking: bleeding, just for the sake of blood, makes no sense at all.

History demonstrates that promotions that saw big upswings in attendance due to the introduction of blood, also saw a bigger drop in paid receipts when bleeding was overdone. But when David Von Erich used his father's Iron Claw for the first time to win a non-title collision with NWA Champion Harley Race in St. Louis, the buckets of blood that Harley donated helped make David and his claw headline news throughout the wrestling universe. Why? Because it seldom happened in St. Louis, except when Muchnick figured the time was right for red to mean green.

Has the "work" changed over the decades? Of course, it has. On the surface, the pace today is much faster, and fans have been educated to expect more bumps. Nonetheless, the basics, the essentials are the same. Success is measured in viewer response. Easy crowd or hard crowd, the goal of the wrestlers is to make the devotees of this spectacle let go of their inhibitions and react as loudly as they can.

Why has mixed martial arts become so successful? One reason is certainly the ebb and flow of real competition. Once in a while, it actually can verge on boring, although promoters hope that a more educated audience will accept and appreciate solid groundwork. Therefore, when the big moments inevitably erupt, the big knockouts or submissions, the audience erupts as well.

In the 1960s, oldtimers griped that the in-ring product was different and poorer from what Strangler Lewis and Jim Londos did in the 1930s. In the 1980s, the experienced hands complained that the product was vastly changed and worse than it was in the 1960s and 1970s. And in 2009, the headliners from the '80s and '90s criticize the current style. When 2020 dawns, current main-event regulars will probably lament how much the work has slipped since their day in the sun.

It's the nature of the beast to prefer the style in which you excelled. Yet time and again events prove that there are fundamentals indispensable to capturing the public's imagination.

Audiences have changed because of the way they've been educated; television's fast cuts and short segments, in particular, have shaped expectations. Of course, those long and tedious promos can test many viewers' attention spans, even if done sparingly by the miniscule few who are capable. Wrestling moves have evolved too, though almost everything has deep roots in the mat history. The so-called rest hold, which was still "working," especially if the trapped grappler played up his agony, has turned into rest punching. Today, performers no longer rely on a move or hold — instead they just wail away at each other with soft-looking blows or even kicks. In fact, what percentage of modern WWE duels start with a kick to the stomach? Maybe that's the new version of the collar-and-elbow tieup.

The dreaded "rest holds" don't have to be dull if executed correctly. The value comes when built into an intelligent context of the battle and sold by all participants from workers to television announcers. Likewise, "rest punching" and cheerleader flip-flops can have some significance within that aforementioned credible context of the duel, provided they are not just random movements for the sake of movement.

Somewhere in the middle exists a common ground with room for the best of *both* philosophies, which would satisfy far more fans from a wider range of backgrounds. Thus, more followers could find something they like and become loyal customers of the phenomenon known as wrestling.

No matter the time period, the crowd needs to take a deep breath and reload emotionally while waiting for more meaningful action. Customers catch on quickly.

Think of the baseball pitcher who has only a great fastball. Blazing away at 100 miles per hour, that's all he throws. For three, four, maybe five innings, the opposing batters have fits. Then, they start catching up. If all that the pitcher has is smoke, but no smart tricks, no curve, no off-speed pitch, soon he's getting shelled by line drives and home runs. Hitters, like wrestling fans, figure it out.

There are dead spots during a baseball game, and incredibly boring moments in football. There are quiet, dull times in an NBA game and down time in hockey. There are passive, reflective moments during both dramatic and action movies. Ballads are worked into rock concerts. Even MMA features slow, strategic engagement. So, is wrestling to be held to a narrow standard of constant high spots for fear that a loud minority, not understanding how drama builds, might start a "boring" chant? Building emotion, occasionally quietly, is always necessary. The idea is to make a worked wrestling match look like a *real* contest so all of the observers can suspend their disbelief.

A rapid-fire sequence of high spots and big bumps becomes meaningless if the recipient never takes time to register or sell any damage. Slowing down allows the customers to absorb the action, and a victim playing up the impact of a bump or attack makes his opponent more credible.

The objective — and it is so important that it bears repeating — will always be the same: get as many people of all ages, races, and incomes as interested as possible. Then encourage those folks, whether crammed together in an arena or watching a pay-per-view intently from their couch, to surrender themselves to the moment and, when the wrestlers go home with the finish, leave them shaking their heads, saying, "Damn, that was fun!" Then the business side is happy as well, because those fans will spend their money again.

The ways of getting there haven't changed as much as some people think. Shakespeare knew a thing or two in the 17th century — and ole Will's stuff still clicks today. Wrestling's no different. The bard had swordplay, humor, violence, and a great climax that tied up loose threads. Doesn't that also describe a good wrestling match, or an outstanding card?

So-called old school shows would build from a solid opener to the pinnacle of the main event. Often there were two major features back-to-back. But the workers in the ring always did what needed to be done to reignite the heat. Johnny Valentine and Harley Race jump to mind immediately, though it applies to any of the major stars of the era.

If Race or Valentine followed another pair of headliners who left fans exhausted after screaming their lungs out, they would likely begin their battle with a big bump, maybe two, and then hook a head or an arm of the opponent. Twist, turn, growl, groan but — and it's an important *but* — give the fans a chance to rest, to come down from the high. Let the folks catch their breath. Wait for them to become restless. Tease that emotion. Then, turn up the dial and try to build to an even bigger climax. At this point, trying to steal the show is acceptable conduct . . . and usually not easy to do.

What WWE and TNA do is a different twist on the same game. The features are split up by what would have previously been considered preliminaries. Hopefully, the performers in those prelim duels don't realize they are being used to give fans a chance to buy popcorn, open the fridge, or go to the bathroom. The wrestlers are working hard, but likely in a losing battle when it comes to making a building really shake.

Same goal: let the audience relax and settle in. Allow them to build up energy for the next big main event. When the studs, the *real* stars, finally come to the squared circle, the fans should be ready to roar. As Stan Hansen once said about his legendary tag team with Bruiser Brody, "We knew where we were going; we just didn't know how we were getting there."

Vince McMahon also knows where he is going and is working the audience to make sure he gets them there when he wants, just like Race, Valentine, and all the rest of those Hall-of-Famers. Vince just does it by manipulating the lineup.

Today's audiences have been educated to be worked by television, the wrestlers, the booking, the finishes, even the atmosphere of wrestling events. A little bump I had with Vince when I began working for the WWF in 1984 demonstrates this. My complaint, partially supported by the drop in attendance that would occur when a rematch involving Hulk Hogan was booked, was that the main events were too short. St. Louis fans grew up with competitive, tight, 15- to 30-minute features. Though "Eye of the Tiger" (Hulk's original theme before "Real American") would thunder during

Hogan's entrance, and again as he posed after a decision had been rendered, he rarely wrestled for more than ten minutes. I complained to Vince that the bell-to-bell action was too short, that there was not time to build anticipation for a return, and that this was hurting attendance figures. Here is the point: I was clocking Hogan's matches from lock up to decision.

Vince countered: "You have to figure the time from Hulk's entry through when he poses afterward as the length of the event." From his standpoint, that meant the match went at least twenty minutes.

I disagreed then, especially when it came to a market like St. Louis. I still think I was correct — back then. Today, Vince is definitely right, because over the years audiences have been educated to see a wrestler's entrance and the post-match frolic as part of the total package. That's what today's fans expect, although they could just as easily be educated otherwise.

As always in wrestling and working, there's another "but." The hottest, funkiest music can blare with the loudest, flashiest fireworks, but if the fans are silent after the hubbub dies down, maybe the wrestler is not over as much as even the producers have been led to believe by the smoke and mirrors. Fooling yourself is pretty easy when you're caught up in the sizzle, too.

For truly big guns, there should be a buzz before the head-to-head action ever begins. It's like an invisible guitar string goosing a live crowd. A million years ago, with not a note of music or a spark of pyrotechnics, that buzz was audible and thrilling at the start of a main event. The buzz is still audible today, or should be, when performers really are getting over.

These days, splashy, loud, staged moments are an integral part of the show. And maybe it's saved some wear and tear on wrestlers — or hidden a lack of talent, in some cases.

Either way, all of this shows that when the chips are down, and it is time to make money, Vince knows how to tell the story. It always warrants repeating. What happens when *WrestleMania* is on the horizon? He puts the right workers in the right situations, minimizes meaningless high spots, maximizes key incidents, and makes absolutely sure that the viewers can grasp what's at stake. While that may mean main eventers take turns laying each other out with their specific finishing moves for a few weeks, at least the premise is established that Triple H's pedigree, Randy Orton's RKO, Batista's bomb, and John Cena's FU/Attitude Adjustment mean a match is about to end.

Vince is selling his story to the public, working the fans, just as the wrestlers have to sell the story of their characters and individual matches.

Another kind of selling might be the most undervalued part of a grappler's repertoire. Knowing when and how to sell — how to make the scene appear real, that a foe's offense is effective and has put the recipient in trouble — can determine whether or not a match works. Once again, selling is an art not easily explained or mastered. Selling also means different things for different wrestlers; it really depends on their style and personality. Many are generous in giving to their opponents; plenty are stingy and give next to nothing worthwhile.

Ric Flair, as both a heel and babyface, spent a lot of time selling, being in jeopardy until it seemed he could take no more. Bruiser Brody, on the other hand, sold damn little . . . until suddenly something happened — then, just by flinching or staggering, being outmaneuvered or even body slammed (once in a great while), he sold being in trouble just as much as the Nature Boy. Both got to the same point in a match, but used different methods of getting there. They understood what worked for them and what was best for their specific characters.

That, of course, is important for every worker. Each has to know his strengths and limitations, what works and what does not. So what if Hulk Hogan could never execute a moonsault? He understood ring management and how to connect with the crowd.

One guy who has never received anywhere near the credit he deserves for his ability to work and sell is Ken Patera. Fans recognized him as an elite athlete — Patera's weight lifting exploits were well known even before he got into the wrestling business. In his prime he snatched almost 400 pounds and was able to clean and press more than 500. Muscled and sleek, he was visually terrific.

Plus there was his attitude. Cocky, sarcastic, and smart, Patera knew, almost instinctively, how to project a classic heel persona. He could pound someone like Bob Backlund, Greg Gagne, or Ted

DiBiase and immediately generate serious heat. When a sensible transition gave the babyface a spark, Patera would sell the come-back in a completely believable manner that culminated in a big pop — whether Patera won or lost — because the story made per-fect sense.

The best workers have been able to achieve the same thing in their own unique way. Understanding themselves and their audi-ence, when fans are at an emotional peak, the finest workers know how to wrap things up. That is what makes legitimate stars.

Thanks to pay-per-views and the strict schedules of television, where everything must fit, no matter what, one instruction book-ers used to give wrestlers is seldom heard now, and it's a shame. Back in the day of the arena show, when there were no rigid time constraints, the booker or promoter would tell the boys, "Go home when it's right." Not at ten minutes, not under twenty minutes, not when the booker stands up and gives some signal — just when it *feels* right. When the performers, in intimate contact with the audi-ence during the height of the magic, know the moment is there.

Finally, one more private and *real* part of the work should be addressed. No fan, no announcer, no promoter — not even the booker — is part of it. It's when the two combatants, face to face in the dressing room, shake hands and say, "Thanks."

Maybe it's not always perfect, maybe there's residual tension or competition, maybe some of the babies in the business don't even understand what it means to shake hands. Or maybe it's one of those nights, after an explosive battle, when every emotion was genuine: however hard the way may have been, the heat was there, and the fans were thrilled.

Two professionals, recognizing their mutual accomplishment: for whatever other work may be going on, for whoever is working whom to whatever end, that handshake congratulates the work that is the most satisfying, for everyone.

CHAPTER SEVEN

BOOKING 101: DOES IT DRAW?

The most important question about booking — the development of plot and motive — is often lost amid the politics and personalities of professional wrestling: *does it draw?*

Perhaps just as important: does it draw *again?* And again? Not *does this or that type of match draw?*, but does business — the wrestling business — continue to draw? Did the sellout set the stage for more big houses? Did what was done to achieve a satisfactory finish leave everyone primed for more? One-hit booking wonders looking to swerve (fool) the fans can do more harm than good, all for the sake of one lonely pop.

Trying to come up with methods of luring customers into purchasing the product is the goal of *any* business, including one as off-the-wall as wrestling. Will spectators, whether casual or hardcore, take money out of their wallets to watch the events that the booker and promoter have decided will be most attractive? Is the planning and thinking short term or long term?

Could anything be more obvious? A wrestling company has to take in more money than it puts out, or good-bye promotion. No matter how many wonderful revenue streams there are, no matter how clever someone thinks a booker is, the only result that makes a difference is how many people pay to see the outcome. Everything else begins, or ends, with that simple consideration.

When enough people purchase an event, it is time for satisfaction and celebration — at least for a while. However, there is always the next show, the next success or failure. Another main event should always be in the works; the next challenger for the champion is always on the horizon. Satisfied buyers are likely to return; frustrated ones do not.

If too few people purchase an event, it is time to figure out what went wrong, but it better be done quickly. Again, that next program always looms, staring a promoter and booker in the face. Redemption, or more failure, is always at hand.

Sounds easy, doesn't it? Like most elements of wrestling, though, nothing is as it appears at first glance. Wrestling people often have an incredible capacity for taking the simplest issues and making them complex.

Make no mistake, not everyone has the ability to spot talent and successfully mix it together. Real foresight and perception are needed to anticipate who will develop into a standout, to grasp what foes work best against each other, to sense which gimmicks will captivate, to understand how television should be utilized, to carefully plan a sequence of matches and — when necessary — angles that fans can buy into. Finally, it takes something special to convince *everyone* involved in the business that this plan is the best for *everyone else* . . .

When egos and aspirations of wrestlers, bookers — even creative committee members — become involved, the process becomes even more difficult. As the wise and cynical Terry Funk always says, "Everyone has an agenda."

Usually the agenda involves a wrestler putting himself into the strongest and most lucrative position, or the booker getting plaudits for being so inventive. The behind-closed-doors juggling gets intense, and the more people that are involved the more confusing it becomes. Wrestlers push ideas that involve themselves. Bookers strain the limits of imagination. The promoter has his own objective.

Before long, power and politics take the spotlight, and the main goal is lost in the shuffle . . .

Does it draw?

Everything else is secondary, or should be.

To keep business prospering, the fact that the booker is building toward something else is no real excuse for excessive referee bumps, interference, or indecisive finishes. Good planning, and having other hot talent ready to step in is paramount. In the best storylines, the best booking, the finish and what happens next are key.

Booking might as well also be called "persuasion." Certainly, as far as making money is concerned, the goal is to persuade fans that they want to see a match — and to see it *now*.

On occasion, a booker also has to persuade his boss, the promoter. Years ago, bookers tried to persuade promoters to try certain new talents or different types of matches. Today's creative teams, similarly, attempt to persuade Vince McMahon to approve specific performers or battles.

It's one thing to plan out a series of matches that lead to a specific end. It is another to get those involved in that ladder of bouts to do their job without complaint. Remember, wrestlers are employees. They are being paid to do a job, even when it includes "doing *the* job" — i.e., losing. Most wrestlers will eventually go along with the program, because that's how they earn their income. It's no different than an auto plant or large financial institution — a fairly high percentage of employees will grump, gripe, and groan . . . but they will do what's required to earn their paycheck. The good bookers, like the good administrators in any business, have the knack of motivating the talent to get the best performance out of them.

Furthermore, the best bookers know how to develop new stars. Of course, that means more than just choosing someone, for political or other reasons, and giving that person a push. The true key is identifying the performer who possesses those intangibles that make a star and providing him the opportunity to *be* a star. All the pushing in the world cannot make a donkey win the Kentucky Derby.

Recognizing who has what it takes is an underappreciated skill. Just as very few performers are capable of being the big money players, not many bookers or promoters are honestly able to spot workers with the qualities necessary for true stardom. On top of which, right or wrong, most of those underneath will complain because they weren't picked for the spot.

But if wrestling is just a work, why on earth would anyone complain? A wrestler is not really being beaten, right? Or is he?

The hard truth is that wrestling is sometimes all too real. The bottom line is money and, guaranteed, unless it's a big main event, the wrestler flat on his back isn't going to make as much money as the guy who gets his arm raised. Someone else decides who wins and who loses, who makes more and who makes less, so someone else is going to be blamed. Especially if the loser believes — as most of them do — that he deserved to win.

Wrestlers at the top of the lineups make substantially more income than the grapplers in the preliminaries. How does a wrestler end up in the feature events? He gets a lot of victories — because the booker and promoter have confidence that he can (a) draw viewers, (b) have a satisfactory match, and (c) make money for the company. "Make money for the company." Repeat that a dozen times.

It is the main event that determines profit or loss. Every booker should get that tattooed to his brain. Main-event stars are the horses that pull the wagon.

Whether a show has one or three features, how those main events are put together and who they utilize determines the size of the crowd or the number of PPV buys. Honestly, expecting three or even four main events to draw — the *WrestleMania* model — is wildly optimistic at the best of times.

Supporting matches have their role. They set the stage. They build up the talent who may or may not some day move into the main event. They add overall entertainment value to a card. But fans — casual followers, in particular — do not purchase tickets or PPVs to see the performers second from the bottom in either WWE or MMA.

Vince McMahon has established WWE as both a touring show and a PPV juggernaut. Except in certain key markets, WWE does not appear often enough to require advertising more than a main event or two — matches which may or may not actually take place. The strength is in the brand. Again and again this is proven by the fact that when injuries put featured performers on the sidelines for lengthy periods, business rarely falters. Because lineups are fluid, defined advertising about who will face whom is unnecessary, and usually minimized. Like the Ice Capades or the Harlem Globetrotters, WWE draws a decent crowd because fans understand, without much advertising, that the stars they see on television will likely be the ones who appear in person. While one of WWE's greatest marketing achievements, this doesn't change one fact: the fans still expect to see the stars.

To put today's schedule in perspective, wrestling's weekly two- to six-hours of television programming have replaced a combination of regular house shows in a promotion's main market and what used to be a one-hour television taping. Today's house shows are yesterday's spot shows. Pay-per-views are the Madison Square Gardens, the Arena/Kiel Auditoriums, the Maple Leaf Gardens, the Omnis, the Reunion Arenas, the St. Paul Civic Centers, the Cow Palaces of today. This is the time to make *serious money*.

For the crucial PPVs, therefore, main events had better have heat or buy rates will sink. Making the supporting bouts attractive by building rivalries is fine, but hardly crucial. If there is a hot angle to be shot, shoot it with main-event talent. Building angle after angle for every match on a show is actually counterproductive. The biggest value in that type of thinking is making preliminary performers feel their role is more important — but doing so may well come at the expense of future main events if some clever angle was already used for talent without serious box office appeal.

Looking back, it's almost ironic that my regular late-night telephone calls with Bruiser Brody and Dave Meltzer in the mid-1980s touched on the idea of introducing more heat to preliminary rivalries. Brody in particular insisted that while this would make underneath talent feel more involved, in the end box offices might be damaged if strong ideas were wasted on performers that would not draw. Naturally, others in the business came up with the same idea, but the trend ran wild. After a while, it seemed like every single bout on a card had to have an angle behind it: fans became so burned out that no single storyline had more impact than another. Main events were the losers. McMahon has refined the concept to some extent, although not entirely, and enhanced prelims have become part of an attractive package. They clearly do not, however, replace legitimate stars in important main events as drawing cards.

Even a *WrestleMania* relies upon the right main event, the biggest stars in the most momentous collision, to do eye-popping business. A potential buyer may consider a strong card, but he is guaranteed to spend his cash if he needs to see that one *big* match. Wrestlers know this, too — that's why everyone always wanted to be booked with Flair, Andre, Hogan, Stone Cold, and the Rock.

When a show does not draw, excuses abound. The weather was lousy . . . The baseball team was in town . . . A big accident shut down the highway . . . The weather forecast called for snow . . . There were big high school football games . . . A rock concert at the other big building . . . The weather was too nice . . .

When a ppv does not sell, there are even more extenuating circumstances. The weather was too good for people to stay indoors . . . There was a boxing ppv the night before . . . The ads did not run as scheduled . . . Breaking news distracted everyone . . . There was a ufc event the week before . . . The basketball playoffs were on . . . It was so miserable that everyone was watching the Weather Channel . . .

The economy is always a good excuse, too!

Hogwash. They stayed away or didn't buy because, plain and simple, they did not want to see the show. Every promoter and every booker has to accept this: when a card does not draw, the reason is that the audience did not care.

Another reality? There will be ups and downs. Sometimes booking is to blame, and sometimes it has more to do with the natural highs and lows of public interest. Following a sellout, or the big ppv equivalent, is always going to be difficult. Entertainments, including sports, which run a regular schedule, cannot always be at a peak. A mid-July series between the Cubs and the Pirates will not draw as well as games between the Cubs and Cardinals with the pennant on the line. A football game between the Chiefs and Lions in mid-November will generate more naps than viewers, especially when compared to the excitement of a playoff duel.

Realizing this, Sam Muchnick actually would build "down" cards into his plans because he knew that not every program could sell out. In 1962 — yes, 1962 — wrestling was big business too. Five of Muchnick's first six shows that year drew capacity crowds of over 12,000 to Kiel Auditorium, and that included a streak of four sell-outs in a row heading into early April. The next couple cards featured solid lineups, but they were not pushed as hard nor enhanced by special angles, nor did they pit the biggest stars in highly anticipated collisions. The attendance produced profitable, though by no means record-breaking gates, gave main event time and money to deserving wrestlers who were not necessarily super-stars, and provided the market an opportunity to relax — on *Sam's* schedule. Then Muchnick and booker Bobby Bruns tinkered with the action, turned up the heat, and St. Louis had another 12,000-plus sellout in June.

It was a philosophy Muchnick held throughout his career. Nonetheless, there was always a card here or there where Sam antic-ipated a large gate that just did not materialize. He would simply say, "The fans did not want to see the main event we presented as much as we thought they would. Maybe the performers are not the draw we thought, or maybe our booking was not right. No excuses."

Vince McMahon has apparently adopted a similar strategy. He does not follow *WrestleMania* with the same type of feud ending, stars-exploding, heavy hype, over-the-top extravaganza. It's not that either promoter, or any promoter, does not want to draw as much money as possible. The fact is simply that the truly observant impresarios know there is a cyclical nature to drawing crowds or buyers.

Actually, those average cards are often the time to judge the kind of box office attraction an individual really is. When receipts exceed expectations, the reasons are usually good booking and, particu-larly, that the main-event performers really do draw.

Any wrestler worth his salt, unless he's a rookie just "paying dues," or a veteran trying to hang on for a few more paydays, believes he is the guy who can draw the most, that he is, in Ric

Flair's terms, "the man." He necessarily believes he can produce the most exciting action. That confidence — the fragility of which a good psychologist could expose — is always on display in a macho, he-man environment like pro wrestling. Role players, so to speak, are vital, but it is not a position any individual easily accepts.

The wrestler looking up at the lights when a match is finished often fears the implications of that "loss": that he might earn fewer important matches and less money in the future. A bank account, after all, is black-and-white, down-to-the-detail, *real*. A bank balance is a shoot.

The booker, therefore, must become someone who can persuade a performer to do something that, on the surface, may not seem in his best interest, and to do it in a meaningful, valuable way. Back in the day that was tricky, because someone who was indeed valuable at the box office always had the option of leaving for another territory. An average wrestler could move around until he found his comfort level, and the true big-market main-event performers could stay fresh by moving between the bigger, well-paying cities.

In a spot like St. Louis, where one defeat did not necessarily doom a talented performer to a career of lower-pay preliminaries, it wasn't a big issue . . .

Or was it?

If Sam Muchnick decided a wrestler was not a main-eventer, one St. Louis main event might be all he'd have. Refusing to "do the job" meant incurring the wrath of a powerful promoter and likely a reputation that would make others shy away too. In the end, Sam or his booker needed to wield little in the way of persuasion because the sheer power of the market and the politics meant it was best to toe the line, and do it as well as possible. Muchnick would respect the effort, and that could lead to future opportunities in St. Louis or a good word put in with the booker from another territory.

Obviously, the market now is different with WWE essentially in a monopoly position. Since there are few paydays outside WWE, how many can say "no" to a booker from the company? And who among them are willing to refuse Vince McMahon himself? Vince, without question, is one of the most gifted men in the history of wrestling at the art of persuasion. Clearly, the days when Bob Geigel claimed, "you have to say *fuck* every sixth word or the wrestlers won't take you seriously" are long gone. Of course, more sophisticated and polished manipulating does not change the desired result.

Somehow in this climate, though, there are performers who have learned how to manipulate the system, how to market themselves, how to save money. Those personalities are going to be more stubborn about "doing the job" if they feel it is wrong for a particular rivalry, or for the character they portray. Consider Hulk Hogan and Bruiser Brody at one end of the scale, or Lou Thesz and Bruno Sammartino at the other.

It's tricky terrain. In recent times, there have been performers, notably Hulk, who command creative control by legal contract and flat-out refuse to do what they do not want to do. This is wrestling's version of the no-trade clause. Is it a good thing for a promotion, whether it's owned by Vince McMahon or Verne Gagne? Can the inmates run the prison?

Who is best suited to decide which wrestlers will bring the most bucks to the box office? Who has the biggest financial risk? In the end, in any venture of any kind, the owner makes the call about the direction of his business.

Wrestlers can balk, and become reluctant or downcast. That's when the booker must cajole and convince, doing whatever it takes to get the correct hand raised. Isn't this the moment when many a truth has been shaded, many a lie has been told, many a false promise has been made?

Numerous wrestlers complain, but few ever stand up. Worse, some who bitch and moan are simply wrong. No, they are *not* that good. They will *not* be that kind of draw. Hard-core followers can critique McMahon's booking up and down, but it doesn't change one fact: he *must* have made plenty of good decisions about talent, and other issues as well. Vince is the one with all those zeroes in his bank account.

Nonetheless, the booker is always smack in the middle. Despite the squawking, most performers go with the program. I can remember telling Nikolai Volkoff that he would be losing to King Kong Brody in a main event in 1983 — and then making the mistake of asking if he was okay with it.

Volkoff shrugged, "No, of course not. But you're paying me, so that's what I'll do. I just hope it doesn't mean you won't bring me back." In the end, that's the response most wrestlers offer. Besides, Volkoff was a pro's pro; he worked just as hard whether he was winning or losing.

Nick Bockwinkel says the trick is to have such a terrific match, generate so much excitement, and make both himself and his foe look so good that when the combatants go home with the finish, both the booker and promoter question whether they made the right decision about who they chose to be the winner.

Lou Thesz, in his superb but sadly forgotten book *Hooker*, claimed, "The 'winner' wasn't always the wrestler whose hand was raised, but the one whose performance stuck in the minds of the fans . . . the one they would pay money to see again, regardless of whether they hated or admired him."

A controversial former booker and wrestler, Buck Robley had a slightly different take on the same subject when he said, "You have to get the opponent over while you get yourself over, otherwise beating him didn't mean anything. You have to make your opponent look like somebody; the other guy has to put some doubt in the mind of the people, that he has a chance. He has to shine, too."

Sam Muchnick was even more blunt when he told me that he didn't want "washrags" who wouldn't fight back on his show.

It's easy to see how difficult the process can become, with the multitude of personalities, egos, promotional mind games, and different goals. Something basic about why wrestling works gets lost in the muddle. If it's just a work, why is it so hard?

The booker can run into other problems as well. Once, when Pat O'Connor was booking St. Louis, a tag match involving Rocky Johnson and Dick Murdoch was slated for *Wrestling at the Chase*. The plan was for Murdoch and Johnson to end up in a melee that would hopefully bring about a lucrative main event.

Muchnick had rigid standards about what he would allow wrestlers to do on television, although he'd bend his own rules for the likes of Dick the Bruiser, Fritz Von Erich, Gene Kiniski, or Brody. Murdoch was another who had some wiggle room and, in this instance, the action was hot-and-heavy on top of the announcer's table, which was overturned and broken. Chairs went flying. Murdoch grabbed the camera cable to choke Rocky, who battled back gamely until O'Connor and other referees could intervene.

Afterward, Sam was livid. O'Connor was reamed out. The former world champion, a remarkable worker in his day, hung his head and moaned, "Sam, I don't have handcuffs on them. I tell them what to do, but once they're out there. . . . " And O'Connor threw up his hands.

Of course, Pat was right. When two dynamic personalities who have a bit of independence get caught up in the moment anything can — and usually does — happen. Plans often go awry, leaving the promoter to question how much latitude he should give both booker and performer. Besides, there have been many wily grapplers who've twisted the finishes they were given to suit themselves, or even found ways to avoid doing certain finishes altogether. Can they get away with it? Ask Kevin Nash, or Shawn Michaels. And don't forget about Cowboy Bill Watts either.

Today there appears to be less latitude than ever, at least on pre-taped shows. McMahon has not been shy about sending wrestlers back in front of the audience to retape a sequence and "get it right." He'll edit out poor parts of matches, too. A few thousand at an arena might have their illusion shattered, but many more thousands, perhaps millions, at home never know the difference. They're still mesmerized.

Terry Funk complained that doing television for WWE was no fun because everything was tightly choreographed. Bump, bump, this, that, go home. Two minutes, three minutes. An innovative booker himself at one time, Terry groused that "this ain't working, and it ain't fun." He, like so many, missed the freedom of improvisation. The micro-control squeezes out any individuality in manufactured personalities.

Vince himself must realize the limitations. A large chunk of his television is broadcast live, not to mention all his pay-per-views. During the "war" years, Vince and I sat once before a TV taping at a darkened Kiel Auditorium in St. Louis, and the subject of live television came up. McMahon said, "There are no mistakes on live television. Just keep going." It's an excellent philosophy — plus it puts some control back in the hands of wrestlers.

The never-ending circle of cause and effect brings everything back to trust. Who can the promoter and booker rely on? Is Vince willing to take a chance on a performer who might undermine what he and his creative team have carefully plotted?

Sometimes, heaven forbid, it's simply a case of who he likes best. And isn't that just like any other business, where the boss will give certain difficult jobs to the employee he feels he can trust, who will get it done? It may leave some young turks chafing, but it's a fact of life — not just in wrestling.

Does friendship become part of the equation? Muchnick used to proclaim that real friendships were rare in wrestling because of its skeptical, suspicious nature. Of all the men who ever worked for him, Sam became closest to Dick the Bruiser, Gene Kiniski, and Fritz Von Erich. Is it surprising that each was among the biggest drawing cards who ever worked in St. Louis? Sam may have gone to dinner with Kiniski, or been visited in the hospital by Bruiser, but the wily promoter was not having beers at the hotel bar with preliminary guys like Bulldog Bob Brown or Ronnie Etchison.

Now throw nepotism into the mix. Consider the Von Erich boys. The Funks. Greg Gagne. Even Vince's son-in-law. In each case a personal relationship obviously affects how business gets done. The car dealer is more likely to groom his child to take over his business than one of his hard-working salesmen. It's another fact of life.

No one should be surprised to learn that the business underwent subtle changes when some *active* talent became bookers, who answered to owners, or eventually became owners themselves. Inevitably, an active wrestler hired as a booker put himself in a feature role. Imagine what an active wrestler in an ownership position would do.

While numerous old-time wrestlers who had retired obviously did become promoters especially in the 1930s and 1940s, they were out of the ring and not active participants in the hijinks. The swing to *active* stars as owners began in the late 1950s and lasted into the 1980s. Verne Gagne, Fritz Von Erich, Cowboy Bill Watts, the Funks, Dick the Bruiser, Jerry Lawler, Carlos Colon, Harley Race, The Sheik (Ed Farhat), and others all wound up owning controlling percentages of wrestling companies. Generally speaking, they were noteworthy performers who had earned good money in main events, and this gave them the financial wherewithal to protect their positions for the future, both in the ring and out. In some cases, they bought out promoters who were never active in the ring, men unconcerned with putting themselves in main events where they could double-dip on receipts.

Is there any reason to think that just because a promoter or booker is not a wrestler he or she can't understand what makes the business tick? After all, wrestling and the booking thereof are not advanced physics. Just because a baseball player makes it to Cooperstown, will he be a good manager or GM? History says, usually *not*. The best managers seldom were the biggest stars — many in fact were never more than fringe players. Numerous successful general managers (the position all but equivalent to a promoter) have little, or even no high-level, on-field experience.

A fabulous performer himself, Nick Bockwinkel is an astute evaluator of the wrestling business. He believes that someone like Muchnick had an advantage over wrestlers when it came to spotting talent and assessing matches. "Sam did not have a stake in what went on insofar as him performing in the ring," the articulate former AWA titleholder says. "No ego was involved, because Sam did not compare what some wrestlers did to what he did. Sam was not a wrestler. Therefore, Muchnick, or someone like him, could make an objective judgment about what he saw in a match and how the crowd reacted. Sam was totally pragmatic about who and what worked."

Wrestling thrived for decades with promoters and bookers who learned and understood wrestling without ever taking a bump. Muchnick, Vince McMahon Sr., Morris Sigel, Paul Bowser, Jim

Barnett, Frank Tunney, Wally Karbo, Don Owen, and many others demonstrated the ability to build wrestling empires because they could discover and book appealing talent. This part of the business deals with the mind and the instincts, not the body.

When all was said and done, guess who got the main events when wrestlers were owners, no matter who was booking? Guess who seldom, if ever, did clean jobs in the middle of the ring? Guess who was portrayed as the best of the best? Guess who got the blame if something did not draw a good crowd? (Hint — try either the opponent or booker who was not the owner.) Isn't that human nature? More wrestlers in the owners' seats, however, added yet another tier of politics to an already touchy situation.

Around 1960, in Toronto, Fritz Von Erich and Gene Kiniski were the top heels. They mashed opponents and were careful about when and how they sold. The lead babyface was Whipper Billy Watson, who, along with promoter Frank Tunney, also owned a large part of the stock in the company. Needless to say, Watson facing either Von Erich or Kiniski, or both in some sort of tag team duel, was common.

Kiniski, who eventually bought into Vancouver and surrounding cities, remembers the bet he had with Von Erich. Watson's favorite comeback move was a nasty Irish Whip that sent hapless foes sailing into the ozone. The heels had a standing wager involving who could fly the farthest to sell the move.

One night in a tag bout, Watson got the hot tag and launched Von Erich — who then launched himself. Fritz rocketed across the top rope and landed in the front row with the spectators. Kiniski jumped into the ring, attacked Whipper, but was soon being battered too. And then . . . whoosh! Watson's Irish Whip hurtled Kiniski upward and onward. Gene went flying past Fritz, who was on his knees selling, and into the aisle *just past* the first row.

Kiniski heard Von Erich snarl, "Shit!" Fritz had lost that night's bet.

Why did they do it? "Hell, Whipper was the boss! He was office," Kiniski explains.

In Japan, during the early 1980s, Bruiser Brody and Stan Hansen sold even less than they did in North America. Many a Japanese rival, and not a few Americans, got their brains scrambled as Brody and Hansen ran roughshod. But when the two collided with Giant Baba and Jumbo Tsuruta, the intense Brody and brutal Hansen sold their butts off. And, on more than a few occasions, the two even sold for the Funk brothers, Dory Jr. and Terry.

Rotund "Crusher" Blackwell had a great understanding of how to work a "big man" match, and the 450-pounder was never knocked off his feet, except by someone like Andre the Giant, in towns like St. Louis. Once when I went to Winnipeg, Canada, to announce an AWA telecast involving Blackwell in a tag bout against Greg Gagne and Jim Brunzell, the exciting "High Flyers" who together did not weigh as much as Blackwell, Jerry warned me that I would see a different "Crusher" than in St. Louis. And my goodness, he was right; that night I saw him bumping all over the place — for 190-pound Greg Gagne!

Why did these things happen? Baba owned the promotion, Tsuruta was his big star, and the Funks were the bookers who opened the door to Japan for Brody and Hansen. What Brody and Hansen did made Baba, Tsuruta, and the Funks even bigger stars to their audience. Likewise, what Von Erich and Kiniski did elevated Watson in the eyes of Toronto fans. Greg Gagne's father owned the AWA, so Blackwell's bumping boosted Greg's standing. Brody, Hansen, Kiniski, Von Erich, and Blackwell all solidified their positions with their bosses. Had these men sold for just anyone, what they did in big matches would have been irrelevant, not strengthening the promotion, and definitely not earning them more money.

Today? The more things change, the more they stay the same. Jeff Jarrett headlined TNA for years, a company either he or his father Jerry owned in part. What happened in his bouts, and where was he positioned on the program?

Think about when Vince or Shane McMahon step through the ropes for a match. Don't Stone Cold Steve Austin, Triple H, Randy Orton, or Mick Foley make sure that the McMahons come across as tough guys?

By all accounts, Vince wanted to wrestle in the 1970s, but his father would not hear of it. Before age started catching up with McMahon (it does, in fact, happen; even to him), it was apparently important to him to take bumps and prove himself to "the boys." Urban legend features many tales of Vince wanting to show wrestlers his ruggedness. The smart ones let him "prove" it, even though he could then use the fact that he risked his own body to justify asking for something from one of his "boys."

Naturally, when he eventually got into the ring as a participant, Vince was also able to pay himself both as the owner/operator of the company *and* as talent. He did exactly what everyone from Von Erich to Watts to The Sheik did, taking their portion of profits and paying themselves for working. It's not wrong; these men did two jobs.

Often lost in the noise is the fact that Vince truly became a major player in the booking plots of the late 1990s, when World Championship Wrestling was tossing around gobs of money and looking to steal WWF talent. Even Shane and Stephanie became characters in the soap opera, and clearly Pop and the kiddies were not going to leave for WCW.

Perhaps the idea took on a life of its own as those involved became addicted to the spotlight. Even now consider that Stephanie is portrayed as a dominant and feared business personality (whoops, that may be true!); and that Shane recently beat up, sort of — if disbelief is indeed suspended — three heels, including one main-event participant. (Who made the decision, and why? Is the whiff of birthright and privilege overwhelming?)

Yet here's something else to contemplate. All examination of ego and the perks of power aside, Vince was and is a great heel, if not a legitimate wrestler like Watts, Gagne, or Baba. He is an excellent *performer* — which disguises his age and lack of athletic ability — who has taken his lumps for other talent. And furthermore, in the end, Vince usually puts over the babyface, for which he gets a tip of the hat. Even Shane was carried out on a stretcher as part of the family feud with Randy Orton, though not until he had "proven" he was just as tough.

Most importantly, if the fans didn't like it, why did they buy tickets? Why did they tune in and fuel ratings? Why did they order pay-per-views? Watson could point to all the capacity crowds for cards he headlined. So could Baba and Watts. If it was that wrong, why did people shell out to see their product? Even those who gripe about it from a creative standpoint — and they are not necessarily wrong — must understand that the bottom line, money, led all of them to book themselves as they did.

In other words, the people who make the decisions have reason to believe it *does* draw — and that is because the execution, and especially the booking, worked.

CHAPTER EIGHT

Booking 102: What's Good for the Business is Good for . . .

Booking is more than just writing down two names and telling them who wins. As important as the political instinct is, the ability to put together the right foes is invaluable. If styles aren't complementary, the results can be awful. Different types of wrestlers can mesh well, but there are no guarantees. Furthermore, some guys — wrestlers who are unable to let go of their egos for the good of the business — just do not want to work together.

When a duel *must* be made, because of the money it will generate for the company, concerns about artistic value and personal sensibilities are generally tossed aside. Once in a while, with the perfect pair, that works out just fine, too. Thus, managing people who can be egocentric must also be part of the booker's skill package.

Bookers are expected to discover the hook that grabs fans, the angles that fire emotions, the storylines that captivate. It really is a science, and some have been better scientists than others. Often ignored in the successes of WWE is Pat Patterson, an imaginative thinker who over the years has tried to meld so-called old with the new. He wasn't a booker, at least in name, but he has had Vince McMahon's ear for years, and his influence should probably not be underestimated.

Wise booking minds like Patterson aren't just integral to pro wrestling. Booking is a key to the success of UFC, and MMA in general. In those cases, unlike in wrestling, the people who book the battles do not pick a winner and loser. The selling point is competition between two studs and that anyone can come out on top —

141

not that wrestling hasn't used that same approach successfully.

In the best of all worlds, the rivals should be equally strong gate magnets, but sometimes that is not possible. The major factor for UFC is that even if one fighter is not a potent drawing card, he must at least be a meaningful opponent, and this is where the booker's expertise comes into play. The booker must be able to evaluate talent and how it all fits together. The competition factor then carries the load, maybe even making a new star with a surprise winner, since UFC/MMA is a business like pro wrestling: it's make a profit or fold.

As in wrestling, an MMA booker tries to blend skills and abilities; the stylistic comparison of potential opponents is a prime consideration because the conclusion should be a scrap that has fans yelling for more and impressed by both participants. The UFC's booking, however, cannot be tweaked to add little storyline touches that might hide a competitor's weaknesses. A future opponent of Anderson Silva cannot jump into the ring and attack him mid-match to juice sales!

Still, opponents can be put into positions on television (the magic word: *television*) that will, hopefully, create conflict, anger, dissension, and controversy, which translates into sales. In *The Ultimate Fighter*, for example, future combatants often coach different teams. To develop the tension, they're put together for interviews where, hopefully, the natural flow of competition develops. Or, clever features contrasting contenders can be filmed and edited to build drama. Overall, UFC does a sensational job selling the personalities and talents of their featured fighters along with *why* a contest between them is important. If one is perceived lacking at the box office, the promotion elevates him by highlighting his strengths.

In the many years of wrestling, haven't the best and the brightest promoters and bookers been able to do something exactly like that, especially since they were blessed with the advantage of being able to add angles and orchestrate what happens leading up to the showdown?

Vince and WWE had their brief flirtation with booking "shoot"

Sam Muchnick, the voice of reason in a
combustible business

Bruno Sammartino, the first WWWF champion,
with Vince McMahon Sr. and Phil Zacko

Old school cross-marketing: Joe Garagiola, Lou Thesz, boxing promoter Hans Bernstein, Joe Louis, Stan Musial, Yogi Berra, and Red Schoendienst

Verne Gagne, AWA owner and champion, prepares to battle Nick Bockwinkel, with manager Bobby Heenan

Vince McMahon, the flamboyant ruler
of a bizarre world

Stephanie McMahon: heir apparent?

Bruiser Brody, wrestling's true independent

Ted DiBiase, a million dollars
worth of versatility

Big John Studd:
did this giant get big enough?

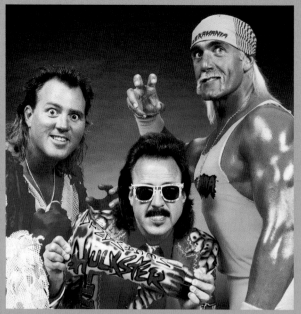

Credit: Mike Lano

Jim Cornette and Dave Meltzer
trade wrestling stories

Hulk Hogan can always count on Brutus
Beefcake and Jimmy Hart

Rowdy Roddy Piper could speak for himself

Jesse "The Body" Ventura, the governor that
wrestling gave Minnesota

Steve Austin — "Stone Cold" discovered his voice

Jim Ross at home with the microphone and Paul Heyman

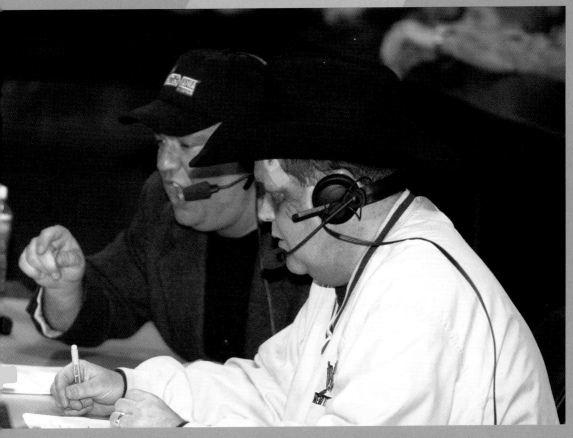

Vince McMahon "proves himself" to Shawn Michaels

Mick Foley knows about
"red making green"

Chris Benoit, freefalling from heaven to hell

Mark Calaway made The Undertaker his own

Who got cheered? Cena or Big Show?

Weapons like ladders have become a commonplace part of the work

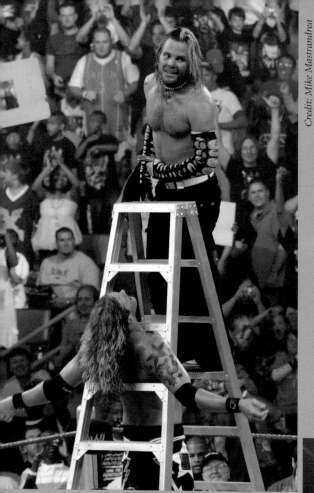

Credit: Mike Mastrandrea

Edge and Jeff Hardy have climbed the ladder of success

If only TNA could always fly like A.J. Styles battling Samoa Joe

How much does WWE miss Kurt Angle and Brock Lesnar?

Bobby Lashley might be a steal for MMA

Credit: Matt Balk

Jeff Hardy has paid his dues and become one of WWE's biggest draws

Credit: Mike Mastrandrea

Now C.M. Punk has his eye on the prize

Credit: Mika Mastrandrea

Batista, a much-injured powerhouse

Credit: Matt Balk

John Cena, the mighty
WWE marketing machine

Can Ted DiBiase Jr. and Cody Rhodes go as far as their fathers?

Credit: Matt Balk

action in 1998, when they allegedly wanted to get Steve Williams in a position to challenge the company champions of the time. Nicknamed Dr. Death, Williams was a real deal character with legitimate credentials in college football, amateur wrestling, and especially the pros, particularly for Bill Watts' promotion and in Japan. The idea was to put together several matches on national cable via *Raw* with no predetermined finish — shoots! — against less-skilled foes; Williams was expected to come out on top. This sequence would lead to a *WrestleMania* special event that Williams could win against a boxer before Dr. Death transitioned back into the fictional competitive world of WWE.

Of course, reality intervened. Bart Gunn, a rugged looking tough guy assumed to be a sacrificial lamb, whipped Williams when Dr. Death tore his hamstring at the very start of the bout and couldn't move, thus becoming a sitting duck for Gunn. Therefore, Gunn was on his way to a date with boxer Butterbean, actually a gimmick performer in the boxing world and one Vince had been assured that Williams would eat for lunch. Except it wasn't Williams, but Gunn who squared off with Butterbean in 1999. And it was Gunn who got his lunch handed to him when he was kayoed in the only shoot match in *WrestleMania* history.

Everyone knows about the best-laid plans. It certainly was enough to keep Vince from mixing shoot and work together again, for obvious reasons. While both forms are dangerous, demanding, and stressful, the training and mindset for the performers is (generally) very different. From a booking standpoint, however, the end result is actually no different.

The natural flow of winning and losing can create rivalries, and rivalries between stars make money for all concerned. This has been done in pro wrestling, too; it dates all the way back to Muchnick and his predecessors. UFC has refined and modernized the package for their purpose — even if they do not realize (and likely would never admit it if they did) how similar what they're doing is to old school pro wrestling psychology. Return matches of hot battles are, always, a blessing: think Couture versus Liddell, or Penn and St. Pierre.

Once upon a time, the responsibility for booking a wrestling territory fell to one person, who got either all the credit or all the blame. Sam Muchnick used just a few bookers, most prominently Bobby Bruns until 1968, and Pat O'Connor through the 1970s. But Sam had a strict formula in place, which the booker had to work within — plus, Muchnick handled all the payoffs.

At the other end of the scale, Jim Barnett employed many bookers over the years, from Gary Hart in Australia, to Ole Anderson in the Atlanta territory. Barnett had a sharp eye for new talent, but he gave his booker plenty of leeway and usually let him make up the payroll. Most territories were run that way; St. Louis was an anomaly.

Like Muchnick, Vince McMahon Sr. ran another stable operation, and it's safe to say that he, too, always had his hand in what the workers were paid. When Vince Jr. and I talked about payoffs in 1983, it turned out that, like Muchnick, the McMahons paid off about 32% of the net house after taxes, with 16% allotted to the main-event workers. Vince laughed about it though: if the percentage meant giving someone more than McMahon thought he was worth, well . . .

"I always have an eraser I can use to change the number," he admitted.

There's always been input from the performers, and even others within the promotion, about upcoming lineups and feuds. (Chris Jericho lobbying to face Rey Mysterio, as he did in 2009, is nothing new.) The good booker listens, maybe even "hears," and uses or remodels the ideas he feels are best for everyone. But in the end, the responsibility usually falls on one person. The booker of the past was powerful, yes, but there was turnover. Many promoters figured bookers burned out, used up their ideas or contacts, and occasionally needed to be replaced to freshen up the product.

Some bookers (and to a lesser degree maybe even today's creative committees) fell into the trap of acting out personal vendettas against certain performers through the booking. How short sighted, how petty. Wrestling is a business. The goal of booking is to draw money and to increase the profit, not get even with someone about past disagreements or play a demeaning "rib" on some-one not in the company's favor. Worse yet, it can become a self-fulfilling prophecy — by booking a wrestler into situations that will never draw, some bookers have manufactured the opportunity to tell the boss, "See, he can't draw!"

The idea of booking by committee became more prominent with World Championship Wrestling, the Ted Turner–funded operation that battled Vince's wwf in the 1990s. The thought was to get the best concepts from several inventive minds. In reality, though, it became a debacle. Having a committee of four, five, or even more strong-willed and self-centered egos added another layer of politics into an already suspect system. One committee member favored a certain wrestler; another liked someone differ-ent . . . and where was that dispute headed?

Wrestlers, naturally, did whatever they could to curry favor with their personal contacts on the committee. The committee members felt the need to outdo one another with what often became bizarre booking, and this, unfortunately, often only confused and drove away potential buyers. Since wcw never really had a strong leader who actually understood the business calling the shots, the com-mittees did more damage than anything else.

Vince has had much better luck with his version of the commit-tee, which is actually dubbed the "creative" team. Obviously, the creative department is just booking with a fancier name. Although more opinions are solicited, at wwe only one opinion has ever truly mattered.

While there's still plenty of internal politics being played at wwe today, the final version of any idea always passes through Stephanie McMahon before it goes to Vince. She is the moderator and gate-keeper. Another issue, of course, is how much say Stephanie's husband, Paul Levesque (Triple H), has. The truth clearly is: a hell of a lot. Apparently, one of the most redeeming qualities Triple H has is that he knows when, if, and most importantly, *how* to push Vince on any idea.

The booking workload is surely more than it was in the territo-rial days: today, it's about more than just laying out matches, winners and losers. That, alone, would be all-consuming. At WWE, the experienced hands of what are known as "producers," including Ricky Steamboat and Arn Anderson, are involved to guide the workers in putting together their matches. The producers have no say in who wins or loses, and are often handcuffed by instructions from creative that only a few minutes are available for in-ring action. Nonetheless, their input is useful for the (often limited) talent.

Anyhow, the creative committee (remember — these are bookers by another name) has more than enough outlets that it influences. Creative tries to work with the characters that have been given to each performer, molding everything from ring costumes to entrances to the performer's victories or defeats to the often weak, time-consuming, and only sporadically amusing skits. They try to find the performer's "voice," scripting interviews and promos, searching endlessly for a "catch phrase" that defines their concept of the wrestler. But exactly whose voice is creative finding? The wrestler's, or the scriptwriter's?

Did Superstar Billy Graham need someone to help him find his voice? What about Hulk Hogan? Dick the Bruiser, Terry Funk, Bobby Heenan, or Bruno Sammartino? Each of these legends were merely being themselves — or letting loose a high-volume version of their actual personality.

The argument would be that these men were "natural" performers, while others today need assistance and direction. Do they really? Does it really help them, if they do not already have an inherent ability to project to an audience? Luckily, John Cena, love him or hate him, has that gift, because there have been more than a few times that he has been saddled with lame material.

And that is only the tip of the iceberg. As the process of composing the script for a show comes together, Vince may have passed down word about the direction he wants followed and developed, but there's plenty of space for wheeling and dealing.

Disagreements and posturing are unavoidable. Frustrating hours are spent waiting for meetings that Vince himself has scheduled but is late to start. Imagine the real-life soap opera scenarios being played out as a wrestler tries to boost his stock or become friends with committee members who might push him higher up the ladder. Everyone tries to influence Stephanie — and even Vince, if they can reach him. Creative team members themselves jockey to get their own pet projects approved. Temporary alliances are formed and disbanded within the committee. Backstabbing is not unheard of. Some stories simply disappear because they lose support or because Vince axes them.

Something else has changed about the way wrestling is booked. The performers, even those who grumbled about bosses who had not taken bumps, used to respect those in control. They realized promoters had risked their own money to make a show happen. The announcer, who at times had also paid his dues in the office and learned the business, was part of the performance and helped wrestlers get over. The same was true of the referee. A successful wrestling card was a team game.

The wrestlers, quite simply, understood. Whether it was Muchnick or Barnett, Jim Ross, Gordon Solie, or Larry Matysik, they were part of the business, physical bumps or not. The shared in the mental and emotional bumps, perhaps the most punishing blows of all. Everyone's body of work helped to draw money. That's not quite the same thing as a writer whose short tenure on a situation comedy gets him an office in Stamford . . . or the guy who remembers Stone Cold and Hulk Hogan only by name, not deed.

Many of those in creative at WWE now are, at best, fans with little sense of what worked or failed over the years. A few have had even less exposure to what wrestling is and how it works best. Regardless, they are in a spot, through their ideas and suggestions, to either make or break careers. It is not that they can't learn to do the job well, but perspective takes time to develop. Some resentment is almost certain to arise. Obviously, experienced wrestlers bristle when the person telling them what to do is so far removed from the business that the fact that "he never took a bump" is just the beginning of the catalog of shortcomings.

Vince becomes the focal point, the voice of authority who must balance creative input with his own knowledge, but tension is inevitable and it influences the behavior and attitude of everyone.

And somewhere, hopefully, amidst all this jockeying, the fans' voices are heard, too. They speak, and loudly, through television ratings and buy rates for pay-per-views, and are ignored at the bookers' own peril.

What happens if the committee is more concerned with pleasing Vince than creating a successful product? What if they're intimidated by McMahon? What if they hesitate to give Vince, or Stephanie, an honest opinion? The process replays itself a few times every week before a finalized version of a show is presented to the boss. Talk about needing persuasive skills!

In the end, Vince says yes or no. Or he changes everything at the last moment — hardly a rare occurrence. There are those who wish that McMahon paid even more attention to the process, but WWE has grown so much and Vince is such a hands-on executive that he usually is not that involved until the final script is written. His attention is diverted in a hundred different directions until he issues a final acceptance or rejection of ideas. Of crucial concern is that McMahon and his underlings remember that to sustain success, they must also remember how that success was built.

At times, Vince has been so distracted that he has had little personal contact with the creative team, which has left them floundering and frustrated. Stephanie may push her writers to develop long-term plans, but at times that must seem fruitless: Vince has a long history of changing, often at the last second, the best laid plans.

So, who has Stephanie's attention? Who has Vince's attention? How can you concentrate on developing, or at least enhancing, personalities that fans would empathize with, not to mention matches that sell tickets, with all that noise? Add to this the need to produce six hours — *six hours* — of first-run television programming every single week of the year, as well as plotting crucial PPVs and even house shows that reflect current storylines. It's a back-breaker even Gene Kiniski could appreciate. Obviously, with the job pressure and the hours spent, turnover of creative staff is high.

Want another frustrating job? Try handling marketing and publicity when lineups change a couple times a week and advertisements have to be placed. Between new directions from creative, Vince's sudden modifications, the inevitable injuries, and last-second changes, particularly to live broadcasts, the folks charged with getting the word out to media sources accurately are more often than not in a frenzy.

Knowing all of this, who honestly thinks he can fix everything that ails wrestling, especially when the guy who runs the entire she-bang has reason to feel the thing works pretty good? Well, who gets these creative spots? While there usually is a strong wrestling influence on the committee, most recently from Michael Hayes, the majority are entertainment writers. A scarily high percentage of them have no wrestling background, by Vince's choice. Being a "superfan" might even be a negative. It's here that the disconnect between fan and product is often born.

If a writer looks at wrestling as farce, and has no real respect for the art form, too much of his influence can alienate the folks who just happen to like wrestling. Perhaps the worst result, whether it comes from boring comedy or bizarre in-ring activity, is that the product insults the fans' intelligence. A perfect example is all the ridiculous wrestling romances that have eaten up TV time over the last few years. Admittedly, some fans like the interplay between wrestlers and "divas," but many others want competition, and find the simplistic, unrealistic romances boring at best.

The other side of the argument is that the "character" skits, which sadly are often not too witty, might lure new people to the product. But if viewers don't already like wrestling, why would they tune in when there are plenty of better comedies on the tube? Does a laugh sell a pay-per-view? Someone might be entertained, but another portion of wrestling's fan base will be switching channels to MMA, a hockey game, or *The Closer* when two prelim performers get into a grade-school game of kissy-face, huggy-bear.

Depending upon whose ideas are getting the most airtime, sometimes angles can go so overboard that viewers are left bewil-dered — in a very bad way. *What was that about? That segment was stupid.* At its worst, the entire production suffers, turning into a fast-paced muddle. WWE is often drastically overbooked, and TNA can go even further overboard. What often gets forgotten or ignored is the attention to detail, upon which so much relies for credibility.

This is where Vince must step in, if he thinks to do so is in WWE's best interest. He knows where wrestling's bread is buttered. When everything is settled, he'll allow some of the silly ideas to air, if for no other reason than to fill time and encourage creative tension. But usually, if definitely not always, he draws the line. When it's time for *WrestleMania* or a major PPV, McMahon has demonstrated the ability to make the focus clearer, to define rivalries, to give more edge to the stakes and the violence, and to make those concerns the priority. The plan is always to grab buyers from all elements of the fan base, but down deep Vince understands wrestling's core appeal.

Not surprisingly, the current trend of soap opera booking looks much like the traditional in-ring booking. Both have the same goal of staging a battle that draws heat and makes money. If the issue is basically believable, if the performers have connected with the audience to some degree and can talk convincingly, and if what happens grabs attention, soap opera booking works. Isn't that just like in-ring angles of yore, when two meaningful combatants butted heads about something that was portrayed as important to them and the spectators?

Like any other angle, if it requires poorly scripted talking about some nonsensical issue by performers who don't mean much under any circumstance, the result is exactly like a surprise donnybrook that looks soft and is conducted by preliminary figures. Soap opera or in-ring, neither clicks with the crowd. Without credible emotion and some logic, understandable motivation, electrifying personalities, or actions that at least look real when they happen, the result is no heat, no money, and no difference whether so-called old or new.

A good example of how modern soap opera booking can work is the recent feud between Chris Jericho and Shawn Michaels. Following a thread that began with Ric Flair's retirement, through a controversy with Batista, the involvement of Shawn's wife, and culminating in hot matches between Jericho and Michaels, the booking sequence held together, did not insult anyone's intelligence (although in the hands of lesser performers it might have), and actually made a personal link for many followers.

Of course, Michaels and Jericho were reportedly calling the shots for the angle, with minimal influence from creative. In the end, the feud helped draw money, though only marginally more than average for the PPVs they topped and with no difference for arena outings. Were the players involved not over as much with the mass audience as everyone thought? Did the soap opera aspect of the angle not work well enough for casual fans? Is the overall context now so dumbed down and goofy that the large body of potential fans do not watch carefully enough to buy into a well-developed angle? Has the audience seen too much packed into each time period and is blasé to most everything? Was it all of the above?

By the time *WrestleMania 2009* rolled around (with a mind-boggling number of issues jammed onto the lineup), the involvement of wives had evolved into some absurdist muddle. After a Road Runner–style cartoon chase one week, Triple H became an even more deranged stalker seeking revenge on Randy Orton for what Orton did to H's wife, the aforementioned Stephanie McMahon — who generally had been portrayed as a heel before, and once actually clashed with her own father Vince in a sort-of match on a PPV.

The next step was that Triple H broke into Randy Orton's clearly fake house, terrorized Randy's fake wife, and finally battled Randy in the dwelling and the yard before being fake arrested. The week following brought a teased rape scene as Randy got his reprisal by handcuffing HHH and attacking poor Stephanie — who did excellently sell a DDT and thus was unconscious when Randy kissed her. WWE creative tends to alternate weeks of the main-event combatants getting the upper hand, but this sequence was close to going over the edge.

The last chapter of this came after Jericho had assaulted and stripped the clothes off of Ric Flair, a scene that, though similar to things Ric himself had done before, was disturbing now at his age and this time.

On top of which, viewers had to be subjected to the supposed marital discord of Edge and his fake wife Vickie Guerrero, who was messing around with Big Show and being secretly taped by none other than John Cena.

How is that for "kid-friendly" television? Maybe more importantly, will any of it grab the gut of some even halfway intelligent viewer? Talk about overkill! When those in charge complain that fans today do not get caught up in the performers, isn't the obvious answer that many potential, clear-headed followers are laughing — or worse, being repulsed — when heat should be building?

Does this angle fall into the classic "hot shot" mold of perhaps providing short-term gain, with long-term harm? Or is it too ridiculous even for that definition? In reality, that particular "hot shot" apparently flopped, since the buy rates in domestic markets for *WrestleMania 2009* were disappointing.

In retrospect, the convoluted TNA storyline involving Kurt Angle's wife Karen and A.J. Styles perhaps isn't quite as ridiculous and silly as it first appeared. Regardless, the idea never clicked in the more meaningful way that Michaels and Jericho did. The TNA plotting failed to work for the larger audience that wants at least a degree of realism involved. The argument could be made that the issue boosted Styles, but he could have been jump-started with other ideas that did not make people laugh. Plus, did what happened perhaps lessen Angle as a serious competitor who draws money in the eyes of fans? The entire scenario made noise, which a lot of things will, but did it help draw money? Were buy rates up? In fact, were ratings even up?

In some of the best booking, the margin between fantasy and reality is slim, and Vince has cashed in on this (Edge and Matt Hardy come to mind), even if most of the casual, transitory audience never know or understand the real roots of the story. Sometimes an ingredient can be added that makes an angle resonate more strongly. The more real it looks, the more money it draws. Even TNA fiddled, quite successfully, with this concept by doing legitimate sports-type, competitive interviews and features leading up to a duel between Kurt Angle and Samoa Joe.

In the end, it all boils down to convincing buyers that what the promotion is presenting is what they, the fans, want. Promoters cannot react to every chirp and burp from fanatics any more than an author can change what he writes to suit the opinion of every reader. The respect of the most hard-core fans can be won with consistent, coherent, finely detailed booking and promoting. And at least some of those vital casual customers will be drawn in when dynamic personalities are involved in situations that make sense. WWE seriously underestimates the hunger many potential fans have for clever and serious angles, which is one reason why when younger fans get older, a significant percentage are gravitating to UFC and MMA.

Sam Muchnick always said, whether the subject was television announcing, publicity, or booking, to shoot for the best and brightest people possible — don't settle for the lowest common denominator, because wrestling will get that group regardless. The goal was always to make the potential audience as large as possible, and nothing has changed. Here is an all-in bet: McMahon, though his methods and his actual wrestling product may be different, has the exact same target in mind.

Vince might protest, endlessly, that what he does is entertainment; that he is a television producer, not a 'rasslin promoter. Therefore, he might argue, the basics of booking do not apply to WWE. Yet haven't successful television programs like *CSI, ER, Law and Order*, and even *The Sopranos* based their across-the-board appeal on a well-drawn plot? And what is plotting, today's so-called storyline in wrestling language, other than booking? Saying it's "just wrestling" (or sports entertainment) is no excuse for terrible execution. Without fail, audiences will leave a shoddy product in either anger or disappointment.

The promoter has to stay true to his vision and believe it will find an audience. His goal is to persuade the fans to purchase what he sells. Without confidence, a promoter is doomed. Trying to give everyone what they claim to like most means giving nothing to nobody. Bookers and promoters must give the best *they* have, not dilute their product by chasing every little market niche. The great promoters have always known how to package and present *their* product to sell tickets. If that product is solid and has enough time and visibility, it finds an audience.

Is booking by committee "wrong?" Of course not. Does it work for Vince? Does it make money? Therein lies the answer. The days of the sole booker are probably long gone. It's just not viable, one man being responsible for churning out six hours of new television every week (not to mention monthly PPVs, weekly house shows, and frequent overseas tours).

Delegating works for McMahon; he steps aside as others battle, manipulate, and play politics. Then he can orchestrate the changes he wants without wasting his time hashing out ideas or, worse, debating about what to do with prelim talent who matter little to his gross receipts. Under his system, McMahon can pick and choose from the best ideas, and then spin things with his own, unique vision.

Why does *WrestleMania* usually draw so well? One simple reason is that fans know there will be fewer tricks, at least in key confrontations. There will be winners. And losers. A climax to the story. Maybe a surprise or two. The hot-shot gimmick, from Mr. T to Tyson to Trump to Mayweather. Nobody plunking down a buck gets taken at *WrestleMania*. Critics may complain that a finish was not inventive enough, but aren't there those who gripe about the Super Bowl, too? Vince deserves accolades, because he's been proven right. His bank account says so.

How many bookers, in how many offices, including WWE, have wondered, "How do I get out of this angle?" It still happens. How do they "get out of" champion versus challenger? How do they "get out" when they're dealing with stubborn stars? Any right-thinking promoter, or student of the game for that matter, should cringe when they hear the phrase, "We can get out of it by . . ." Run for the hills, because what follows is likely to leave everything in ruins and waste valuable, limited resources such as good talent and good ideas.

The utterance almost always indicates that no thought was given to the most important part of booking and plotting — the ending, the climax, the finish. That decision should have been made when the match was booked! Scrambling like this can also lead to the type of finish that solves a headache for one night, but creates a far bigger problem when business falters because fans are unhappy. This is not to say that the babyface has to win, just that the finish has to make sense and not insult the customer's intelligence. A touch of unpredictability, some tension about what is going to happen, is good for the audience, but the booker/promoter should have determined long before how that final scene was to be played.

The simplest and best finish is, to some minds, the toughest to pull off. Anyone can bump a couple referees out of action, miss a clear pin, run in a few bellicose wrestlers, miss another pin, add a couple chair shots, before implementing a confused ending that, supposedly, will hurt no one. Oh, those dreaded words: "We got out of it without hurting anyone." They mean, in reality, we got out of it without *helping* anyone — and thus not helping the business either.

Naturally, there's room for mixed-up mayhem when it leads to a real payoff. The risk of doing it too often is that fans simply become immune to the heat that is supposed to be generated. Worse yet, relying on another referee bump or yet another run-in for the blow-off is, to put it bluntly, cheap. It cheats the paying customer who wants and deserves a resolution. Somebody clearly and cleanly wins the World Series, the Super Bowl, a heavyweight boxing match, and a UFC clash. In wrestling, the onus is put squarely on the talent and the booker — they need to correctly sequence the ring action to tell the story, and suggest that the outcome could have gone either way, preferably without the clichéd extra activities to "protect" people.

Fabulous competition, a gut-grabbing story, a clean one-two-three pinfall: even in defeat the challenger should still be a viable contender, and a dethroned champ should remain a real threat to regain the crown. A worthy main event property should be skilled enough as a worker to avoid being devalued by a memorable defeat.

That's a *real* finish — not running in half the dressing room or having outside interference hide the fact that the promotion did not have the courage to pin somebody cleanly. It might amaze some bookers, but there are plenty of examples throughout mat history to prove that fans will buy the product again and again knowing they'll get a real finish.

Buck Robley is a cynical old school warrior who knows the ins and outs of all the backroom politics. A smart, though contentious booker in several different territories, Buck makes no bones about it: "If I'm not smart enough to put together a finish with two talented performers, I shouldn't be doing the booking. Stuff like ref bumps and run-ins are to camouflage one of two things — the booker doesn't know how to put in a finish, or the wrestlers aren't good enough to do a finish."

Some bookers have been known to place praise for how "imaginative" they are ahead of the right finish, something they may not even understand in the first place. A committee can become insular, with the members eventually booking and offering bizarre ideas to impress each other rather than the fans.

Not all ideas are good ideas. Drawing heat the hard way, putting key talent into explosive situations with meaningful conclusions despite the politics and personalities, always works best in the long run. That type of heat, rather than "getting out of it" or being "creative" for its own sake, leaves an audience excited for the moment and wanting more in the future. As Robley points out, everything in wrestling today is a rehash of something that has been done before. In the end, what matters is whether the superior talent can put on an irresistible performance.

For example, a run-in is a run-in, nothing more. Even the overdone "distraction" leading to a decision in the ring counts as sort of a run-in, because it has become "blah." Generally, no particular athletic skill is needed, no lightning charisma is required, no intricate psychology is at play. Don't be surprised to see the day come when a crowd chants "booorrr-ing, booorrr-ing" during another repetitive run-in and beat down, which also signals "no finish that matters here." In the end, the talent needs to put on on a compelling performance, within a storyline that is not patently ridiculous, and that fans have not seen over and over.

Do booking/creative teams think that explosions, pyrotechnics, and set collapses are the only ways to get anyone's attention, now that chair shots, sledge hammers, and gang attacks are passé? After all, machine guns and axes are politically incorrect.

Is the beloved hot shot at risk of becoming ordinary?

The hot shot has been a long revered term in wrestling annals. Generally, it involves blood or some particularly violent outbreak. In the 1970s, The Sheik used hot shot after hot shot to draw huge crowds in Detroit and Toronto. But he used the technique so often that, before long, both towns were dead as a doornail and had to be rebuilt with different booking philosophies.

During the past two decades, wrestling has had more than its share of hot shots. At times, the barrage has gotten to the point where the creative sorts think nothing short of car wrecks and supposed broken bones will move spectators. The trick of a hot shot is to pick the perfect moment, which is very rare, and to do it right, with the correct performers and as much of a new twist as can be reasonably added without encouraging fans to scoff, "Come on, get real."

Sadly, sometimes hot shots are booked in desperation. Lack of planning can leave any promotion, including WWE or TNA, in a spot where nothing can draw a house or sell PPVs. When panic sets in, a hot shot of blood, gore, ladders, tables, and garbage can lids is sure to follow. Too many panic situations? Well, then nobody cares about hot shots anymore. Repetition makes even the hot shot boring.

There is another kind of desperation, and Robley dealt with it when he started booking in Kansas City during the territorial era. Talent was weak, business was bad, and Bulldog Bob Brown was just about his only established performer. Unfortunately, Brown had been there so long and done so much that he hardly drew. Buck invited in his longtime buddy Skandor Akbar. Akbar promptly threw a fireball and burned Brown on television.

Surprisingly, all of the territory towns drew well for the showdown between Akbar and Brown. "Brown had been there so long that what Akbar did shocked everybody, so we got something out of nothing," explained Robley. "But we couldn't do it again."

Even with hot shot booking, though, there eventually has to be a finish. This is where so many bookers flounder, falling into the "get out of it" trap. Isn't it telling that the biggest crowd reaction still occurs when a worthwhile championship changes hands after a fabulous struggle?

In wrestling terms, shady finishes with referee bumps and outside interference are known as "screw jobs." They call it a screw job for the reason that one participant, usually the babyface, is being screwed. The truth, though, is that the fans are the ones getting screwed, and a sad part of modern wrestling promotion is that a percentage of the fans, especially newer ones, have been conditioned to accept being screwed. Remember what Wild Bill Longson said about finishes and sex? Well, a referee bump, a run-in, and a dirty one-two-three are just another tease. There's a politically incorrect phrase for this kind of thing, and it can apply to booking as well.

Movie critic David Ansen, writing for *Newsweek*, once bemoaned that "special effects have become the crutch for lazy dramatists." He argued that special effects have become "a substitute for a dramatically coherent ending." Ansen is apparently not a pro wrestling fan. . . . Imagine how he'd feel if he'd been subjected to countless run-ins, telegraphed referee bumps, nasty weapon attacks, and frustrating missed pins. He'd clearly be appalled by inept, insecure bookers (or committees) who repeatedly use their business's special effects to satisfy political ("Keep his heat!") or personal ("I wouldn't do a job for that guy!") agendas at the expense of satisfying paying customers. Lazy dramatists, lazy bookers — who says wrestling is not part of the same entertainment culture?

Jeff Jarrett, a guiding light in the ring and behind the scenes with TNA, talked about gimmick matches and finishes during an online interview for *Between The Ropes*. He acknowledged complaints, but then explained: "The criticisms come from people . . . without them knowing the full hand we've been dealt."

Isn't that a knock at his company's own talent? Years ago, that comment might have made sense for Memphis, the territory Jarrett came from, because the level of talent was nowhere near what New York, Minneapolis, St. Louis, Toronto, and other markets had at their disposal. Imaginative booking was needed to hot shot talent that on big market cards would have been far beneath the top hands and involved in preliminaries.

Shouldn't TNA be held to a higher standard with a former Olympic titlist and great performer like Kurt Angle on its roster? When Angle dropped the TNA crown to Samoa Joe, the company nailed it. Unfortunately, TNA immediately fell back into old habits with crash TV programming and "special effects" booking that have again left the promotion spinning its wheels. Luckily, TNA has been able to make some financial headway by tapping into alternate revenue streams like licensing, because their PPV buy rates remain stagnant.

Yes, there are readers who will now accuse me of being stuck in the past, of being old school, of not realizing that clean winners and losers no longer work. Well, for decades Major League Baseball and the National Football League have seemed quite successful. Those businesses are all about victors and the vanquished. Isn't there a storyline in a season of winning and losing, of ups and downs?

Aren't there definitive finishes, varied but satisfying, in movies as diverse as *Indiana Jones and the Temple of Doom*, *The Dark Knight*, *Michael Clayton*, *Slumdog Millionaire* or any flick where Will Smith saves the world? Absolutely. Storyline, or plot, or booking, led to a final triumph and, for viewers, the *real* payoff.

When it comes to combat sports, whether they're "real" or not (or whatever the murky ground in between might be), what's been the hottest item to the highly sought after young adult male demographic? It's the UFC, where somebody wins and somebody loses. Because fans accept wins and losses as an enjoyable selling point, they realize the loser is an outstanding athlete who may well have won on a different day. Their only real storyline, based on victories, right now lures more domestic PPV buyers on a consistent basis for UFC than for any other sport, including WWE.

Apply the UFC's booking philosophy to wrestling and all sorts of thrilling options are opened for the worked sport. UFC, the "hot new thing," actually follows traditional wrestling promotion and booking — the old St. Louis way — to astonishing success. Terry Funk explains it like this: "UFC is us. It's what we used to do . . . manipulating, and putting the stars in the right spots. Vince is something else."

Whether wrestling is a work or shoot is not the point. Without a winner, where is the climax, the payoff? When bookers ignore the history they themselves have created, wrestling is compromised. Can you imagine George Lucas sending out postcards informing his audience that Darth Vader is actually still alive? Well, that's tantamount to what some bookers have done when, whether it's something that happened last week, last month, or last year, they tell fans that something they watched happen, did *not* happen. No wonder everyday wrestling enthusiasts, where the bulk of a promotion's profit comes from, turn away in disgust after seeing stipulations disappear like dust in the wind.

What if one of the performers in a match is not good enough to tell the story without creating chaos in and around the ring? It happens often, and it surely brings up the question of what in the world he's doing in the role to begin with. Usually a great worker can pull up a mediocre but willing wrestler to make a terrific match. How many duels did Gene Kiniski, Pat O'Connor, Ray Stevens, and Harley Race save?

If working involves a performer knowing what he can and cannot do, booking means plotting while understanding the limits of everyone. Two average workers who understand their characters well (Hulk Hogan and Andre the Giant fall into this category) could stick to the basics and put together a memorable battle, because fans wanted to see that collision so badly. Critics may scoff, but the attendance figures have told the tale again and again for years. Catching lightning in a bottle with two great workers who could "blow the roof off the dump" like Dory Funk Jr. and Jack Brisco makes the story even better.

The phrase "getting your heat back" — which means protecting the character of heels — has been bandied about for years. The babyface gets the win, but then the heel beats the living daylights out of the winner. The idea behind this, theoretically, is that the heel will still be able to draw because fans are angry with him. Well, maybe it works once or twice. At one point a few years back, the pendulum had swung so far that in almost every match won by a babyface, the heel would "get his heat back" in a beatdown after the decision was rendered. And bookers wondered why fans were tuning out?

Carried to the extreme, this also meant a babyface could lose a bout and then work over the heel following the bell. It's the reverse of getting heat back for a heel, and just as useless in accomplishing anything worthwhile. The entire idea is more about protecting someone's ego than it is about strengthening the business. Obviously, that's bad for the bottom line.

All that type of booking does is diminish the result and cheat the fan out of a chance to cheer or boo.

A truly gifted performer does not need to "get his heat back" when he drops a decision. In defeat, he should have also been able to create enough doubt as to who the best truly was, regardless of who was cheered. He can "get his heat back" in future outings if he has legitimate talent and charisma.

Heat is a funny thing. Buck Robley recounts a time during the mid-1970s when Dory and Terry Funk asked him to help book Stu Hart's Stampede Wrestling in Calgary, a difficult territory where no established performer wanted to work for long. The weather was brutal, the trips were arduous, and the pay was lousy. Robley felt obligated — the Funks had given him an opportunity to help book in Texas. He also was friends with The Stomper (Archie Gouldie), who at the time was a Stampede fixture.

In typical wrestling fashion, Buck was promised $500 per week; he says he was never paid more than $300. When he arrived, Robley found the territory light on talent, except for a couple youngsters, and he had to use Stu's kids on a regular basis. He tried to create some heat, though, and naturally introduced himself as a key heel getting ready for The Stomper.

One evening, after an eight-hour drive in ice and snow to a tiny town not even on most maps, Robley was in the ring trying to generate heat for a dinky crowd. As Buck pounded some green grappler, he suddenly realized that someone else was kicking his opponent too. Shocked, Robley realized the referee, Stu Hart's son Smith, was putting the boots to his fallen foe.

"What the hell are you doing?" Buck shouted.

Smith Hart kept on kicking and yelled, "Hey, I gotta get my heat too!" Robley threw up his hands, laughed, left the ring, and went home.

That incident fits in with the despicable "cheap" heat, which is prevalent today because many performers have never mastered the nuances of smart working and legitimate ring psychology. What is cheap heat? Cheap heat can be grabbing the ring microphone and insulting the home town, or wrestler's promos being flat-out rude to fans (a favorite and numbingly redundant theme in scripted promos from the creative staff, with WWE heels calling spectators hypocrites, fools, cowards, or whatever). It can be a groin shot delivered to the babyface. It can be the disgusting tactic of playing to racial stereotypes. It can be the routine run-in — which of course most have become. It can be the desperate begging for applause or the frantic arguing with a ringside spectator to incite jeering.

Actually, cheap heat does have its place in getting a momentary reaction from the crowd. Nothing is wrong with that, although even the ring announcer could get cheap heat by sticking out his tongue, dropping his pants, and mooning the audience. Fans would make noise for sure! Heat that is cheap is ultimately pointless. It doesn't mean a doggone thing, nobody remembers it, and it won't draw a dime.

Cheap heat does not require the passion of performance, the projection of personality, the development of the story, or the clever exhibition of outstanding athleticism. Cheap heat is not like REAL heat, earned the hard way. *That* makes money.

The bottom line now is that generating genuine heat, the hard and legitimate kind that draws money, is next to impossible. Spectators have been bombarded with so many angles — way too often involving performers who just cannot cut it or ideas that insult the intelligence — that the customer base is now reluctant to suspend disbelief and emotionally invest in a character. Furthermore, they are often watching a promotion that has made no pretense of saying the action is real, so why should they care? Whether or not they actually knew better, they have been deprived of the opportunity to believe, if only for a few minutes.

Doesn't it seem odd that after all the effort Vince and company have expended trying to position WWE as not a sport but a safe entertainment of some sort, so many angles revolve around injuring someone, crippling him, and putting him "out of the business?"

By his own public statements, Vince has told the world that the promotion is *not* going to deliver on the very promise WWE dangles as bait for pay-per-view buyers. Common sense suggests that angles reliant on wins and losses or capturing a valuable championship would be much more likely to satisfy the audience and keep them coming back for more. In other words, the twist of the plot, not someone being maimed — which isn't even going to happen, even though stiff, physical contact is definitely appreciated.

For those relative newcomers who have been indoctrinated by Vince's vision of pro wrestling as merely entertainment, the soap opera aspect may hold their interest and patronage for awhile. But isn't it interesting that many of these same fans get suddenly extra-enthusiastic when they think an "accident" happened and Chris Jericho *really* hit Shawn Michael's wife by accident and now Shawn is "really" irate? More to the point, isn't it even more interesting that on occasion Vince and his creative team attempt to devise a feud that has the tinge of "now this — *this* is real"?

The perception of real still moves ratings, tickets, and PPV buy rates. That feeling, even momentarily, stirs an emotion that makes it so much easier to get worked up about what is still a staged event. Somehow finding that fine line, and letting a fan believe for an hour or two if he or she wants to regardless of what they know, is the task of a booker. And good heat makes doing that easier.

Even Smith Hart would admit that, truthfully, the best heat a heel can get is by winning a close, sensational, *clean* verdict. What's better? Fans want to see that heel whipped, and now his heat comes from the fact that he really is *good*. It is like the Red Sox coming to Yankee Stadium, or the Yankees at Fenway Park.

The same concept holds true in a babyface versus babyface duel. Fans will still pick a favorite, and they'll jeer the man they want to see lose. It's the John Cena dilemma. wwe has been hell-bent on making everyone root for Cena — but no matter what they do, there will always be a segment of their audience that wants to see him trounced. Why worry? At least people are buying the product, living vicariously, and making lots of noise. That's heat, and it's all that matters.

When Dory Funk Jr. was becoming hot in St. Louis during the mid-1960s, the same thing happened. Dory, along with his father Dory Sr. and brother Terry, was often involved in feuds with Dick the Bruiser or Fritz Von Erich. A small but very vocal minority, probably not more than 10% of the St. Louis audience, resented Dory's push — and especially the Funk family dynamics — against the likes of Bruiser, and they booed the babyface. Eventually, Dory won over most of his critics, and later became an excellent title-holder — one who got booed in certain circumstances.

Today, discussing Cena, there are those who maintain that there are no longer heels and babyfaces — that such thinking is obsolete in an era when characters are drawn in shades of gray, when truthfully wrestling has thrived with stars like that for decades. The rationalization of wwe would hold up better if both marketing and booking did not go out of their way to portray good guys and bad guys, quite often for purposes of selling merchandise tagged by the perceived fan favorite. Vince and his entourage look at Cena as a babyface. wwe spent countless hours trying to make everyone cheer Cena because John was supposed to be the babyface, before they finally accepted the situation as it was. His image still sells gobs of merchandise anyway.

Part of the problem — Cena is not alone in this — is that many of today's performers begin a match with a kick or a punch, immediately, perhaps because they are not polished enough in more subtle forms of working psychology. Starting that way is not exactly a babyface tactic. Actually, no matter how extreme the heat on a heel, there always was a crossover between heel and babyface, because the best in both roles made that powerful emotional connection with the fans.

Years ago now, long before Cena donned jean shorts, Muchnick and I talked about the reaction Dory Jr. received. Sam said he was never concerned: "We didn't care if they booed or cheered as long as they bought tickets and got excited. Empty seats do not make noise."

There are those who believe that wrestling's characters and the reaction to them are a reflection of society as a whole. With many today preferring anti-heroes or rebels, this means that traditional clean-cut babyfaces like Jack Brisco or Bob Backlund will probably get booed. And while this is a fact of the new reality, it's not necessarily true for every part of the potential audience, especially if the perfect performer is cast in the clean-cut babyface role.

If older fans or young girls like someone, is there something wrong with collecting their money? If the crowd is split in their allegiance, doesn't that make for a torrid atmosphere? Anyway, in time, the little girls who cheer for Cena will grow up to be big girls, and the boys booing Cena now may just discover that cheering for Cena is a smart move after all.

Whether by necessity (because of the lack of polished new talent), or by conscious decision, Vince has played off this dynamic recently and found success. The best versus the best, no matter who is cheered or jeered, has worked. Isn't that the goal of both legitimate sports and serious drama? And isn't it intriguing that Sam Muchnick did the same thing? Once again, the old and the new can make for strange bedfellows.

Vince reportedly talks about the year between *WrestleManias* as a novel with approximately 14 chapters. When one *WrestleMania* ends, it's time to write a new book. There are planned peaks, obviously, like *Summer Slam* or *Survivor's Series*, that are supposed to draw big business, and the burden of stockholders and Wall Street anticipating quarterly profits is ever present. There are the resolutions of feuds, tests for new talent in important positions, and digressions to keep the true superstars strong and at odds. But in theory, everything builds toward the final slam-bang chapter, the next *WrestleMania*. And then it all begins again.

In the 1950s, through the red-hot 1960s, and into the 1970s, Sam Muchnick's sportswriting background led him to favor a season for wrestling. Of course, back then there were no PPVs and a promoter's money was made at big house shows, of which there were perhaps 17 a year.

Sam would take July off for baseball, the racetrack, and family pleasures. The season for wrestling began in August and ended the following June. There were some peaks to cash in with big business during October, late November, and January into April, comparable to the modern PPVs. Feuds were made and concluded, new talent was tested in high-profile slots, and proven superstars were kept strong and at each other's throats. The finale of the season in June was a blow-off, big bang show that would sell out. Then Sam would go on vacation for a month, recharge, and get ready to start a new season.

Vince McMahon has the novel. Sam Muchnick had the season. The similarities are fascinating. Both men grasped the natural peaks and valleys of the wrestling business cycle. In different times, with different tools at their disposal, they ended up with essentially the same philosophy.

Booking, clearly, has always been a huge part of it all. Sam was just as guilty as Vince of letting some ideas burn out. Look at the Texas Death Match, hardly a term that would find a home in today's politically-correct version of family-style, PG-rated entertainment that WWE claims to be, but is not. For Sam, the no-holds-barred brawls started in 1960 when Whipper Watson and Gene Kiniski settled their feud with a win for bad guy Kiniski.

The rules were simple: anything goes, except choking. Falls do not count toward winning or losing. A fall only means a brief rest period of around 30 seconds. The winner is declared when one man concedes or is ruled unable to continue. At first, a Texas Death Match meant an obvious winner and, better yet, a jam-packed arena. Think about last-man standing brawls, or I-Quit collisions, but a bit more structured.

Did losing hurt the star who did the job? Well, Dick the Bruiser could not continue after sustaining a knee injury and getting carried out of the ring in 1965 when he lost to Fritz Von Erich. Seventeen years later, after more sellouts against different foes than even Dick would remember, a main event between The Bruiser and Ric Flair lured over 19,000 fans.

Killer Kowalski was unconscious for minutes in the middle of the ring after a sleeper from Johnny Valentine, and Fritz Von Kiniski was escorted out by the ringside doctor after Gene Kiniski destroyed Fritz's claw hand. For the first ten years that St. Louis used the occasional Texas Death Match, there was a cavalcade of Hall of Fame standouts who lost, definitely unable to continue at the end of the match. All came back to draw big crowds in other main events, and in the case of heels, to have major heat. None needed to be protected; none were unable to "get their heat back."

But the Texas Death Match itself had long since fizzled by the time Flair and The Bruiser clashed in 1982. In different territories, and even in stand-alone St. Louis, the match was used so often that it was no longer unique. Worse yet, as grapplers who did not want to lose cleanly began to balk or bookers got cold feet, the rules shifted — to the point that a ten-count between falls was added.

That usually meant that fans paid expecting to see one star or the other beaten and unable to continue. Instead, they got one man on his knee and counted out at ten while the winner barely managed to beat the count himself. Acceptable once, maybe — if it was the babyface who won. Twice, and the gimmick lost its power.

The Death Match fell victim to the "how do we get out of it" mentality, even in St. Louis. Either performers could no longer be persuaded to do the right thing, or bookers got the "soft ear" and could be talked into a different finish. The fans balked, because the match meant little more than a regular bout. (Think about what happened to the hard-core duels in recent times.) In fact, Muchnick stopped allowing O'Connor to book Death Matches for some time, until he was finally persuaded that a contest between The Bruiser and Ivan Koloff could be done properly. My, my, more persuasion.

The finish was a mess; the contest officially ending when Koloff was counted out, outside the ring. The problem was that nobody realized the match was over. Joe Schoenberger, a former referee, was the timekeeper seated next to me, the ring announcer. We both knew Dick was getting his hand raised, but neither of us knew how. When it supposedly happened, we had no clue. Neither did the fans. Joe began timing the 30-second rest period between falls. Bruiser came to the apron and yelled at me, "Aren't you going to announce it?"

"Announce what?" I answered.

Bruiser shouted, "It's over. I won!"

Startled, I think I responded, "What?"

Dick rolled his eyes and then started brawling with Koloff again while the referee explained to me that the match was in fact over and Bruiser victorious. The fans were generally happy to see Bruiser win, but there was no big cheer and plenty of boos because the people couldn't understand what happened. The paying audience felt cheated. Neither man was disabled — they were standing toe-to-toe and slugging it out.

It was a fiasco. And afterwards, Muchnick announced that Bruiser-Koloff was the last Texas Death Match he would ever promote. Sam believed the bout should only end when one man concedes or is physically unable to continue. He believed it should never finish with doubt and confusion. Of course, what was unsaid at the time was that O'Connor was to blame: the booker had once again okayed a finish that just didn't work.

It was four years before Sam allowed another Texas Death Match to be booked in St. Louis. When Jack Brisco beat Ken Patera on September 11, 1981, I was involved in the booking; and Sam still didn't give his okay until I promised the finish would have Patera unable to continue after losing a fall to Brisco's figure-four leglock. Fortunately, Patera was a true professional and sold it perfectly.

The bottom line was that booking, in St. Louis like everywhere else, killed the Texas Death Match as a guaranteed attraction. Over the years, handicap bouts have turned into squashes, first-blood duels have culminated with trickles of the red stuff, cage matches have been plagued with outside interference, I-quit affairs have featured non-combatants conceding, battle royals have run for a mere few minutes, last-man standing collisions have ended in a draw, and stipulations have been piled on stipulations until no one cares — name the gimmick match, and the operators of wrestling have demonstrated an undeniable talent for running the concept into the ground, usually with the classic bait-and-switch and a failure to deliver on the promise.

Consider another wrestling term, the so-called Dusty finish, which is basically any variation of the following scenario: the first referee of a title match is bumped and knocked down or out of the ring. A second referee hustles to the ring, but while he's on his way, the champion does something (usually throwing the challenger over the top rope or hitting him with the title belt) that would normally lead to a disqualification. That DQ, of course, meant that the champion would keep his title. But since no referee was available to make the call, at least as far as the energized fans can see . . . By the time the second official is in the ring, the two wrestlers are back at it, and then the challenger pins the champ. The second referee then makes the three count and proclaims the challenger the winner and "new World Champion." The crowd, naturally, pops.

The "Dusty finish" became almost the exclusive end to title matches under Dusty Rhodes' watch as booker for Jim Crocket in the 1980s. The repetition of the scenario, again and again, was bad enough. But here was its true major flaw: audiences were never told that the second ref made an incorrect call — they went home thinking they'd seen something momentous, a title change.

Then, on the next television show, a disconsolate announcer would explain that the first referee had called for a disqualification and therefore, while the challenger was declared the winner, he did not get the title.

Think the fans felt screwed? How else could they feel? Frustrated ticket buyers, especially from the critical casual base, decided they had better places to spend their money than on an operation that continually screwed them. Fans today would react exactly the same way. With slight variations, Verne Gagne overdid the same thing when he had Nick Bockwinkel as a heel champion for the AWA. Even Vince himself has fiddled with the concept.

On the other hand, done once, correctly, the "Dusty finish" *could* spark another big crowd. On February 6, 1981, in St. Louis, challenger Ted DiBiase and champion Harley Race perfectly enacted the feat. In this case, however, as ring announcer, after the turmoil had ended, I explained from the squared circle what had happened regarding the decision and the title, with both DiBiase and the original referee, Charles Venator, right beside me. Working marvelously, DiBiase portrayed dismay and anger — but then shook Venator's hand, because the correct call had been made.

DiBiase earned a rematch after a string of other victories, a little angle was shot, and Race and DiBiase tangled again on June 12, 1981, with over 16,000 fans on hand and paying record gate receipts. After a scintillating duel, the champion won cleanly in the middle of the ring. Win or lose, because it was booked and performed correctly, DiBiase secured his place as a major player in St. Louis. Race, a heel champion, had the best heat possible to draw money in future title defenses.

Naturally, treating the primary championship like the Holy Grail and protecting the throne's legitimacy has been of awesome value. Obviously, Muchnick and Vince's father were proponents of that philosophy and cashed in on booking built around a prize that was elusive and thus more precious. The title itself became a drawing card, particularly so when the right performer (and it seldom required the same style or personality) was on the throne. The wrestler who had the honor gained in stature, and that stayed with him even after his reign was finished. Championship duels were premier events, the chase of eager challengers was engrossing, the rare change of the guard was stimulating, and everybody made money because of all that.

At different times, VKM has done a wonderful job of making the crown matter, thus the argument of old school versus new school is once more shown to be baloney. At other times, he has fallen into the trap of short-term gain at the expense of long-term strength by making the title look like a bouncing rubber ball.

Finding the happy medium between "anything can happen at any time" and "it's a BIG deal when this happens" is not easy with often-changing theories of booking influenced by factors like overnight television ratings. Where is the confidence in a promotion's booking philosophy?

Multiple combatant matches where the champion can lose the crown without even being beaten were cute a time or two, but the appeal wore off quickly and failed to increase revenue. The tactic, naturally, allowed a champion to lose his crown without being defeated. In fact, in any such bout, whether or not titles are involved, certain pieces of talent can also be protected. One criticism might be that lazy booking has reared its ugly head . . . or that politics are being played . . . or that a shallow pool of headline talent is being extended. Nonetheless, battles that allow a championship to change hands without the titleholder himself losing do little or nothing to make the promotion's main prize more precious as a drawing card.

Having the title switch every few shows surprises fans for a bit, until it happens so often that the title itself loses meaning, and once more business flattens even when the championship is involved. Cheesy finishes also chip away at the meaning when applied too often in title duels.

The rationalization, of course, is that such booking tactics can extend the box office life when fewer true main-event performers have gotten over or even exist on the roster. The response to such an argument is that intelligent booking, good planning, and the ability to look backward as well as forward allows a star to be a star until the fire simply extinguishes. A meaningful goal that fans care about and for which everyone strives can bind the entire package together.

As detailed, political, and mysterious as booking appears, the truth of the matter is simple. Salty characters, from Buddy Rogers to Dick Murdoch, all agree: it's the "KISS" theory. Keep it simple, stupid. The easier it is for fans to understand what is happening, the bigger the audience will become. Persuasion is much easier under those circumstances. Please recognize that the word "stupid" refers to the performers and bookers, and that simple does *not* mean dumb.

In the end, it does come down to talent. People get behind stars who are battling for something perceived to be important, be it a championship or personal pride. Fans want to react for a winner and a loser. They accept a favorite's defeat if it makes sense and they're left with hope. Good, consistent booking makes the process much more effective.

Some critics complain about so-called even-steven booking in WWE, where the loser immediately scores a victory over the wrestler who defeated him only days before. But once again, the resemblance between the way Sam Muchnick operated and Vince McMahon works is surprising.

Muchnick quite often had leading stars trade wins and losses — but it was usually done over a longer period of time, as much as a year or more. The only headliner not part of the equation was the NWA champion, who battled top hands coming off triumphs over other leading men. Over time, though, a parity among the ranks of the best of the best was established.

In St. Louis, it took four years for Jack Brisco to get a victory over Gene Kiniski, who defeated Brisco three times during the period. Brisco was the NWA king by the time he whipped Kiniski. Of course, that is an extreme case, but it did lead to an absorbing story about how Brisco's reign was in jeopardy because he had never gotten a decision over "Big Thunder."

Vince has a tendency to turn victories around much more quickly, with yesterday's loser becoming today's winner, sometimes as soon as the *Monday Night Raw* following a PPV. Actually, he has deviated from a pattern he was obviously exposed to as he grew up in the business, a time when his father fed challengers to the champion. There would be a rematch or two in the top WWF towns, if business was strong. Then the challenger moved down to meet and, eventually, lose to the number two babyface throughout the territory, maybe participate in a couple tag bouts around the horn, or a few duels with the third-from-the-top star. And then the one-time challenger moved on to another territory.

Muchnick, in comparison, generally relied upon six to eight stars in the main event and championship mix. Over time, he rotated who was in that treasured group, because he could pick and choose from the comparatively large number of performers able to deliver the goods. The talent pool today, especially at the top, is much smaller. And due to this reality, Vince has in essence adopted the Muchnick system, but has added his own variations to its timing and finishes. The end result, however, is virtually the same: A beats B, then B beats C, but C beats A. Equality! Parity! Unpredictability! Excitement! Money!

Now work backward with the same talent for a different result. B beats A, C beats B, but A beats C. Throw in a champion, who defends against each of A, B, and C at the right moment. Perhaps blend in a young newcomer like D, to both win and lose. Suddenly an entire year or more of a booking outline that will grab fans emerges, clean and concise. Include just a small surprise here and there, booked and sold well, and predicting a winner becomes both intriguing and complex. The shelf life of existing talent, at the same time, is extended, plus there's space for new stars to emerge. More equality, parity, and, most importantly, money!

Vince has done a remarkable job of building a brand that in and of itself as WWE will usually draw a profitable crowd for house shows, thus keeping the boys busy and making a few dollars. Certain major PPVs like *Wrestlemania* or *Summer Slam* will do strong business based on the name alone, or at least have so far. Yet his gigantic shows, with a so-called famous label or not, the ones that set records and make the entire world blink, happen because true stars have been established, something perceived to be valuable is being fought for, and the outcome is in doubt . . . all thanks to good booking.

Many successful bookers started planning at the end. That's right, begin with the climax, the final resolution. Build backwards, with matches or angles, over several shows, so that the heat intensifies. Be flexible, however; adjust for surprise developments like crowd reaction to a new performer.

It's just as important to initiate other story threads a show or two into the sequence, as well as later on, so that there are various peaks along the way toward the finale. Don't get caught empty-handed: there has to be something to follow up with. There's absolutely no good reason for a booker or a creative team not to have a main event for the "next" program; there should never be a need to resort to panic matchmaking.

This is not old school or new school. This, my friend, is simply common sense.

Booking is an enormous obligation, even more complicated than what this lengthy consideration of booking philosophies examines. The continuity of the matches from show to show alone requires constant attention, if it is to be accomplished correctly and keep fans interested. In addition, much rests on managing the so-called small details efficiently and tying them into the in-ring excitement, the television production, and the promoting and marketing. Done wrong or poorly, all of those details can undermine the entire effort. Imagine the pressure.

Yet when all is said and done, whatever the personalities, politics, history, and manipulation in the backroom, booking always comes down to very, very simple points, even if getting to those questions is torturous in the best of circumstances: Does it draw? Is there somewhere to go next? Is business left healthy?

If the answers are yes, yes, and yes, that is good booking.

CHAPTER NINE

THE VOICE

Nobody had a clue who I was in 1972 when I became the play-by-play announcer for *Wrestling at the Chase*. To viewers, Larry Matysik was just a fresh-faced young man with enthusiasm for pro wrestling. At the time, I wasn't analytical enough to grasp how important the announcer was to the product. But I learned. Otherwise, I just got on the horse, and off we went.

Like Jim Ross, Gordon Solie, Gene Okerlund and Rodger Kent, Lance Russell, Dick Lane, and all the others who called the action in a particular territory, I discovered that when a show was a hit, a competent announcer went along for the ride. And what a ride it was. Even today, more than two decades after I was last on the air, I'm regularly stopped by folks of *all* ages who have a story to share about how they or their family invited me into their homes every week. *Wrestling at the Chase* had the right people at the right time, and left a cultural and historic footprint in the community.

Though few other promotions, if any, have achieved the national cult status of St. Louis, in countless other cities, over a period of some 25 years, wrestling gained similarly large and loyal groups of followers. It's still happening today: Vince McMahon's televised wrestling extravaganzas draw some ten million viewers on a weekly basis. The only difference is that wrestling was much more localized back then. Now it's a national production. Years from today, people will still talk about watching wrestling, maybe with their parents or their kids. They'll smile about how they enjoyed listening to "Good Ole JR" and "The King."

It's an often-overlooked fact, but the announcer really is a critical part of what makes a wrestling program click. Consider this: Vince McMahon used to be a commentator for his father's show. If anyone knows, Vince should.

When I got started in St. Louis, I had a boss who had confidence in me, and a television station that was willing to give a green but talented kid with the gift of gab a chance. I followed the popular George Abel, who had been involved with various St. Louis television programs for years, and briefly worked with Sam Menacker, who was little known in St. Louis but was respected throughout the mat world. These were big shoes to fill. Fortunately, partly through growing up following wrestling (and later learning from Sam Muchnick), the business had somehow become a part of me, so I was ready for the opportunity.

The fellow who started it all, though, was Joe Garagiola. For many of the very same reasons that would be applicable today, Joe Garagiola was the perfect announcer for Muchnick's *Wrestling at the Chase*. Wrestling was a seldom-seen TV entity in the late 1950s, but the success of Sam's wrestling show with Joe on the mic pushed televised wrestling ratings through the roof. Promotions and television stations around the country jumped on the bandwagon with their own wrestling shows after they saw the resounding success in St. Louis.

It was 1959, a conservative period in social history. Here was wrestling, always a shady proposition for a large part of the general public, moving into the gorgeous Khorassan Room of the Chase-Park Plaza Hotel. Wrestling! Imagine. With its rowdy practitioners and its Gorgeous George characters, wrestling was sharing an ornate room at a fancy hotel that also housed balls, banquets, concerts, and high society dances for the elite of the community. That fact alone made everyone take notice.

On top of that, wrestling was going to be a prime anchor for the fledgling television station KPLR that, like the Chase itself, was owned by Harold Koplar.

The fact that Sam Muchnick provided a much more sports-oriented product than most wrestling operations would likely have garnered at least a modicum of respect and attention in St. Louis with any professional announcer. Joe Garagiola, however, helped make it special.

Growing up with Yogi Berra on St. Louis's hallowed Hill, Joe had been a Major League Baseball player, too, and that really meant something in a ball-crazy region like St. Louis. When injuries took their toll, Joe's wit, knowledge, and personality led him into the broadcasting field. By the time *Wrestling at the Chase* premiered, Garagiola was a broadcast fixture, sharing the microphone with Harry Caray and Jack Buck for Cardinal baseball on then-mighty KMOX Radio. Many in the industry thought, correctly as it turned out, that Joe was destined for even bigger things.

Wrestling at the Chase may not have seemed like a big move, but it ended up being great for all concerned. Like so many in St. Louis, Garagiola and his brother Mickey had grown up as wrestling fans. Joe knew all about Strangler Lewis, Lou Thesz, and Wild Bill Longson. He might coyly tell you that he can't tell a toehold from a headlock, but Joe understood and *liked* professional wrestling.

Koplar wanted someone to add entertainment to the wrestling show. (Sound familiar, maybe like someone named McMahon years later?) Muchnick wanted someone to add credibility in the sports universe, someone whose presence alone would attract viewers not normally interested in wrestling. Joe Garagiola was the perfect choice, cross-marketing at its best. Koplar told Garagiola to say whatever came into his head, and Muchnick encouraged him to go at the job like an athlete and not to worry.

He came across as a charismatic, colorful, almost playful presence, someone who had legitimate affection and respect for what professional wrestling was. Furthermore, Garagiola was able to play off the incongruous marriage of wrestling and the society locale without being snooty. He was funny — not funny like a grade-schooler snickering at a dirty joke, but amusing in a way to which viewers could relate.

One of Garagiola's *Wrestling at the Chase* duties was a live-on-tape commercial for Busch Bavarian beer, a product of main sponsor Anheuser-Busch. The trick was Joe had to describe the beer and pour at the same time, so that the foam ended just above the beer's label on the glass. Remember that this was around 1960, the early days of video tape. Nobody wanted to do anything over, which meant lengthy delays for rewinding, erasing, and cuing the tape. It was get it right — on the first take. Talk about working! Garagiola was afraid he would mess up the spot, so the producer told him to buy a couple cases of beer, go home, and practice.

Joe did just that, though he took the cases to his parents' house on the Hill. His father asked what he was going to do with all the glasses of beer he would pour. Joe said, "Dump it down the sink, I guess."

Dad said to wait a bit, and within 15 minutes a few of his father's friends had appeared — to drink the beer as Joe practiced getting it just right. "It took almost the entire two cases before I got it down," Garagiola laughed, "but my pop's friends were in a really great mood by the time I finished."

Garagiola, with his engaging personality and sharp wisecracks, was the glue that held the KPLR show together. That's what a good announcer did in 1959, and it's the same 50 years later. Clearly, if the product goes too far off the deep end, no announcer can save it; but by the same token, even if the wrestling is at least decent, an overbearing, carnival-barker screamer can drive viewers to switch channels.

Wall-to-wall action. Clever jokes about patrons dressed in fine gowns or suits and ties. Sweaty grunt-and-groaners under sparkling chandeliers. Joe mixed the elements together so fluidly that an entire metropolitan area fell in love, discovering the delights of wrestling in the process.

The athletic stuff came easy, because Joe truly admired what the wrestlers did in the ring. Even when he might poke fun at a personality or a move, it was done with respect and, yes, affection. Garagiola recognized the effort and emotion wrestlers put into their craft; he had been the same way with baseball.

What really clicked was Joe's banter with the likes of Gene Kiniski and Rip Hawk. For viewers, it was like watching and hearing baseball's bench jockeys trying to get under each other's skin. Once, the volatile Kiniski even jumped out through the ropes and chased Joe around the ring. It wasn't planned, and certainly not choreographed; that it was spontaneous, the natural instincts of two professionals letting themselves become lost in the moment, made it even better. Muchnick had a small spasm about it though, pointing out that no money had ever been made by a wrestler beating up an announcer. More importantly, he did not want his friend Joe hurt. But Sam felt better once he talked with everyone involved. When he later ran into Garagiola, Kiniski, and Hawk out bowling together after a show, Sam really relaxed. Muchnick's original instincts were correct, and so were those of Harold Koplar, and they trusted Garagiola and the ring warriors to make everything work smoothly.

Joe eventually used *Wrestling at the Chase* as an audition tape for NBC, where he later became the host of the *Today* show as well as a substitute for Johnny Carson and the play-by-play announcer for baseball's *Game of the Week*. Wrestling helped Joe, and Joe helped wrestling. Garagiola added tremendous crossover appeal, some 24 years before Vince McMahon melded rock and wrestling.

Just as Muchnick planned, Joe Garagiola lured casual fans. The overall audience was enlarged. If McMahon had Joe Buck or Bob Costas do *Raw* or a pay-per-view, would the same thing happen?

Garagiola brought credibility to wrestling, something Vince still covets today. The definition of credibility may vary with time, but WWE wants its productions to be considered slick, cutting-edge, and professional. McMahon wants wrestlers recognized as artists. Sam Muchnick might have defined credibility in different terms, but the principle is the same. And in the search for credibility, an announcer can certainly make a difference. Good company, professional, sharp, he's someone fans would enjoy having a conversation with. He helps performers tell the story in a way that makes sure viewers are not embarrassed, insulted, or aggravated. He educates. Whether it was Ross in Atlanta, Tulsa, or for today's WWE; Solie in Florida and Atlanta; Russell in Memphis; Okerlund and Kent in Minneapolis; Lane in Los Angeles; or even myself in St. Louis, the role of the announcer cannot be diminished. He's the link between audience, performers, and the promoter.

Over the years, I've chatted with several of the fellows who did the same job. While there were often small differences, certain basics always seemed to work. Of course, every promoter wants the job done his way. Jim Ross, for instance, once related that Cowboy Bill Watts, as both the owner and an in-ring star, would critique him after every taping. Since Watts was a big fan of Solie's style, he liked a very descriptive account of the action; Ross learned to provide him with this.

I had been influenced by Garagiola and Abel, but Sam Muchnick insisted that I should find my own voice. Knowing I could never be as funny as Joe, and wanting to be more colorful than George, I relied on my knowledge of the talent and the angles. I let my enthusiasm show. In the end, if I followed anyone, it was Bud Blattner, the smooth and effective voice of the St. Louis Hawks pro basketball team, or Jack Buck, who provided a superb mixture of fact and drama when it was called for. That worked perfectly in St. Louis, where wrestling was more of a sport than a circus sideshow.

In St. Louis it was definitely soft sell: subtle and cool — with the occasional burst of red-hot emotion. I always tried to avoid using the word "great," for the simple fact that it was too easy to fall into the habit of anointing every upcoming main event as "great," meaning that, eventually, "great" wouldn't mean a thing, because viewers would recognize it as just another sales pitch. "Great," in St. Louis, was saved for, well, *great*. Lou Thesz was "great," and so was maybe one star-studded Checkerdome lineup per year.

Is this the only way to do it? Of course not. The best way to judge success or failure is by the size of the audience. Some promoters wanted their announcers to be more aggressive and direct in selling a show. From my own experience, however, the St. Louis approach worked successfully for a quarter of a century. It was equally successful in the beginning, and later, when conditions caused wrestling to change.

Sam never really critiqued. I was working in his office, daily, so his relaxed, low-key, knowledgeable manner rubbed off, and it showed in my announcing. Ironically, the only two specific pieces of advice I remember Sam giving me had little to do with actually calling a wrestling match. Once, I and Mickey Garagiola, who did the ring announcing and occasionally chimed in during the bouts, laughed about some inside joke. I can't even remember what it was, but I believe it involved some interplay between Dick Murdoch and the show's director, Jim Winkle. We laughed, the technical crew got a kick out of it, and even Muchnick was amused. But the next day, Sam said, "It was okay, once, but don't tell inside jokes on the air. The viewers don't know what you're talking about. They'll feel left out. Stick to what they know." He was 100% correct. During the past few years, I noted a few times when an announcer is working a "rib" on the boys or the production crew during a broadcast, and it's irritating. Some announcers have, in coded fashion, poked fun at a wrestler's social habits. Worse yet, others have referred to backstage politics that, at best, had surfaced publicly on some miniscule blog. Usually, it is the booking that puts the announcer in this unenviable position. A vast proportion of the audience just shakes its head. All it does is drive viewers away and build a gulf between the fans and the announcer, the person they're supposed to trust the most.

Muchnick's other criticism was funny, but it also demonstrated how the wise old promoter never missed a trick that might sell a ticket. On this occasion, Mickey and I somehow got talking about our wives — Adele in his case, and Pat in mine. It was a brief exchange, and actually tied to wrestling, since we brought up what the wives thought about a rivalry that was being pushed. Quietly, as usual, the next day, Sam said, "You're a nice looking young fellow, and I'm not saying you should lie about being married or not wear your wedding ring. But there's no reason to bring up your wife. If some young gal wants to believe something, let her believe it. She might buy a ticket." My wily boss wasn't going to lose any opportunity.

Educating the fans was actually Muchnick's most important concern. He wanted wrestling enthusiasts to understand strategy, why wrestlers attacked as they did, why holds and escapes mattered, what was at stake, and how championship matches were earned. He also wanted them to at least get some inkling of who the wrestlers were, personally, to grasp the referee's job, and to fully understand the story that was being told in the ring and at the microphone.

For Vince McMahon, education is just as crucial. Although his product is assuredly different, making sure that fans understand the issues and philosophy he's selling is probably still the most important job of his announcers. Vince might not be worried about what to call individual holds, but he wants to make sure the plots are explained in understandable fashion. Of course, in Muchnick's time, what was at stake and how feuds developed could have been called *storyline*, too.

But schooling fans is not just the chore of the announcer. He is at the mercy of the booking, which has to be consistent and paced well enough for the lessons to be absorbed. No announcer, not even a Buck or a Costas, could save a mish-mash of ideas with all the connection of diced linguini. Thus, an announcer needs to understand the booking so that he can explain what is going on in entertaining fashion. I'd grown up with precisely this style. My brain was steeped in it, from watching televised wrestling since kindergarten (does anyone else remember Vess Box announcing *Texas 'Rassling*?), and from reading every scrap of news available about wrestlers and the sport. Being in the office with talking encyclopedias like Muchnick, and even to some extent Wild Bill Longson, it came naturally to me — and I think to many of the best announcers over the years.

It was also because calling St. Louis meant emulating the style of sports announcers like Blattner and Buck. Jack once did an interview with Marty Brenneman, the voice of the Cincinnati Reds, which touched on a very basic aspect of success at the microphone. It fit, and still does, for wrestling as well as baseball. Buck pointed out that sports are not brain surgery, that most fans understand the action and have a good grasp about the players and the strategy. Then he explained that he and Marty were just fans who were lucky enough to have more access to strategy, information, and news. Jack concluded that it was the announcer's job to share as much of that knowledge as possible with the folks who watched or listened to the event. The same held for wrestling — for Ross, Solie, me, or whoever else called the mat action. The more data the fans could understand and become intrigued by, the more likely they would be to get deeply involved and buy tickets.

A good announcer paints the picture with the glowing color of details. He can clarify a character with only the words used to narrate a moment in a match. A heel struggling to escape a predicament that could lead to submission might be portrayed as desperately grabbing the ropes to force a break, giving the impression that he somehow cheated or lacked that last little bit of courage. Put a babyface in the same situation, and going for the ropes can be represented as a clever way of saving himself for later in the match.

That tactic was fairly common for articulate announcers in most territories, even though the pictures they drew were much more black-and-white, bad guy versus good guy, than what we did in St. Louis. Today's WWE draws the lines between good and bad in graphic detail. It's not that St. Louis failed to distinguish between hero and villain — I most surely did, in colorful fashion, too — but there was usually a nod toward the competitive, sporting elements of the confrontation. Blatant cheerleading was not part of the equation. In St. Louis we explained *why* Gaylord Perry used the spitball and why Bill Belichek secretly filmed opponents, why Harley Race cut corners to keep his crown and why King Kong Brody had such a short temper.

One way is not necessarily better than the other. On *Wrestling at the Chase* I once explained a heel forcing a break in the same terms usually reserved for the babyface. I gave credit to him for saving himself and using good ring psychology. It was also a chance for me to put over what a devastating move the babyface had, and that the heel knew it. Afterward, Sam, who had a more subtle take on wrestling than most, said he really liked how I alerted the fans to the fact that heels can be smart, too.

Another critical and undervalued aspect of announcing is the need to vary your volume. If the announcer is already screaming during a bout featuring guys who are essentially preliminary talent, why would anyone pay attention when he yells for the main-eventers? The audience can't distinguish between what's important and what isn't if the volume is cranked up, "carny style," for a full hour.

It actually applies to interviews, too. Gary Hart, a wily booker and also a top-flight manager, explained it best. When everyone else is shouting, he once told me, speaking softly and carefully is what catches the attention of fans. Because it's different, it's recognized as serious.

During a typical television show, an announcer should run through all the registers of his voice. Like JR or Gordon Solie, I tried to follow the fans' reactions. My style was different, but the rhythms are basically all the same. If holds were being traded, technical and quick moves being made, I would try to stay right with it and explain what was happening in detail, naming the maneuvers and explaining the why of what was happening. When the crowd was quiet and engrossed, it was time to talk about a wrestler's background, about the history of a certain feud — maybe even to drop in a plug or two on behalf of the station. If something funny happened in the ring, I'd acknowledge it. If the fans chuckled, I'd laugh with them. Or I'd pick up on the natural humor that certain ring personalities displayed. All the while, I'd be paying attention to time cues from the floor director or following instructions from the director communicating through the headset.

An experienced hand can protect the talent — to an extent. Say a move backfires or looks sloppy. A quick explanation about how the wrestler on the receiving end managed to avoid disaster, or is perhaps "playing possum," can help keep the illusion alive and healthy. Similarly, when a blow or bump is particularly stiff, run with it! That's always worth turning up the volume a notch for.

As things warm up, when the heel draws some heat for example, the time is at hand to add urgency to your voice. Get on the roller-coaster, and ride it up and down. If the folks are shouting, something similar from the announcer is appropriate. Find the tempo of the struggle, and let it guide you. But always remember this: it's the stars who draw; their angles are what count. And know, too, that all of the wrestlers are significant. Help everyone look his best, while keeping in mind who really packs the house. If the volume scale runs from quiet to the intense roar of ten, saving ten for that one earth-shattering moment that occurs once a year when the two top stars collide is wise.

Vince McMahon, in the role of television producer, has added a twist to broadcasting wrestling that works well — because it's different. During a big angle or moment, his announcers often go silent and let the images and crowd reaction carry the load. With the expert camera people he employs, it can really be effective. But relied upon too often, the tactic can also fail. A few times, spots designed to build major heat for the heel actually saw the heat dissipating — because setting up a bump took so long the live crowd lost interest, and no announcer was covering the hole for the viewing audience.

A skilled announcer can help make a weak match tolerable, and a good match nearly great. He can also add something special to a great match, but it's the wrestlers, not the announcers, who matter. The broadcast table is no place for ego. If an announcer is trying to get himself over, he's hurting the show. Being articulate, syntactically playful, and reveling in the beauty of the language is wonderful, but it should never overshadow what's occurring in the ring.

Today's wrestling product does not necessarily reward a good announcer. Most matches are so short and drastically paced that there is no time to sell the jeopardy or paint the picture. Another difficulty is posed by the huge number of promotional elements that need to be worked into the commentary. Marketing responsibilities often make the announcer a pitchman, especially in a shorter duel: plugs for websites, pay-per-views, music, T-shirts, books, other television properties, and even a commercial break are often included at the expense of calling a match or developing a character. This necessarily works against younger or new in-ring talent, who no longer benefit from the "shine" or rub an announcer was once free to give them.

Wrestling is no different than any other television property. Take local news shows, for example. How much "news" is actually nothing but promo? Granted, much of the content is still as it should be, but is hyping an upcoming network program an anchor's main responsibility? Count how many plugs for the station's website are inserted. And how many "news" breaks tease a story, but never give a hard fact? Promos, promos, everywhere! Television and radio broadcasts of baseball are similarly cluttered with announcements, either paid or self-promoting, masquerading as part of the game's description. Wrestling is hardly alone in suffering this plague.

At the risk of being typecast as old school, things were different in this important area back in "the day." In the 1960s and 1970s, the Federal Communications Commission kept tight control on the amount of commercial content on any television show, wrestling or otherwise. Only so much advertising time was allowed in any single hour. Unregulated cable did not exist; programming was strictly governed by FCC rules. Constantly selling an upcoming PPV within the body of a TV show was impossible in the past.

An upcoming date could not be specifically hyped, except during the two or three minutes of clearly separated commercial plugs for auditorium programs. While we as announcers could discuss upcoming matches (a "soft plug"), the promos had to be subtle and clever — even subliminal — without mentioning dates or buildings.

An announcer was limited to saying something like, "By this time next week, the title could belong to . . ." Or, "In just six days the long-awaited collision between these two superstars will finally happen." Even, "What a fabulous night of wrestling is on tap when DiBiase and Brody write another chapter in their bitter feud, the master scientific wrestler against the vicious back-alley brawler . . ." Or, finally, "Kiel Auditorium is a fabulous building for sports, including wrestling. Kiel has been the site of many historic showdowns, which might be the case again when Funk tackles Brisco."

Rivalries and angles could be explained, but even wrestler interviews had to tread carefully with respect to advertising restrictions. All sorts of hell could be raised about a future opponent, but the rant was not considered a commercial as long as the date of a bout was not mentioned — though that information was occasionally slipped in during the heat of the moment. (A lot of old hands are winking right now.)

Another complication was that the same tape might be telecast in four, six, or even ten different markets. Each had different dates for their non-television cards. In those cases, the interviews would often include the date, and that meant different interviews had to be recorded and inserted for each town. Usually the deals with the stations noted that these interviews were commercials (for which some financial consideration between promotion and station existed), so that the station could list the interview as an advertisement to satisfy the FCC requirements.

Back then, television stations actually had to "log" the commercial time in every hour of broadcasting under threat of censure by the FCC. By the 1980s, the rules were becoming more flexible, but restraint still needed to be exercised. Now the restrictions on promos as commercials have generally disappeared.

Cable, of course, changed things completely. Regulation became a dinosaur, which has proven both good and bad — and not just for wrestling. Commercial and content can now be blended seamlessly. In typical wrestling fashion, however, most shows went overboard with blatant, loud, and nearly constant plugs for the next big event or the plethora of other items they wanted to sell their audience.

This is not a complaint. Actually, as a former announcer, I am jealous of today's freedom. But the other side of the coin is that promoters — especially the big one, who fancies himself as first and foremost a television producer — began to do less wrestling and more pitching. Talk, talk, talk; plug, plug, plug. Doesn't that show a lack of faith in what happens inside the squared circle? Wrestling has slipped far past the point where action and acting are balanced.

Once upon a time the focus was the battle in the ring, the gladiators colliding. That still occurs, but generally only once or twice per program. Many bouts are only a couple minutes long, or *less*, after the introductions. The opportunities for the announcer to perform his brand of magic are dwindling, except perhaps on pay-per-views, and the lack of time definitely works against him. It's hard to be subtle any more. And to a very real extent, the fact that there's really only one game in town means the announcer pool has shrunk just as radically as the one that spawns talented wrestlers.

Calling a wrestling match is hard work. Taking a time cue and getting out, or in, at the exact second is just one precise action an announcer must handle smoothly. So is nailing a clever segue into, or out of, a pre-taped video package. There's so much to learn, so much to understand; there's subtle psychology in play, and you need to be quick thinking *and* have real verbal dexterity. Finally, there's teamwork: to be most effective, the announcer must mesh with everyone from the cameramen and light and sound crew to the wrestlers themselves.

An announcer must develop his own style, and it's advisable to project an honest account of himself that viewers can learn to trust. Not every announcer can be a character — nor should he try, unless he really is one. Wrestling's already a zoo; the announcer does not need to be another circus animal. If he's not comfortable, the audience senses it, instinctively, and ignores him. This is even harder than it seems, on a national stage, when the stakes are so high, and the pressure of working for a demanding organization like wwe is so great.

Ever notice those headsets JR, Lawler, and Michael Cole wear? Guess who is usually in their ear while they're trying to talk to the audience? Yes, of course, it's Vince. The old announcer in the boss has strong opinions about what should be said. And *when* it should be said. And *how* it should be said. More challenging yet is the fact that Vince's concept of what works and what doesn't work changes on a regular basis. Apparently, he's not shy about barking commands during the show.

Say this. Don't say that.

No, say it *this* way.

Throw the director's voice into those headsets, too, and chaos can reign while there's a match to be called. A rookie announcer would be eaten alive. Mick Foley was lucky when he landed a seat at the *Smackdown* announcers' table; he arrived with his own reputation and style and it bought him some leeway until he got tired of being pressured by Vince and finally said goodbye to the job.

Under Vince's regime, the role of the announcer has become more and more homogenized, to the detriment of the product. When the likes of Ross and Lawler finally disappear from the scene, it will become obvious that a mistake has been made. (Pity poor Todd Grisham and Michael Cole: they've had anything unique about their personality squeezed out of them.) A bland disembodied voice chirping promo spots does nothing to put icing on the cake.

A story once leaked that Stephanie McMahon, Vince's daughter and the head of the creative team, was handling the communication for a few shows. The announcers probably expected a bit of breathing room. Instead, as it turned out, Vince was in the control room telling Stephanie what to tell the announcers. Same old story, but with another layer of pressure added!

Yet Vince, of all people, should understand the job. After all, he called the action for many years in a successful promotion. While he spoke to me all the way back in 1983 of wanting to remove himself from the announcing position so he could concentrate completely on the monumental production and booking chores behind the scene, it was not until 1997 that Vince turned over the commentary duties. He realized how critical it was to get the message over, and it took him time to trust anyone other than himself.

Whether some viewers liked Vince's style and some hated it, the bottom line is what counts. People watched; people bought tickets. Vince must have been telling the story in an acceptable fashion. With his own strong ideas about how his company's angles and characters should be presented, Vince understandably wants things announced in a certain way. It's a burden his announcers, who could go in varied directions and be equally effective (and perhaps reveal more of their own personality), must accept.

There are other challenges. Changes in a show's lineup can be made abruptly, dramatic moments can erupt from out of nowhere, with no build and little follow-up. There is so little time for the announcer to fit everything together, especially on a live broadcast like *Raw*. Even experienced hands are hard pressed to keep the ups and downs from becoming too jarring.

Today's announcer has less and less rope. McMahon has at one point even apparently ordered his staff to get away from naming holds — likely figuring that many viewers don't care what they are, or that those who do already know. But telling the in-ring story without some certain descriptors is not always feasible. The names of finishers, like Whisper in the Wind, Figure Four, Iron Claw, STFU, or Pedigree; or the endless list of basic wrestling moves like reverse chinlock, hammerlock, vertical suplex, head scissors, or stepover toehold have always added color to the spectacle.

Look at those words again. It's vivid language, making it easier for an announcer to build the drama as he explains personality, rivalry, stakes, and strategy. Plus, fans *like* calling a move and having a name. It can also be bread and butter for an announcer as he puts the package together before a viewer's eyes. Doesn't it make sense to utilize all facets and report the action in a manner that satisfies those who are serious about watching?

In turn, potential new fans might actually find their appreciation of the event increased. Trust the viewers to sink their teeth into the meat of the spectacle. My experience is that fans end up calling the match in their own heads, and that makes what excites them even more tasty.

Perhaps an even sillier edict from Vince regarded that piece of hardware the many champions in his menagerie wear around their waists. Maybe, since some finishes were repetitive (not unusual!), he got tired of hearing an announcer shout, "The champ hit his opponent with a belt shot!" Or, "he nailed him with the title belt right in the head."

For whatever reason, Vince told the announcers not to use the word "belt" with "title" or "championship." In fact, don't say "belt" at all. Who knows what that thing is called that someone buckles around his or her middle if he or she is a champion? Thus, when a victim was whacked with the belt, the announcer was forced to describe the action a different way or say, "He hit him with the championship!"

Huh? No wonder some commentary often sounds stilted. Of course, it is Vince's dime, but doesn't that verge a bit on some sort of weird censorship or something? After all, Vince has also at times banned using the referee's name. What a gimmick! The nameless referee. *That* should add some PPV buys.

Technological advances may have given announcers some unexpected breathing room. The WWE rings are miked so expertly that what's said inside the ring can often be overheard. Allowing these ambient sounds to take over can provide a few seconds of silence for the harried announcers. Dick Murdoch was born too early: he would have been perfect in a televised bout today. Murdoch always kept up a running conversation, totally in character, while he worked. Of course, Murdoch was always in character, because he was the character, for real. His verbal hijinks, on WWE television, would have been priceless.

This naturally brings up the issue of color commentators, in particular the so-called heel announcer. When Roddy Piper began ranting on a regular basis with Gordon Solie during the Atlanta Superstation show, the heel announcer was essentially born. When Vince later began featuring Jesse Ventura and Bobby Heenan, the position was officially formalized. How many others have tried to copy them since, with far less impact?

Over time, Heenan and Ventura became popular *because* they touted the bad guys. Maybe society was moving in the direction of championing the anti-hero, but the unique personalities that "The Brain" and "The Body" flaunted were so entertaining that they, in fact, became babyfaces!

Nobody today really considers Jerry Lawler a heel. Fans like him. He is funny, bright, and grasps the role he plays in the whole production. That's the key: so what if he cheers for the bad guy once in a while? Compared to the announcers, wrestlers have relatively short, louder promos, or tightly scripted lines to recite; the wrestling broadcaster often has only himself to rely upon.

Viewers get to know *you*. Of course, to some extent, announcers are playing a role, too. But the role of announcer is much closer to reality than anything else in the business. You cannot fake yourself — not fully — especially with the amount of airtime to be filled week after week.

Viewers are generally smart. They can see though scripts and make-believe characters. Piper, Ventura, and Heenan hit the jackpot because fans could tell, for all of the baloney and bluster, they were distinctive individuals and fun to interact with. The more outrageous they were the better, because Roddy, Jesse, and Bobby were in reality pretty eccentric.

There have been countless bland heel commentators, only able to yell and shout, who did not click with viewers because what they did was forced. For Heenan, Ventura, and Piper, it was free flowing and came naturally.

Although the vast majority of what a wrestler now says on TV is a scripted promo or storyline element, once upon a time, announcers and wrestlers regularly did interviews together. Of course, calling it an interview masked the fact that it was actually a promo for an upcoming show. There was give-and-take, with the advance planning mostly limited to how long the chat would last and perhaps a couple of bullet points to be emphasized. Then, as now (again, nothing is really new), the ability to talk could really get a wrestler over with the audience.

Even with a script, though, not everyone is created equal. A large majority of the talent recites lines written for them by someone else, and their cadence, their rhythms often sound unnatural. For the most part, it's simply not the way fired-up, emotional athletes talk. Worrying about getting your lines out correctly takes something away from a performer's energy. And where is Elmore Leonard when the business needs someone to write realistic, gut-grabbing dialogue?

The growing reliance on scripts certainly hurt someone like Ric Flair — when he was allowed to say something more than the obligatory "whooo!" Somehow, somebody decided that the 1980s style promos The Nature Boy excelled at no longer work, although the theory was seldom if ever tested by simply letting him go, full steam ahead. Ric Flair looked and sounded like he was handcuffed when he worked from a script.

On the other hand, scripted scenes are fine for John Cena. The ultimate company man and a marketing machine, Cena's personality somehow manages to break through, despite what is at times the most dismal and stupid material. Similarly, Chris Jericho, in the finest tradition of Nick Bockwinkel, can meld what is written for him with the freedom to use some of his own words and his remarkable intonation.

Sadly, some of the newer guys appear to be held back by the scripts they're given. It clearly prevents them from developing their own personality, because they stop thinking on their own. Everything is handed to them. Unchallenged by having to ad lib, another small but important skill is being lost. And when it comes time for legitimate, off-the-cuff interviews with mainstream media outlets, it's no wonder many of today's wrestlers struggle.

Long-winded wrestling monologues are almost always tedious, a more dangerous trend since practically all interviews have now been turned into promos done solo by the performers. Talk, talk, talk, talk, talk. Fewer minutes of action, and more talk, talk, talk. Talk about booorrr-ing! Numerous shows are much more junior high bully and smart-aleck talk rather than athletic activity. On the other hand, all that talking can hide a lack of in-ring talent.

Terry Funk, and others like him, could get what needed to be said over in under three minutes. If the preacher cannot deliver his sermon quickly and effectively, the congregation tunes him out. It's the same thing for wrestlers. In his time, Funk and most of the others in main events could also deliver the goods when the bell rang. They could live up to the promise of what they said. Sadly, that could also signal a difference between "then and now." There are those in the spotlight today who would probably be better served just wrestling, letting their actions tell their story. One thing is certainly indisputable: if a wrestler can't talk, he's not suited to an improv promo or comedy skit. The honest, down-in-the-gut fire will be absent, and he'll fail. Give the fans credit for knowing the difference.

That viewers recognize they're engaged with a real person in the midst of the occasional madness of a wrestling show has helped make Jim Ross close to irreplaceable for WWE. He's that good at what he does. And make no mistake: Vince has *tried* to put others into his role. They've always flopped.

So you think you want to be on WWE television? Try getting down on your hands and knees to kiss Vince's ass, or letting Linda McMahon kick you in the groin. Yes, it's all a work — but performing those acts had to be difficult for JR, knowing his family and friends saw them, even if what happened was not "real." (What is real again?) Was it all in the name of entertainment, or was it, perhaps, just a ploy to see how far Vince could push and control another employee? Was it Vince's mean streak surfacing as humorous storyline? You could argue that Vince has allowed similar or worse things to be done to him — but, then, he was always royally compensated (as the boss who decides who earns what).

Wrestling and TV, so intimately intertwined, share a ravenous appetite for young, fresh, new faces. Vince has been futilely searching for someone of that description to replace Ross for quite some time, which of course is a logical way of preparing for the future. But he'd be wise to note that David Letterman, NBC's Brian Williams, and even Al Michaels and John Madden have huge, devoted, followings that cut across all age demographics. And for crying out loud, how long has Regis Philbin been a star? Finding the *right* person to fill the role is more essential than just tossing anyone young into the announcer's chair.

The WWE philosophy is apparently that youth and appearance beat age and experience. But one critical element gets lost in this equation: ability! It does make sense to have someone young and handsome announcing — if that person has both the knowledge and the chops to carry the ball. But young, blandly good-looking, and not too sharp is definitely *not* better than charismatic and smart as hell, no matter how old an announcer might be.

Jim Ross, for wrestling fans young and old, fills a critical role for Vince and WWE. He sounds different than the other announcers, and in fact is different, without insulting the current tastes or intelligence of fans. Today, he is the voice of authority in wrestling, and he also reinforces the tenuous link between the present and the past, just as Ric Flair once did in the ring. For the mass audience, and critically all those casual viewers who determine how much money WWE will or will not make, JR as an announcer is a key part of the formula.

When Jim McKay, celebrated host of *Wide World of Sports* and twelve Olympics, passed away in 2008, Bob Costas explained why he was so successful: "He brought a reporter's eye, a literate touch, and above all a personal humanity to every assignment."

Now, I understand that this discussion is about wrestling. I understand wrestling is the bastard child of sports. I understand the truth is that wrestling draws fans from all demographics no matter what anyone says. I understand the announcer has to help sell tickets and garner ratings. I understand some elite media powers would snap at me for making this comparison. I understand Vince would most likely disagree with my stance on the subject, too, but . . .

I also know from my own experience that there are intangibles — like believability and trust — that cannot always be replaced by a pretty face.

None of us may be at the level of Jim McKay, but the qualities Costas described are what a wrestling announcer must strive for to be truly effective. Being a reporter in the eyes of viewers, having command of the language, and most of all being *real* allows JR to accomplish that goal. The longevity of someone like Jim Ross proves that no matter how much the sport and the way it is marketed has changed, the announcer it still critical. And if, somewhere within all the dazzle and bluster, the announcer can use some part of his own personality to develop a legitimate relationship with the viewers, the odds are that a lasting connection will be established. Those are the connections that sell wrestling, draw fans across generations; those are the connections that become part of wrestling's true legacy.

Isn't it funny that the one announcer Vince liked the most was . . . Vince McMahon? Despite whatever shortcomings he might have had behind the microphone, Vince was incredibly effective at selling his own product. Could it be that viewers, instinctively, sensed his emotional attachment to, and investment in, what he was talking about? However much he might protest now, Vince himself has proven how much the announcer means to wrestling.

CHAPTER TEN

CONTACTS, CONTACTS, CONTACTS

Legitimate news about pro wrestling was once as difficult to uncover as the secrets of the federal government. Items slipped out rarely, and in drips and drabs. Most of what emerged was gossip — interesting and entertaining, but usually not the real nuts and bolts of how the business operated.

Then along came a young squirt named Dave Meltzer.

Before long, it seemed, pro wrestling was a sieve. The flow of information could not be stopped, and it generally flowed through Meltzer and his baby, the *Wrestling Observer Newsletter*. Unlike others who came before and many since, Meltzer actually took the time to educate himself about more than just the dirt and feature material. He came to understand both the business and the psychology. Seven point type, jammed into tight columns on anywhere from twelve to eighteen pages, with piles of wrestling news and notes, is the weekly result.

Before Dave Meltzer, kayfabe reigned supreme. Whether it was matches being predetermined, or wrestlers' salaries, or the actual attendance for a show, the truth was hidden. It was a bucket with no bottom; an endless sea of gossip, lies, and protected secrets. The mantra went: tell anything but the truth. When Meltzer began, his most difficult chore was separating what was both real and important from what was, truly, nothing but bullshit.

Believe it or not, more than a few folks out there wanted serious wrestling journalism. The truth was absolutely fascinating, if anyone could figure out what the truth was. Dave discovered this, and because of him so did those who would become his followers. His

Observer mixed together the wacky day-to-day politics of wrestling, the engrossing booking patterns, the colorful personalities, and a dose of scandal; it proved an addicting concoction.

The young squirt built an empire out of the facts he chased down, and in the process almost single-handedly opened up wrestling to the type of scrutiny it often would rather not have. His newsletter was disparaged by the industry as a "dirt sheet" — and there were elements of that to it — but promotions and promoters, particularly Vince McMahon, eventually learned it was a type of exposure they would have to endure.

For a while, it seemed there was just one thing that both promoters and wrestlers could always agree on: "Meltzer's damn dirt sheet is exposing the business, and it's killing us." In reality, however, the people who made these complaints most likely had subscriptions — taken out in the names of relatives or friends. Furthermore, a pretty high percentage of them were probably talking to Dave on a regular basis, feeding him the very news and gossip they complained about going public.

Dick Murdoch once told me a great story from when he was with World Championship Wrestling. The big shots met with the wrestlers and warned them in no uncertain terms: "Don't talk to Meltzer. He's tipping off finishes. He's exposing us. If you talk to Meltzer and that damn dirt sheet, you're fired!"

A legitimate rebel, Dick left the room and headed for a pay phone to tell me about the threat, knowing I was tight with Dave. "Only problem was, I couldn't find a phone that wasn't busy," Dick griped. "Every wrestler was trying to call Meltzer and tell him what happened!" Very wise about the ways of wrestling despite the image he liked to project, Murdoch added, "Hell, those suits probably went right to their office and called Meltzer themselves. Probably bragging to him. And he's laughing at them. Bunch of dumb shits!"

The *Wrestling Observer* was born in 1982, but Dave's first newsletter was actually published in 1971 — when he was *ten*. (My first article on wrestling appeared in *Ring Magazine* when I was twelve, so I understand what Dave was doing.) He had become a wrestling fan in fourth grade, thanks to a best friend hooked on the sport. Soon, Dave himself was in love with both wrestling and roller derby, another big deal in his native San Francisco Bay area of California. He soon became friends with many of the regulars at the shows, but his first time out, some older kids asked, "You know it's fake, don't you?"

Dave and his friend thought about it until the next show a couple weeks later, when they saw the midgets put on a hilarious and obviously staged battle. Looking at each other, Meltzer and his buddy agreed: "Yep, it's fake." And they didn't care one iota. It was simply never an issue. Obviously, that's not an uncommon story for wrestling fans in general. He quickly grew up on the sport, schooled by classic, great workers like Pat Patterson and Ray Stevens, just like I cut my teeth a decade earlier watching Lou Thesz, Pat O'Connor, Gene Kiniski, and Johnny Valentine.

Meltzer took his enthusiasm to the next level. Soon he was trading results with like-minded fans around the country. His list included legendary wrestling fan Diane Devine, then in St. Louis, and Mike Tenay, who would later work for wcw and eventally become the television voice of tna. He went to cards all over the Northern California territory. It was a compact region, so Dave had only an hour or so ride to San Francisco, Stockton, Watsonville, or Sacramento. "It was the Roy Shire promotion, so we would see the same show, the same matches, and particularly the same finishes in different places," recalled Dave. "I figured it out pretty fast."

It wasn't long before he was on the mailing list for the *Wrestling News*, which I was writing from St. Louis. I knew we had several subscribers from outside the area, but I had no idea who Dave Meltzer was except for a name on a list of 4000 until years later. He would also call the Atlanta and St. Louis hotlines to get wrestling results. "It was a bitch to get through the busy signals, especially in St. Louis, because wrestling was such a big deal," he recalls.

As vcrs became popular, Meltzer was among the first to trade show tapes with fans from all over the country. One fan after another would turn Dave on to the action from another area, so Meltzer would seek someone from that location to trade tapes with. As a teenager he was eventually surveying tapes of Japanese bouts.

He thought it was "the coolest thing ever, to be getting all that wrestling news in the early 1970s." Meltzer's dream was to become successful enough as a sportswriter that he could take time off and fly to St. Louis for a show at Kiel Auditorium, to Atlanta for an Omni spectacular, and to New York for action at Madison Square Garden.

Then cable invaded the Bay Area, exposing Dave to the matches from Atlanta on Ted Turner's Channel 17. Almost all the top stars eventually came to work on this national show. "Even then, I understood that would change the wrestling business," explained Meltzer. "I figured, sooner or later, wrestling would be down to two or three companies."

There were, however, frustrations. "I felt my timing was always wrong," Dave said. "When I was finally old enough to drive to all the shows in our territory, Shire's promotion had died, and there was no territory. We had some spot shows from Los Angeles, but they were terrible. The same thing happened with roller derby, because it was gone before I was able to drive on my own. Then I could see the local flavor disappearing in wrestling, because the territories were all dead or dying. If I flew to different towns, I'd have seen pretty much the same lineup in every place. When you're young, you think that the things you like will never change. It started me wondering why at a pretty early stage. Eventually, I figured out nothing lasts forever. When the bosses fuck up, the business dies."

Most of his old wrestling friends would drift away and lose interest. The few who still enjoyed it often hid their interest in such a "low-brow" activity. Dave was always different. He stood tall and kept trying to find out everything he could about the esoteric sport.

Since grade school, Meltzer knew his dream was to become a sportswriter, though he didn't know in what particular field. Even now, he daydreams about being a pro football writer. So why wrestling? "I don't know," he says. "I guess I saw nobody else was doing it, and I had some ego in that I thought I could make a name for myself." He graduated from San Jose State with a degree in journalism in 1983. While in college, he did PR for the San Jose

Earthquake professional soccer franchise. After school, he moved to Wichita Falls, Texas, for a year to work in the sports department of the local newspaper. In typical journalistic fashion, Dave bounced back to the Bay Area to work for the *Oakland Tribune*, then moved to the *Turlock Journal* for a better position in sports. He was with that publication until 1987.

All through this period, that old devil, wrestling, ate up his time and stirred his passion. The *Observer*, published weekly, grew rapidly. I first met Meltzer, with Mark Nulty, at a show in Houston in May 1983. I was gearing up for the promotional war in St. Louis and had gone to Houston where another wrestling squabble was going on. One night, I went to a Joe Blanchard bill, and the next night I was at an event run by Paul Boesch's more established promotion. I was looking for talent willing to buck the system — which was about to change forever — by working for an independent St. Louis promotion. Dave seemed like a bright kid, eager and surprisingly knowledgeable about what was going on. He said he'd put me on the mailing list for his *Wrestling Observer*.

What I discovered was always fascinating, and packed with news and results. In those days, there were even a few pictures. It reminded me of my youth, except the results were from *everywhere* (including Japan), and were coupled with Dave's biting analysis. It was grassroots journalism and editorial comment at its best. If Dave felt a match stank, he said so. If a promoter falsified a lineup, he'd blast them. Even then, Meltzer kept a close eye on attendance patterns — which were not always easy to substantiate. His publication started everyone, including insiders, using terms like "work rate," and made attributing stars based on match quality commonplace.

Something else really caught my eye: when Dave got something wrong, he would acknowledge his error in a later edition — and try to correct it. That wasn't something practiced very often, especially when it came to wrestling. Yes, Dave published the rumors and gossip, too, but usually they were called just that. It was the same with his opinions: they were his. He didn't slap anyone in the face with it, but Meltzer was clearly not observing the sacrosanct principles of kayfabe. Instead (gasp), he was covering wrestling like a legitimate journalist.

At any rate, I closed my new promotion when Vince McMahon and the WWF snatched KPLR-TV out from under me — just as it appeared I was going to land the area's prime television station. Reluctantly, I accepted an offer to work for the WWF. While Vince, to his credit, welcomed me with open arms, I could never shake the anger I felt after his maneuvering. Worse, I knew I'd never again have the hands-on satisfaction I'd come to enjoy under Sam Muchnick. I was frustrated and bitter: the transformation of wrestling occurred just when I felt I was on the verge of showing the world what I could do on my own. But somehow, it also felt like *my* fault, like I'd opened the floodgate that allowed the gut-wrenching change that transformed the entire industry to take hold in St. Louis. It wasn't realistic, of course, but that's how I felt.

For all these reasons, I guess, just about a month after I had begun working for Vince in the winter of 1984, I did something I'd never done before: one night, out of the blue, I called Dave Meltzer. We had only ever spoken once, that night in Houston. After all these years, remembering what we discussed is nearly impossible, although Dave told me I was very respectful about the early success Vince was having and the sellout he'd recently drawn in St. Louis. Maybe because our backgrounds were similar (my college major was also journalism), we clicked. I'm sure I slipped him a few juicy tidbits about something inside the WWF, but whatever it was, it wasn't important enough to remember 25 years later. If Dave sensed my resentment, he was wise enough not to play on it, and just listened.

We began chatting on a regular basis. Dave was generous about filling me in on inside manipulations from the old-line promotions that were still fighting McMahon. It took a few months, however, before I was truly comfortable talking about breaking kayfabe. After all, I was Muchnick's protégé, and who was more closed-mouth about wrestling's secrets than Sam?

More and more, we'd talk about the way the business works, what really matters. Somehow, after all those talks and all these years, I finally understand that, in many ways, I was justifying what Vince was doing even as I complained about him doing it. It has helped me accept reality. When I had parted company with Vince in 1993, and after Brody had been murdered in 1988, it was Dave who helped keep my love for wrestling alive. Apparently I was able to give Dave another useful perspective, while his take on wrestling rekindled my interest in figuring out what, in wrestling terms, worked.

Of course, I was not the first and hardly the last source to speak with the *Observer*, although I like to believe I might have been one of the better ones. Sooner or later, nearly every old school promoter subscribed to Meltzer's publication. Some, like Eddie Graham in Florida, Paul Boesch in Houston, Jim Crockett in North Carolina, and even Jim Barnett did not even bother using aliases. The WWF had a number of people subscribing — so Vince could monitor Dave's work. Office staff and even announcers were also subscribing. Dave wound up speaking with most of them, often in great detail, getting large contributions from the industry itself.

Wrestlers, naturally, were a wealth of information. Dave quickly understood that many had their own agendas, but he said, "Common sense made it possible to weed out the stuff that was just baloney." Sources usually did not lie (that would have been easy to discover and dismiss), but they had their own version of events, which Meltzer learned to recognize and make allowances for.

One thing I did was tout the *Observer* to Brody, who quickly became a fan. Like Meltzer and me, Frank Goodish had also majored in journalism. Frank had also worked in the sports department for the San Antonio newspaper before getting into wrestling. Meltzer has always credited Brody with paving the way for him to find acceptance as a legitimate journalist in Japan, where Brody was a superstar and wrestling was covered on a daily basis in several popular publications. Meltzer loved Japanese wrestling for its stiff, believable style and depth of talent. At that time, in Japan, pro wrestling was on a level with almost any other sport. When Dave went there for the first time, he discovered that what Brody had said about the *Observer* made both the talent and the media treat him with immense respect.

More important, perhaps, was that Brody reinforced what I was telling Dave and what he already had a good handle on. Wrestling was a business, pure and simple. A tough, hard, nasty business. All three of us could become hypnotized, talking about angles, talent, and political manipulation. And sure, that was fun. But in the end, what counted was making money. Brody, in particular, drove home that it was really all about who got rich, the wrestler or the promoter, and that the promoter held the best cards. He was extremely intelligent, well-read, rebellious, and cynical, and could explain the "cons" from a wrestler's perspective. After my years with Muchnick, I could describe the promoter's viewpoint. Dave soaked it all up, asked the difficult questions, and learned. My guess is he was like that with everyone.

How many hours did we burn up in the '80s, talking? With my knowledge of the wwf and other nwa contacts, Brody's status as an independent giant who worked for almost every promoter and knew almost every wrestler, and Dave's incredible work ethic and endless list of sources (most of which he still protects to this day), we used to joke that outside of McMahon himself, nobody had a better handle on when house shows were, when taping dates were, who was upset and why, and what talent was moving where — in effect, the entire wrestling business — than we did. We probably overestimated our reach, but still . . . we were pretty damn good!

The *Observer* got to the movers and shakers. Mostly, they hated it. If Meltzer made a mistake, they jumped him, but then they conveniently ignored all the hard and true facts he regularly presented. They certainly did not like being called to task for unethical business moves or poor revenues. It had to disturb them when Meltzer would break stories about somebody jumping to the wwf, or that wwf was having trouble with a certain star. Dave says, "The old school promoters hated what I did, but they never seemed to hate me. Vince didn't like the idea that someone other than him could do something, that he didn't own it. It bothered him when I knew his moves. None of them were used to being covered like this, even if it was only for a niche readership. I really never had problems, except with Vince."

The old criticisms die hard. Even today, he's foolishly blasted for discussing storyline directions and likely finishes, because, some argue, it drives fans away. Forgotten is the fact that those who subscribe to the *Observer* are the most passionate and committed followers of the sport — how could he drive them away? These fans love the inside perspective Meltzer provides, and can be relied on to attend almost every show or buy practically every PPV, *unless the promotion itself does something to destroy their interest.* The argument that says Dave exposed the business and killed fan interest in the process has clearly proved bogus: Vince himself has exposed the business in the most public of forums, anyway . . . and some would argue interest even grew!

By 1987, Meltzer found himself faced with a difficult decision. He was putting in 60 hours a week with the Turlock paper, and probably another 60 hours for the *Observer*. His newsletter generated only a couple hundred bucks a week for all that effort. But Dave took the chance: he quit the newspaper and decided to try to make the *Observer* his full-time occupation. He's never looked back, and the gamble's paid off.

"I worked my ass off; still do," he says. "It takes too much time, but I wanted to do it. I made a reputation in wrestling that I am proud of. Maybe it is ego, but I didn't want to give that up. I wasn't lucky, but I lucked into several things." The *Observer* served a purpose, he maintains, both within the industry and for serious followers, and still does today.

Just getting out a weekly issue — between 25,000 and 40,000 words — requires amazing effort. Before actually writing, Meltzer must get the information — which means spending hours on the telephone every day and cross-checking stories as much as humanly possible. If anyone has a cauliflower ear from being on the telephone, it's Dave Meltzer. He also must watch and review not only every televised show, but also the numerous tapes that become available. The subscriber list must be regularly updated. Printing and mailing have to be supervised. Monday and Tuesday are generally long days of writing, with mailing happening on Wednesday. The *Observer* website is a daily chore. For objectivity and accuracy, the *Observer* Hall of Fame is the best in the business, utilizing independent voting, by everyone from retired and current wrestlers to serious historians, to establish its inductees.

"The goal is always to do it right," he insists. "Money was never a concern. I *never* expected it to be this successful." It all fit together to make the *Observer* more influential behind closed doors than anyone would ever admit. In public, call it a "dirt sheet." In private, pore over every word.

Irv Muchnick, Sam's nephew and author of *Wrestling Babylon* and *Chris & Nancy*, got to know Meltzer during the '80s as well. He went to Dave's apartment in 1986 and found vhs tapes of wrestling matches piled everywhere, from floor to ceiling, in every room. "But Dave never seemed to have trouble putting his finger on the one he was citing to make a point," Irv pointed out. Bryan Alvarez, operator of f4wonline.com and author of *The Death of wcw*, recounted that Dave once told him, "I had so many tapes, I didn't have room for furniture."

Another time Irv drove with Dave to Los Angeles for a television programmers' convention and a Cauliflower Alley Club dinner that Irv was covering for *People* magazine. They roomed together, with Dave sleeping on a sofa since *People* was picking up Muchnick's hotel expense. On the six-hour-plus drives between the Bay Area and Southern California, Dave talked non-stop about whatever wrestling stories Irv wanted him to tell. "I mean, he just never stopped!" Muchnick says. "Talked until he was hoarse; then talked some more."

Kit Bauman, a highly respected sportswriter, then living in Texas, had similar recollections of Meltzer's early days. "When I first met Dave at his tiny two-room apartment in Wichita Falls, what struck me is there were tapes everywhere!" Later, Bauman joined Dave at the Texas Stadium show where Ric Flair dropped the nwa title to Kerry Von Erich. "Fritz comped us, which I thought was classy because I knew that Fritz didn't like the *Observer*."

Dave and Kit spent the entire afternoon together. "I don't think Dave stopped to draw a breath," Bauman says. What impressed him the most was when it came time for the finish, Meltzer called it. "[It was] like Dave already knew when and what it was supposed to be. I remember thinking I'd never develop sources like his."

Dave's zeal has never diminished, and it's a major reason why the *Observer* is still relevant today. And his tape collection? Dave is married now, has a son, and owns a house. But he still has all those tapes, every single one from the '70s and '80s, of wrestling from long-forgotten territories as well as Japan. "Nobody else would want them, probably," he says, "but each one was like a lesson about wrestling for me."

Those lessons served him and the *Observer* well through the tumultuous upheaval in wrestling during the '80s and '90s, and dealing with Vince McMahon, specifically. Quite clearly, Meltzer has tremendous respect for McMahon's accomplishments, although Dave's esteem is tempered with the critical eye of a journalist who lived through McMahon's quest for dominance and grasped all the complexities of what eventually transpired. On a personal level, Meltzer found McMahon "charming and very, very smart." He stresses, "I admire Vince's ability. He did exactly what he needed to do to make WWE so strong."

But, Meltzer adds, "One of his problems is that when he gets in trouble, he responds in such a way that he creates more trouble. He takes everything as a personal attack. Vince does not realize that he is the luckiest guy in the world because he's doing wrestling."

As an example of Vince's good fortune, Meltzer points out that Congress, when it delved into hearings about steroids and sports such as baseball, knew what wrestling was and what had happened to its performers, but because it was wrestling eventually let the issue slide. Dave also lists several controversies that the media has ignored, because, again, it's "only wrestling" — scandals they would have blasted other companies and sports for.

Consider what's happened to other businesses and sports when representatives were discovered using vile racial slurs — which is why Michael Hayes was given a 60-day suspension from WWE in 2008. Hayes was a WWE vice-president, an important member of the creative team, and, of course, once the most famous part of the "Fabulous Freebirds." Investigation into the comments, things

Hayes said out of insensitivity and ignorance, would have found even more offensive racial epithets being uttered by wrestling insiders as a matter of course. (The wrestling locker room mentality is a carryover from less enlightened and educated days.) No matter what the excuse, general media attention would have opened a nasty can of worms. Vince reacted with the suspension, but in most circles that would be considered little more than a slap on the wrist. Any business not labeled wrestling would have been crucified by the media.

Arguing that wrestling is entertainment, not sport, is again, fatuous — all sports are entertainment. Wrestling, though, dodged the light of interrogation because it was wrestling, all to Vince's benefit. What happened to baseball's Al Campanis, and Marge Schott? Or what about Jimmy the Greek? What would have happened to WWE's stock with a public outcry about its racial attitudes? What might a high profile racial lawsuit do to its bottom line?

"The key to Vince's success is that he got there first [with television contacts and national expansion]," Dave says. "Vince wore everyone down. Vince changed the rules. But he still wasn't a worldwide success — although WWE is now trying to go in that direction to expand their market." Meltzer adds that Vince's failures demonstrate that he really only succeeds with pro wrestling; the bodybuilding and pro football debacles that cost his company millions prove it.

Furthermore, Meltzer believes that World Championship Wrestling could have won the Monday Night Wars. A long string of inept managers, who either failed to acknowledge or were unable to convince the parent company that they were in a fight for their very existence, something Vince obviously grasped, eventually led to its demise. All of these men spoke with Dave at different times while demanding varying degrees of anonymity. "Eric Bischoff finally got them to fight," he says, and gave WCW hope, but Bischoff's flaws likely accelerated the promotion's implosion. Vince, he believes, was on the ropes and vulnerable on a few different occasions.

While relations between Meltzer and McMahon can be described as cordial, the fact that information about his promotion leaks out can still drive Vince to distraction. At one point, Vince had his daughter Stephanie attempt to plug those leaks. She was checking cell phone and e-mail records, hoping to discover who might have been in contact with the *Observer*. Storylines leaking to the public makes the McMahons batty. It's funny: Dave has written in the *Observer* itself that 80 to 90% of the rumors he gets are dead wrong (and thus not printable), but that doesn't prevent other "news" sources, usually on the Internet, from picking up and running with the gossip as fact.

"Vince helped me enormously," Meltzer concedes. "By making wrestling mainstream, he made me mainstream, and the number one source about wrestling for the mainstream media. Vince once told me, 'As I go, you go.' I did not want to believe that. But in the end, he was right." Indeed, Meltzer's landed on national television shows and has been quoted in the most prominent newspapers whenever Vince gets attention — whether it's positive, or more often than not, negative.

That's the thing about the *Observer*. Over the years, many influential media and business types outside of wrestling — those who still have a serious interest or stake in the industry — have devoured Meltzer's data. And rest assured, Vince is aware of the fact. When Dave reports or analyzes something, it's not just "rasslin' fans" who are weighing his words.

As to the future, Meltzer believes that "Only Vince can bury Vince. He's closing in on his mid-'60s, and when he's gone, all bets are off. Likely, Stephanie and Triple H will be in charge. They've been taught by Vince, especially Stephanie, but there's a big difference: they know some of what he knows, but not everything."

Over the years, the shocking wrestling deaths and tragedies have taken their toll on Dave Meltzer. They've made him cast a jaundiced eye toward a business he's loved as ardently as anyone else. Some have been worse because they've also been personal. He was very close to Brian Pillman, and suffered greatly as Pillman battled drug abuse and injuries before the final curtain. Dave liked Eddie Guerrero and was numbed when he overdosed. The horrible Benoit suicide and double murder cut Dave to the quick. Brody's murder traumatized him, as it did me. "It still bothers me how misunderstood Brody was, and still is today," he laments.

Something else inevitably happened: the *Observer* spawned numerous imitators. Meltzer, though, has been the only one to really make a good living from it. Those without his skills and scruples have done damage, or ripped off fans. In the end, only a couple have survived or achieved any real success. Bryan Alvarez, with *Figure Four Weekly*, and Wade Keller, with the *Pro Wrestling Torch*, may be the only two truly in his league. They, too, have the journalistic touch and a solid product; they have the goods and, like Meltzer, have stood the test of time.

The Internet has added yet another chapter to this story. Meltzer is convinced that both WWE and TNA pay too much attention to the hard-core web audience, which only represents a small percentage of the overall potential audience for wrestling. "For instance, the Internet loves mixed martial arts but hates Ultimate Fighting Championships. But UFC is the one getting hundreds of thousands of buys for their pay-per-views, while the others struggle or fail," Dave explained. Wisely going with the trend, the *Observer* naturally gives extensive coverage to the MMA world. Meltzer's also covered it for the *Los Angeles Times* and FoxSports.com, and he serves as MMA consultant for Yahoo Sports — adding another few thousand words to his weekly output.

He notes a similar situation for pro wrestling, where a tiny promotion like Ring of Honor needs only 500 followers to survive financially between small live shows and DVD sales. WWE, and even TNA, need far, far more fans to thrive. If WWE lost the USA Network, or TNA lost the Spike Network, the Internet would not save either business, he claims. "No new fans are made on the Internet. No new stars are made on the Internet."

What does the future have in store for the *Observer*? "The market will determine that," says Meltzer. "I'm prepared for whichever way it goes. When WCW sold out to Vince in 2001, I really believed the *Observer* would be dead by 2003. Instead, I had my biggest year in 2002, and it's been strong from there."

Bryan Alvarez says that it would be foolish to underestimate

Meltzer's impact on the business. "A huge influence, immense! I cannot overstate what Dave has done," he emphasizes. "Promoters have changed the way they operate because of what Dave has reported. Every website existing today traces back to the way Dave covered wrestling. Even now, most of the information others use is first reported by the *Observer*. No publication in any field has covered their business to the extent Dave has, when you add up all the words — millions of words! — he has written about wrestling over more than 25 years."

Kit Bauman, like others, agrees. "I feel like I owe Dave a big debt," he says. "It was Dave that Lou Thesz approached first when Lou had decided he wanted to write his autobiography and wanted professional help. Dave politely turned him down, telling Lou that he really didn't have the time, and then he suggested me. I cannot thank him enough for that."

Still, Dave knows that it's more difficult to get new subscribers now. "The business emphasis goes over their heads," he says. His ability to retain the so-called old fans, however, is excellent. They learned what wrestling was through Dave. As much as he enjoys the action and plotting, Meltzer never loses sight of the fact that wrestling is a business. He wants to know if it's building or rebuilding, whether it's the same, up, or down. And then he wants to explore why.

"There is a knowledge I acquired," he says. "I learned 30 lessons (with 30 different philosophies) every week, looking at those tapes, going through the results, seeing the marketing, finding out what made money." With sheer persistence, Meltzer came to know what works and what doesn't, based on the crowds drawn after different shows have tried different angles. He came to grasp the various philosophies, some of which would work as well today as they did years and years ago. He also knows what's failed in both the distant and recent past, and what will likely fail today.

"Now they don't learn from anyone. Thirty-year-old bookers talk to thirty-year-old bookers. All they know is WWF-style booking. They can't learn. Maybe they learn two lessons if they pay attention to TNA, but TNA can't even learn from themselves. They do something right, like Samoa Joe beating Kurt Angle on pay-per-view, and then screw it all up on television the next week," Meltzer points out.

Today, Dave finds UFC much closer to the wrestling of his childhood: "The titles mean something. Winning a preliminary bout moves the guy up the ladder — unlike WWE, where a performer is locked in a role seemingly forever. They take it seriously and do strong, specific promotion." Of course, UFC is a shoot, but Dave knows that pro wrestling does quite nicely when it embraces that cloak of reality.

Even though he sees wrestling as a business, Meltzer still loves the action: "I *love* watching a great match, like when Samoa Joe won the TNA title from Angle. I really enjoy *WrestleMania*. Some Japanese stuff is excellent, just like the smaller groups in the U.S. I still find enjoyment in really terrific bouts. It's fun! Just because you know some of the secrets doesn't mean you can't enjoy the action."

Meltzer says doing the *Observer* is "just journalism, and I get to do it on my own terms." And he still enjoys sharing and explaining the facts and the secrets, just as much as when he was that young squirt who irritated the establishment by telling the truth.

CHAPTER ELEVEN

LIFEBLOOD

Wrestling needs fans of every ilk and persuasion. Wrestling needs them because they buy what it's selling, just as those who purchase cars, televisions, and computers make companies that produce those goods profitable. Welcome to Wrestling Economics 101.

But fans are important for another key reason: they're critical to the spectacle. Fans make it fun. Fans bring everything together, just as they blend together from all aspects of society. Not only do they fund the promotion, their energy feeds the show itself. If the promotion is the brain of wrestling, fans are its heart and soul. So remember:

- Each fan has his or her own reason for being a fan. They're not just numbers, statistics, ratings points, and certainly not "marks."
- The total audience for wrestling today is not the same as it was during the territorial era, in terms of either the percentage of the total population or raw numbers. The numbers make it clear: there are fewer fans today.
- The audience is divided in the same way as it's always been: intense, rabid fans, very knowledgeable fans, generally attentive fans, and casual fans.
- In the end, the percentage of fans who buy pay-per-view events and go to house shows is less than what it was when attending a live card was the only option.
- The Internet is a way for fans to come together. The web also provides an excellent opportunity for marketing, whether it's by a giant promotion like WWE or a small, cult operation like Ring of Honor (ROH).

• Because of the Internet sites, discussion boards, and chat rooms, fans can have their voices heard by more people who share their passion than ever before.

• Thanks to the Internet, and one dominant promotion like WWE with superior marketing techniques, the audience looks bigger than it used to be (though it's not). This is good for wrestling, because it finally calls attention to how large and varied wrestling's following has always been.

• The Internet creates very few new fans, if any, nor does it make new stars. Television does both. Fans go online with their minds already made up. In wrestling terms, the Internet has more perceived influence than it deserves.

• Rapidly changing technologies provide an inventive company like WWE, or an upstart promotion like ROH, with a unique opportunity: to perhaps grow the audience while maximizing the income generated from fans the business already has (mainly by selling wrestling-related merchandise).

There's more to it, of course; but to understand the big picture, you have to dig into the gritty, messy, and often confusing details first.

Wrestling fanatics live and die for every prelim as well as for the main event. This type of fan was damn serious back in the day — almost every promotion had a legendary "Hatpin" Mary, usually an older lady, who wasn't above attacking a villain with an item from her purse — and nothing's changed. That hard-core base, obviously not all as extreme as dear Mary, includes those who "know" everything and criticize almost anything. But there's also another large portion of wrestling's fan base who take it just as seriously, without being quite as critical. This fraternity is tremendously knowledgeable. They appreciate the atmosphere and enjoy action, good booking, and hard-working talent. Their criticism is more reasoned and specific.

Another much larger, though more fluid, number of fans watch pretty much every television program and are generally attentive. They know who they like and respect, but it's the booking and who is battling that determines whether or not they attend (or buy via

PPV) a particular show. These folks take it "kinda" serious, enjoying the "wink-wink" elements of wrestling's alternative reality. Some, though definitely not all, are hesitant to openly admit how much they enjoy the sport.

Finally, wrestling has a huge group of casual followers, including a fair amount of those notorious closet fans; they're rarely serious, but cannot resist the game's delicious lure. They openly resist being categorized as the stereotypical wrestling followers. This crew watches much of the television, can identify who has star power, and is influenced by great booking and good ideas.

Within this segment, there is a stunning amount of turnover, as there is among the generally attentive folks. The change is primarily, but not entirely, driven by kids and young adults. It's not just a modern trend — people have always grown up and away from the interests and hobbies of their youth. There are endless competing entertainments and diversions, after all, especially today. Some veterans of the business believe this type of fan is replaced or replenished every three or four years. The turnover may be even more rapid in the second decade of the 21st century.

Regardless, the number of potential buyers at any one time is both impressive and, with all the comings and goings among casual fans, pretty much the same as it's always been. How is it possible to claim the audience is essentially the same size today as it was 30 or 40 or even 50 years ago? Simple, although as wrestling proves, simple does not always mean easy.

Look at the question like this: how many viewers watched wrestling on television in the territorial era, and how many watch today? Using general numbers, and not trying to account for those watching more than one show, WWE plays to a total of about ten million people every week. The figure might jump to twelve million during the winter, or drop to eight in the summer (and thus cause much consternation for poor Vince, who recently brought in Donald Trump for an on-air hot shot and has even given away money in the hope of boosting his ratings), but the average number of viewers tuning in barely budges. This audience watches on national channels. DVR users, who watch at different times, may skew the final totals a bit. And the fact that some people watch every possible broadcast can also complicate things, but an average of ten million is realistic (and easier to use as a comparison).

Wrestling Observer's Dave Meltzer believes there are so many repeat, habitual viewers watching more than one program that in 2009 WWE may reach only an average of six million unique individuals. But giving WWE the benefit of the doubt, acknowledging that their ratings have been higher in the past and could be again, we'll stick with ten million for purposes of this discussion.

In 1979, and even in 1969, there were approximately 30 individual promotions around North America. Each had television syndicated in every town where they ran a live show. Some, like Vince Sr.'s WWWF in the Northeast, or Verne Gagne's AWA in the upper Midwest, reached many good-sized markets. Some, like Don Owen in Oregon or the Kansas City office in the rural Midwest, or a Southern operation such as the Crocketts', had smaller towns but a large number of them.

If each of the 30 promotions reached an average of 40,000 viewers weekly in each of 10 towns, then the grand total (300 markets multiplied by 40,000) would easily reach or exceed twelve million. Remember that some markets were much bigger and naturally had many more viewers, but even the smaller towns had good ratings; also note that these were local programs: they only played to discrete, individual viewers.

Do the math: WWE has about ten million viewers today; the territorial promotions could reach twelve million — or more — years ago. Take this logic another step to evaluate the rest of the business, the territorial house show attendance of yesteryear against modern house show attendance, *plus* those who buy "live events" on pay-per-view, since PPV has replaced a large part of "old school" house show figures.

WWE can generally expect an *average* of 200,000 domestic (United States and Canada) buys per PPV. A great buy rate for *WrestleMania*, or a strong *Summer Slam*, can balance figures of 140,000 or fewer for lesser events. It must be said, too, that a large majority of those discrete buys have multiple viewers in front of the television. You can reasonably double the PPV numbers, because each person watching at home would be buying a ticket for himself and a companion or two if they were attending a traditional live show. When all is said and done, let's say WWE's special events draw over 400,000 fans/buyers per month.

WWE runs a semi-traditional house show schedule that offers approximately another 20 North American programs each month (including the PPV site). Informally (but generously) estimate the average attendance at 6,000 or more, and the total is at least 120,000. (Sold-out television tapings and the PPV arena ticket sales help move the average up.)

Adding the two numbers — in very round figures — WWE draws some 550,000 to 600,000 paying customers in a good month, and obviously more each spring when *WrestleMania* inflates the numbers. Tours to Europe, Mexico, and elsewhere are a bonus. It's smart business, but difficult to figure into a meaningful discussion of past and present (though the practice is clearly reminiscent of the old territorial spot shows).

Now, make this comparison: if each of the 30 territories ran an average of 25 shows per month, there would be 750 live cards, monthly, during the territorial era. (The figure is probably low — most territories ran something somewhere, even if it was just a small venue, every day.) What a difference for the culture of the business — 750 live programs versus 20 to 30!

It is safe to say, conservatively, that the average attendance in the territorial era was around 1,600. Madison Square Garden could draw 17,000 in the same month that Amarillo, Texas, drew less than 1,000 for each of four cards; or Minneapolis might have topped 12,000 when Lexington, Kentucky, had a couple shows that pulled in just 600. With many more shows in smaller auditoriums running more often, and with large cities running every few weeks and quite often approaching capacity, the grand total (750 shows multiplied by 1,600) comes to an eye-opening 1.2 million customers each *month*.

There's plenty of room for minor errors in these common sense calculations, but no matter how rough the figures are, something important leaps out. With a vastly different method of operation and a revolutionized television situation, *fewer* people pay to see wrestling today, but the combination of ppvs and other marketing revenues brings in boatloads of money. House shows are not nearly as crucial as they used to be. Regardless, the contrast in live attendance is still staggering, especially as it indicates overall interest in the product.

Dave Meltzer's research estimates live attendance for 1983 — the year before the wwf "revolutionized" the industry — was nearly thirteen million. Today, the annual figure is closer to two million. The fan base is clearly *not* bigger than it was before. What is bigger is the *perception*, by both the general media and the public, that wrestling's audience has grown.

Maybe it's only fair: wrestling fans were once underestimated; now, their numbers are inflated. And bravo to Vince McMahon for this — he's certainly used it to his benefit. To the winner go the spoils.

wwe is far more profitable, efficient, imaginative, and varied than any wrestling company before it ever was, although many of the tools it utilizes today simply did not exist in the territorial era. During a recent quarter, wwe derived more than 25% of its profit from licensing products such as video games; over 12% from dvd sales; and some 3% from merchandise sold at house shows. That's roughly 40% of the company's profit — from so-called secondary products.

Pay-per-view and ticket sales combined for the same quarter brought in a little more than 36%. So, what kind of business is wwe, really? While the figures might vary a bit from quarter to quarter, they clearly demonstrate how clever Vince has been about making money.

A closer look at wwe's 2008 profits indicates that approximately 38% came from live event and ppv purchases. Roughly 54% of profits were generated by licensing, television rights, and dvd sales. Throw in Internet activity for another 6%. While these figures might vary from quarter to quarter and year-to-year, the bottom line is Vince has cleverly devised ways to make money from more than just "putting asses in seats."

Very few old school promoters could have even dreamed of building such a diverse empire. After all, how many of us imagined Video on Demand or Playstations in 1974?

The goal is certainly not to imply that Vince is a bad guy, or that someone else was an angel. Hopefully, you realize that the point of this sermon/history lesson is not to say there's a right or wrong way to "run" the business of wrestling, but simply to point out that times have changed, that the business has evolved into something else. And yet, while things are clearly different, in some ways they are virtually the same. The product still must make enough fans *care* enough to make them spend their money.

Vince McMahon has done a marvelous job, not only of adapting to change, but also in driving that change. Wrestling's audience is looked at in a different context now, but the fanbase is still the key.

No fans = no wrestling.

The rabid and the knowledgeable have always been wrestling's foundation. They've never missed a show, live or on television, then or now. Once upon a time, they were the 4,000 faithful attending every single card in St. Louis; the 8,000 who had a regular seat at MSG; or even the 500 familiar faces in Kansas City. Today, they come from every corner of North America to order pay-per-views 140,000 times each month.

The second tier, the attentive fans, were the ones who jacked the numbers up to 8,000 for a card in St. Louis, over 12,000 at MSG, and pushed K.C. close to 1,000. Today, they'll boost a WWE PPV buy rate over 200,000 a couple times a year.

Hooking the enormous casual audience a couple of times a year, St. Louis would get sellouts of more than 11,000, the Garden would draw 18,000, and Kansas City would see 1,500 paying customers. For the WWE, these fans can push a PPV's domestic numbers to anywhere between 250,000 to a phenomenal 600,000. Figure in the rest of the world — a tribute to the marketing and television might of Vince McMahon's corporation — and WWE can achieve well over a million buys for something like *WrestleMania*.

But these are just numbers. Together, fans create a culture of their very own that has little to do with statistics or dollars and cents. The vitality they contribute matters as much to wrestling as their money — well, almost as much. When they congregate across racial, social, and economic lines, when they collectively suspend disbelief to get lost in the moment, wrestling becomes magical.

The promoters and the wrestlers may stage the show, but it's not magic unless there's someone watching and, more, embracing the spectacle. So what if there are those who don't care for it? Not everybody likes opera or football, theater or tennis. Yes, much of the media looks down at wrestling fans, stereotyping them, denigrating them, trying to make them, somehow, of lesser value. But maybe opera fans are boring and stuffy; maybe NASCAR followers are rowdy rednecks; maybe football worshipers are boozers; maybe rock fans are disrespectful stoners, and maybe sitcom-watchers are dim-witted zombies . . .

It's all bunk, of course. Enthusiasts for any activity or entertainment can't really be confined to one subset or category; membership in any fandom is never static. At different times, different people like different things. How many times have you heard something like this? "I used to follow tennis, but then . . ." Or, "I used to go to the repertory theater, but then . . ." Or, "I used to love baseball, but then . . ." Or "I used to have season tickets for [fill in the blank], but then . . ." In a diverse society, every single element energizes the popular culture — even, oh my goodness, wrestling! Each niche influences, through its language, preference, or product, the whole to some degree. Just as Muhammad Ali, James Brown, and Liberace borrowed from the outrageous Gorgeous George a generation or two before, culture still appropriates from the red-headed stepson now called sports entertainment. Society might sneer, but then it mimics, copies, and steals.

Every time a sportswriter or talking head describes a lopsided game as a smackdown, wrestling shows its influence. Where did the NBA get the inspiration for its high-energy introductions, with the kind of hot music, glaring spotlights, and fireworks that unnerve Commissioner David Stern? How many big league arenas are filled with Ric Flair "Wooooos!" to stir passions for the home team? And wasn't Jesse "The Body" Ventura the Governor of Minnesota?

When the major candidates for the Presidency of the United States are featured on *Raw* — as Clinton, McCain, and Obama were — utilizing wrestler catchphrases, no further argument is necessary. Snobbish pundits can sniff, but facts are facts.

Technological advances have also meant that wrestling's most enthusiastic fans now have the perfect place to congregate and communicate — the Internet. With a user-driven forum from which to state their opinion, their voice seems much louder now.

Less than 20 years ago these loyalists still traded results via regular mail. These were the people who understood how the mat world was structured, what titles were floating around, and how wrestlers moved from territory to territory. If there had been legitimate wrestling talk radio, these folks would have been calling in regularly.

How many were there like this? Each town was different. Maybe St. Louis had 40. Kansas City maybe a dozen. New York probably had a couple hundred, so did other big cities, like Los Angeles or Boston. Tampa likely had 30. Amarillo 20; Toronto another 60; Minneapolis 50. Maybe there were three in Waterloo, Iowa; in Salem, Oregon, two.

But because wrestling played everywhere, the ranks swelled, though they were hidden from national attention. The sum total was likely close to what it is now: and each of these men and women, then as now, had his or her own opinion about how wrestling *should* be booked, or what was wrong with the product.

Put the fanatics and the knowledgeable together and they comprised a true specialty audience. They would trade complaints about why one wrestler was getting a push over another. They had clear favorites, and they weren't always the popular choice of the bigger, more casual audience. They could also loathe wrestlers the casual follower adored!

(Hey, WWE creative, sound like anyone you know?)

Fans promoters knew couldn't be chased away with a baseball bat, these dedicated folks had something they enjoyed, needed, even loved, in wrestling. They'd be there for the lousiest of lineups on the worst of days. Maybe they complained, but their loyalty always helped pay the rent.

Today, live wrestling hits the biggest markets only a couple times a year. Some towns see wwe caliber events just once a year, instead of once a month. Most never even get a live event in their hometown.

Thanks to cable and satellite companies, however, more fans — including more casual fans — watch the *same* event at the *same* moment, everywhere. The national network show is where the passionate affair with this crazy, glitzy, razzle-dazzle business begins. It's where you fall in love with wrestling in the 21st century.

Without question, many newcomers (especially the youngest among them) become infatuated with wrestling as it is now. For them, there is nothing else, no other way; they've never had access to other styles or philosophies that generate just as many, if not more, thrills. When they do get to see and appreciate another product, be it old school wrestling or ufc, their world is expanded.

The diehards of today influence the product online. Instead of small enclaves picking apart what they like and dislike about the product, the specialists use the web to air their ideas, complaints, and evaluations to anyone and everyone. They play virtual booker: why not The Undertaker versus Triple H? The wwe champion should face tna's best . . . Was making C.M. Punk the champion a good idea? Why did they beat Jeff Hardy or give Chris Jericho so much play? They hate John Cena, think Santino Marella is hilarious, and cannot understand a finish without a run-in. Nothing is wrong with any of it; it's all they know and feel.

Not every potential ticket or ppv buyer is online, though. Not even anywhere near the potential majority, at least not consistently. And just because someone isn't monitoring the Internet doesn't mean he enjoys wrestling any less, or that his opinion is any less valuable. Nonetheless, wwe and tna acknowledge and exploit the medium — it's become essential to marketing the business.

Analyze further: from a total television audience of approximately ten million, only 2%, just 200,000, buy the average pay-per-view. Add in the multiple-viewers-per-buy factor and the percentage is still under 5%, and a clearer version of the big picture begins to emerge.

For a monster show like the 2008 edition of *WrestleMania*, for example, nearly 700,000 of the over one million buys came from North American fans. Even with the multiple-viewer consideration, only 10% to 12% of the domestic viewership bought the event.

Now ask yourself, realistically, how many of these 2 to 12% are rabid, even knowledgeable fans?

How does TNA figure into this? In a good week, maybe as many as two million viewers tune in to their program. Their usual pay-per-view buys come in between 20,000 and 30,000. Figure two viewers per buy and perhaps 60,000 customers watch a PPV by TNA. At best, only 3% of the viewing audience cares enough to buy their premiere events. None of this threatens WWE's position as ruler of the industry.

Comparing past and present once more, consider that Hal Protter, at the time the General Manager of KPLR-TV in St. Louis, sat with Muchnick and me in 1980 as we worked out the formula for how many of our usual television audience of approximately 100,000 bought tickets for the average Kiel Auditorium card. The simple math showed 8% were actually buying tickets for a normal Kiel card (which, as noted earlier, on average drew 8,000 paying customers). A sellout of 12,000 meant that 12% were purchasing tickets. It wasn't the same people for every big show; it was a different part of the overall 100,000 every time.

Dave Meltzer adds some insight into all of this, pointing out that in the days of the territories, fans had to actually buy a ticket and travel somewhere to see the big show live and in person. Today, enjoying the comparable WWE event is as simple as relaxing in an easy chair and punching a button on the remote. How many fans in the time of Sam, Vince Sr., Gagne, and all the rest would have paid to watch if it had been that simple?

These numbers clearly dispute one of Vince's biggest claims: that he made the wrestling audience bigger by taking the game into the mainstream. The data just doesn't back him up.

Still, it's not significant enough to detract from the fact that some ten million pairs of eyes watching, and some 600,000 folks spending money, is indeed an accomplishment.

And isn't it interesting that adding UFC's and WWE's numbers together would essentially equal the number of people paying to see *wrestling alone* back in the day? It's particularly noteworthy since so much of UFC's appeal unwittingly recalls old school style of promotion — not to mention WWE's public posture that UFC is not competition. The figures tell a different story.

What is true is that Vince, with sensational marketing and promotion, has made the whole thing look bigger than it ever was — which is pretty damn amazing. He's called attention to a wrestling universe that's immense and enthusiastic.

Naturally, every forward-looking company is looking for new ways to boost their sales. WWE is doing just that online. Some of the claims arising from their experimentation, though, cannot help but invite a certain amount of skepticism.

Realistically, at best maybe 5% of today's domestic viewing audience is online regularly, checking sites, following gossip, complaining, talking about expected finishes, or whatever. Plenty of speculation, lots of noise — from maybe 500,000 fans. There may seem to be more noise than there used to be, but that's just because of the volume of the medium, all of it coming through one giant speaker.

Sure, a goodly number of the more casual fans will stop by once in awhile. In 2008, for instance, WWE.com claimed 4,700,000 unique visits were made to their website during a relatively short time period. That's certainly impressive, and it demonstrates both the growth and the potential for Internet traffic of a dominant company. And it's practically 50% of their television audience.

What must be frustrating for WWE, however, is why, if half their audience clicks onto the website, are only 5% buying their pay-per-views? A vexing riddle, indeed.

More mind-boggling is when WWE.com claims to have thirteen million plus unique visitors each month. That's more than watch their television shows! Who are these people? Where are they coming from? Why are they there? Are they like the curious rubberneckers who slow down on the highway to look at the wreck in the opposite lane?

Another frustrating fact must be faced. If 175,000 domestic buys represents an acceptable PPV draw now, and if only 5 to 10% of the general viewing audience have historically bought tickets to see wrestling events, why celebrate a figure that is .014% — not even two-tenths of 1% — of those who click on the website?

I'm sincerely confused. Businesses turn a profit from customers who stop and *buy*, not from those who merely zip in to glance at the gaudy sign. (Maybe it's just the cynic in me.) But if those one-clickers represent just the marginally curious, and not the casual followers, the effort is probably worthwhile. If just a few become hooked, enough to buy a few items, anything from a PPV to a T-shirt, their dollars represent new profit.

Something, though, still just doesn't compute. This is the outfit that supposedly paid Floyd Mayweather Jr. twenty million bucks, correct? And hasn't WWE argued that their drug testing policy is the equal of any other program in sports? (WWE has improved, but still . . .) Thirteen million clearly sounds better than four million, for PR purposes. One symptom of the wrestling disease is exuberant exaggeration.

In St. Louis, the reliable 4,000 with season tickets, the people who had the "Wrestling" news sent to their home, represented just 4% of the folks watching *Wrestling at the Chase*. It was a dependable base that required no overstatement. Most of them would have logged onto the wrestling sites if the web had existed back then. Again, there's little variation between fans of different generations.

The fanatics and the serious fans from the territorial heyday of St. Louis, New York, or Chicago were the predecessors of the same group within today's much larger national audience, following every bump, burp, grunt and groan. Does it really matter if they figure out a finish or hate a headline performer a promoter's pushing? They certainly do not stop the other 95% of wrestling's audience — the people who are paying *no* attention whatsoever to online gossip or griping — from buying a PPV.

One thing is becoming apparent, however. The fandom online skews younger, and it's a safe bet WWE figured this out long ago. Shading its product toward them is a good way to build, they hope, both for the present and for the future. The work wwe does on its website has become fairly progressive — which might be the fine hand of Howard Finkel, the most loyal employee Vince McMahon will ever have, now that he concentrates on this area.

And no matter what, you gotta love the hard-core fans. They watch the shows, they get the ppvs, they purchase the magazines, they buy the dvds, and they even watch tna as well. They care. They argue. They complain. Maybe just as important, they provide the best advertising of all: word of mouth. Now, as years ago, only the most miserable promotion and height of arrogance could make these people stop loving the pageant.

In turn, because these types of fans do form a vocal community, they have influence. wwe and tna monitor their every thought, mood, and word, but they're just not as all-important to wrestling's bottom line as everyone might like to think. A big-time promotion can't get caught up in Internet games and gossip. The online audience has already bought the product — it's everyone else that must be sold. To change a finish or pull a swerve because of online noise makes no sense if it disrupts well-planned booking: the people being fooled will buy the ppv regardless.

And besides, why wouldn't the sophisticated minds at wwe plant stories or make "anonymous" comments in an effort to achieve their own goals? After all, it's a company that loves to try to manipulate fan reaction. (But let's not become too cynical — *wink, wink!*)

Where the passionate clique matters most is as a kind of canary in a coal mine. If they start to dwindle and disappear — if they lose interest — the promotion is doing something wrong. So listen to them, definitely, but keep everything in perspective. A promotion can count on the true believers, through thick and thin. If *they* go, it is an indication that casual followers — the folks who can silently change the channel and simply stop watching — are already gone. When a promotion has confidence in its booking and its stars, the action will find and retain an audience . . . including a generous number of outspoken critics.

Whatever kind of fan a person is, whether in 2009 or 1959, they are *not* marks. Almost every one of them knows full well what they're buying. Tricking, or swerving, them is a good way to alienate them — and damage the revenue base. Disrespecting them — and numerous promotions have been guilty of this — is as pitiful and shameful as it is foolish.

Sam Muchnick hated the word "mark," and it's an opinion Vince shares, to his credit. That it's a holdover from the old carnival days of wrestling hardly makes it respectable. I honestly cannot remember Sam ever using the term, even in the privacy of his office, where there was no reason to guard his language. What he probably objected to most was dismissing wrestling's audience as people who could be easily fooled.

Instead, the size and the composition of the St. Louis universe demonstrated that wrestling had wide appeal. Fans came from all walks of life, rich and poor, male and female, black and white, college graduate and grade school dropout, policeman and thief.

Why? Like so many others, my own interest is rooted in family history; my father, as a teenager, saw the historic battle between Strangler Lewis and Joe Stecher at the Coliseum in St. Louis on February 20, 1928. Everything begins there.

Stories like these, each with its own personal twist, apply to millions of wrestling fans, of all levels of interest. Because of our history, we're more than a dollar sign, number or rating point. The inter-generational transmission of the wrestling bug has occurred for a century. As a first-grader, I heard colorful tales about battles involving Lewis, Londos, and Kampfer, and they sounded like ancient warriors, battling in mystical buildings. I was a sitting duck when wrestling was broadcast in the 1950s. Even before *Wrestling at the Chase* got rolling in 1959, I was hooked. The action televised from the famous Khorassan Room of the Chase-Park Plaza made it even more enthralling.

After wrestling on television closed the deal for me, it was not long before I was trading results with fans I'd discovered through searching for pen pals in wrestling magazines like *Wrestling Revue* and *Ring Magazine*, where I was also fortunate enough to have my descriptions of bouts in St. Louis published. The two best were

Diane Devine, then from Springfield, Missouri, and Larry Lewis from Waterloo, Iowa. Like me, both had other correspondents from all over the country. Diane and Larry would list all of the results they had and send them to me; I'd do the same for them. What a high, to know what was happening in New York, Philadelphia, and Pittsburgh, as well as Atlanta, Tampa, and San Francisco! Then, I could browse through the results from Vancouver, Los Angeles, Dallas, Tulsa, and Minneapolis. At its peak, I was probably trading with a dozen others. It was an early lesson in the booking patterns and philosophies that I would come to grasp much more fully when I began working in the business.

We really had no idea who or how old each other was, or what background any of us had. We knew one thing — the common bond of our love for wrestling. The members of this little clique — hundreds of us — were scattered around North America. Eventually, I met Diane when she moved to St. Louis and became one of the area's most ardent fans. She now lives in Denver and is still loyal to the sport. Before losing track of him, I heard that Larry Lewis actually promoted some spot shows for the Kansas City office.

I was doing odd jobs for Sam Muchnick by the time I was sixteen. But I was still a fan — even though Sam had begun educating me about the fact that wrestling is a hard, cold business. I could relate to that feeling of trembling excitement when walking into a building like Kiel. The rush of adrenaline watching a great match (it doesn't happen often; I'm picky) between two gladiators who really rock and roll is still a part of who I am, even if there's a different vibe now that I understand more.

Ironically, over time, I found that I was the same as folks like Jim Ross and Jack Brisco, who both became famous in the business. JR and Brisco, like me, got hooked on televised wrestling, and then began reading the magazines like *Wrestling Revue*. Like me, they found their way into the areas of the business where they excelled. And we are hardly alone.

Fans, no matter where they're from, find their way into the legion of like-minded people. It's particularly rewarding for folks like Ross and me to still be part of that family. Because of wrestling, many great friendships have flourished for years.

Cathy Jackson and Darla Taylor, two lifelong St. Louis fans, are like many from around the globe, except for one surprising twist that involves a mutual pal. Darla probably got hooked when she saw Pat O'Connor dethrone Dick Hutton as NWA champion at Kiel on January 9, 1959. (Of course, she was nine months old and asleep on her mother's lap, so her memory of the match is a bit foggy at best.)

Cathy became interested watching *Wrestling at the Chase* on a black-and-white television. At 16, she discovered she could get a ticket to the Chase Hotel to see the action in person. Going by herself and transferring between two different buses, Cathy fell in love with the scene. Probably the first person she got to know was a peppy and funny gal named Juanita Wright, who, Cathy recalls, "seemed to know everyone" at the matches. Along the way, Darla became friends with Juanita and Cathy, as well.

Approximately two decades later, after years of being buddies, Juanita called Cathy at work one day and was so excited she could hardly speak. Juanita had been invited to the WWF headquarters in Stamford, Connecticut, for a meeting with Vince McMahon. "Mr. McMahon wants to see *me!*" Cathy remembers her friend saying.

At first, naturally enough, Cathy didn't believe her pal, but when she picked up Juanita from the airport on her return, Juanita had a contract with what was then the WWF. She became "Sapphire," the partner/manager of Dusty Rhodes. Juanita was *fifty* when she started working for Vince.

Juanita was one of the genuine characters on the St. Louis scene, always happy and energetic. She knew everybody, and everybody knew her. Over time, the wrestlers came to like her, and they trusted her for help getting rides to the airport, and knew her as a sympathetic ear when they were down. Just for fun, Juanita had started to wrestle on small independent shows in the early '80s. She knew the ghost of Mildred Burke was not threatened by her wrestling exploits, but Juanita could do a couple things in the ring, have fun, and connect with other fans. Aside from her family, she loved wrestling more than anything.

When the spot for that managerial role with the wwf popped up, Terry Garvin was working for Vince, and he knew Juanita from when he used to referee in St. Louis. He brought up her name, and apparently Vince remembered her, too. *Boom*, just like that, a life-long wrestling fan got to live her dream.

Wrestling gave Juanita the opportunity to meet more people and go places than she ever dreamed possible. "Sapphire" became a celebrity who loved signing autographs. Juanita, after all, had been on the other side; she understood. She even got to work *WrestleMania VI*, as she and Dusty defeated Randy Savage and Sensational Sherri. To top it off, the lovely Miss Elizabeth was in their corner, too.

The boys looked out for her, with Greg Valentine and Bob Orton in particular always telling Juanita to save her money. Dave Hebner, an agent for the wwf during that time, explained that most wrestlers back then asked for a couple hundred dollars advance on their pay each night at every card. Juanita only rarely asked for one hundred. "She never lived high on the hog, even when she started making money," Darla adds. "She just didn't change. Juanita was so happy! I think she had every penny she got in the bank when she died."

While she was disappointed when her run ended after a couple of years, Juanita enjoyed every day she was with the wwf. She knew the game and realized from day one that it wouldn't last forever. She embraced every moment. Cathy said, "People can say what they like about Vince, but he allowed 'Nit' (Cathy's nickname for her friend) to live her dream." Cathy and Darla know that Juanita never tired of the business; she was still wrestling a bit, managing, or making appearances at independent shows until her sudden death in 1996.

Juanita certainly discovered the answer to the one question every fan has. For those on the inside, it certainly *is* real.

Wiser, better writers than I (the number is infinite) have learned that a book, fiction or non-fiction, has a life of its own; that writing a book takes you in directions you never expected to go. It's true; it happened to me writing this chapter. For a moment, I stopped gathering facts, theorizing, examining stats, explaining and revealing history, and trying to prove savvy enough to interpret it all and still be entertaining. I began to ask myself, "Why? Why do you like it? Why do you stick with wrestling?"

I quickly realized I've been asking myself that question for longer than I care to acknowledge.

Talking to fans has made me understand that analyzing the business of wrestling and its countless secrets can make you cynical. I've been there, and likely I still am — as cynical as the devil himself. Having made a living from it, having been both triumphant and battered by it, and having been a key part of the creative process has surely skewed my viewpoint. But I see, now, how everything fits together — a perfect jigsaw puzzle — to create the mesmerizing illusion. Good, bad, and everything in between pale in contrast to the loyalty and, dare I say it, *love* that fans have for wrestling.

And, hell, I *am* a fan. For all the ups and downs, I'm still a fan, and I always will be. I have been on both sides of the fence — watching from the cheap seats, and performing, or helping to perform as the announcer, booker, promoter, or whatever. It's a position of privilege and responsibility. Juanita Wright probably came to understand this, too.

Jim Ross understands this as well, I bet. And many wrestlers do. Wasn't John Cena a big fan? What about a young Paul Levesque, before he was Triple H? Even a few promoters were fans — when they weren't obsessed with making as much money as possible.

Vince? Vince knows; Vince gets it — when the corporate executive in him isn't calling the tune. Wrestling works best when those doing the show are fans at heart, whether they admit it or not. After cautiously and privately putting aside the harsh realities if only for those few moments, almost all of us in the industry strive to become part of the illusion we cherish.

CHAPTER TWELVE

WHAT NEXT?

No matter how wrestling changes, and it certainly has, the basics always seem to endure.

Critics knock the success of old school promoters, arguing the NWA and its brethren exploited a monopoly. These self-appointed "experts" like to argue that fans were exposed to only one local promotion — one style of wrestling. Folks in Minneapolis, they say, could never compare the wrestling product they watched with the product from Florida. According to this theory, each town was educated to believe that the wrestlers it saw were the "real" stars.

But how are things any different today? WWE stands on its throne, with TNA a mere gnat buzzing around the fringe. To the overwhelming majority of fans, wrestling *is* WWE. Aren't current fans told who they should recognize as stars?

Vince McMahon has modernized a system that worked for years; and it still works because there is no real opposition. TNA tries, but it's little more than an imitator, even to the extent of pushing talent that WWE has decided no longer fits into their long-term plans. Vince surely understands TNA is no real threat — it lacks the over-the-top hullabaloo and pageantry of his company.

Yet TNA, through its mere existence, somehow protects Vince from monopoly charges. The audience for the upstart promotion is now flat, and some ridiculous booking decisions have played a part in that disappointment. In the end, TNA might be compared to a Las Vegas tribute show that mimics "real" stars. Why watch the imitation when the original is on a couple channels down the dial?

Ironically, modern wrestling itself has opened the door for

mixed martial arts. It's clearly cut into wrestling's market, but that might not be the only factor that triggers the next change in the wrestling world. When it comes to PPV domestic buys, UFC has already surpassed WWE. (TNA is but a blip on the radar.) And what's the appeal of MMA? Violence, skill, an ability to develop personalities who become stars, and . . . it's real. (Whatever "real" is.)

MMA is a "shoot," with no predetermined outcome. Winning actually matters. What a remarkable selling point in a culture of competition! The same simple concept — winning and losing — could once again become effective in the "work" of pro wrestling, if it's presented with intelligence.

Smart booking matches styles and skill levels so that, hopefully, the *right* competitor (the fighter who sells the most tickets) can score the victory, but the MMA promoter is not overtly dictating who wins and who loses. If, every so often, the two most charismatic stars also happen to be the two best competitors, UFC in particular seems satisfied to let the chips fall where they may, but they always have a plan for what happens next, no matter who wins. That philosophy also provides ample space for new stars to develop.

UFC has learned, and is perfecting, the ability to promote the main events — its championships and the rivalries that mean big box office. In fact, some of its most successful booking and promoting has been unintentionally and surprisingly reminiscent of the best planning of top "old school" wrestling promoters. UFC builds its promotion around fighters moving up the ladder by winning or rebounding after defeat, with titles carrying importance, just like Sam Muchnick once did in St. Louis.

Not that many years ago, shoot-style promotions caught fire and chopped the legs off traditional Japanese pro wrestling organizations like All Japan and New Japan. Eventually fans no longer viewed pro wrestlers as the toughest of the tough, even though the wrestling-crazed country had always understood that wrestling was as much show as it was competition. Nonetheless, the shoot promotions became big money makers, New Japan fought for its existence, All Japan nearly crumbled, and other, smaller pro wrestling groups simply disappeared.

Terry Funk, who knows the culture in both Japan and North America, expresses concern over the prospect of the same thing happening here. To some extent it already has, as many of UFC's PPV buys surely once belonged to pro wrestling. A segment of the market that was unsatisfied with the hijinks of WWE was eager for what UFC had to offer. Similarly, MMA appeals to a demographic advertisers love — young adult males. And, at least so far, MMA has not been tarred with the brush of illegitimacy that makes many well-heeled advertisers ignore wrestling.

Maybe, though, Vince insulated his business from the same degree of crisis that sank Japanese pro wrestling when, years back, he "exposed" wrestling as a work. The vast audience in America has come to accept this; and clearly, therefore, a distance and difference had already been established when UFC hit the jackpot. Wrestling wasn't held to MMA's standard, and it would have been if the old school mentality, that their product was more real, still held.

Consider the irony, then, of McMahon getting up before stockholders and saying he wanted to make his product more realistic. He brought up his longtime pet peeve: how bad it looked when someone in trouble simply took repeated blows without covering up — which happens, particularly, when heels get heat by pounding the babyface. It's difficult to have things both ways, even for Vince. So, the statement also seems like a tacit admission that he realizes looking realistic is important if pro wrestling is to succeed. Maybe. After all, it is Vince . . .

McMahon has also repeatedly claimed that MMA is not wrestling's competition; the UFC he says, is sport, WWE is entertainment. Does he mean that sport isn't entertaining? Since neither MMA nor WWE will ever cure Alzheimer's or bring about world peace (basketball, hockey, and football won't either), they're both entertainment — no different than movies, music, and television. Was Vince just trying to wedge a little more space for his product against other similar sports-oriented entertainment pursuits? Whatever he says, or believes, nothing was going to stop him from spending serious bucks buying advertising time to ballyhoo *Wrestlemania 25* on *ESPN Sports Center*.

Sometimes Vince McMahon is almost too smart for his own good. After issuing an edict directing announcers and WWE media outlets to stop referring to wrestling as *wrestling*, but as "sports entertainment," he went a step further late in 2008, ordering that WWE events be called "entertainment" and wrestlers called "entertainers." Unbelievable. Just imagine trying to be Jim Ross or Jerry Lawler and not being able to use the word wrestling.

Some felt McMahon was reacting to the possibility of state athletic commission regulations that would require drug and steroid testing — by calling his employees (whoops, independent contractors) entertainers, they would not be tested for performance-enhancing drugs. Likewise, he may have been trying to avoid paying specific state and local athletic taxes, which actually have been a burden on wrestling for years. (In St. Louis, over 17% of the gross gate goes to pay various taxes.) But let's put everything into perspective. If WWE's wellness program is meaningful, why be concerned about a test administered by the state?

Now, does the general audience, the casual fan in particular, pay any attention, or even have any interest in these issues? When they hear that wrestling is no longer wrestling, that wrestlers are now "entertainers," what are they to think? What's next, song and dance?

Maybe there are justifiable business reasons to argue the product is scripted entertainment, but to say so in public, on WWE's primary outlets, is a slap in the face to the very fans the company wants emotional support and hard-earned dollars from. Reading that John Cena considers himself "an actor" in *ESPN The Magazine* must make many possible followers cringe. Seriously, should the magicians spoil the illusion?

Fans simply want to suspend disbelief for a few fun hours, which is a chore under current circumstances. They want a touch of taboo, of crazy excitement that feels real in the moment, which is difficult when the producer says, "This is all scripted baloney."

Clint Eastwood, acting as Dirty Harry or the Man With No Name, or even as an Oscar-winning director — how often did he break the barrier? How often did he *tell* the audience that the films weren't real, even though, down deep, everyone already knew. The answer is: never.

The smart ass insider skits Triple H apparently enjoys, and is actually quite good at, may entertain a certain portion of the crowd, but I truly believe the mass audience wants to think of him as a rough, macho, hard-nosed scrapper. In truth, Hunter might be the best worker the company's had for the past few years, but goofy vignettes do nothing to enhance this fact. Casual followers, considering whether or not to buy tickets or PPVs, are looking for vintage Clint Eastwood — but with all Triple H's campy material, they get Vince Vaughn instead.

Was telling the entire audience, prior to *Wrestlemania 25*, that Triple H was Vince's son-in-law (when the vast majority, aside from hard-core fans, did *not* know) helpful or hurtful to both the product and Hunter's image? Was the payoff big enough? Maybe folks prefer *not* knowing.

Has the arrogance of nearly total dominance somehow undermined the passion and made WWE forget what made dominance possible? Is future wrestling, or "entertainment," on the national scale, doomed to play to fans who cheer flashy tricks but couldn't care less about the tricksters? Has cold, corporate, authoritarian, and manipulative replaced passionate, spontaneous, edgy, and rough around the edges?

The more Vince McMahon moves away from his roots, the more WWE denies its history and the reality of what it is, the more fans leave their arena — forever. If Vince begins to forget the history he himself has helped write or loses respect for the realities of his product, if key performers do not respect what they do, why should anyone else care enough to spend his or her money? With all the challenges and uncertainty, what may come to pass seems even more unclear.

Right now, establishing a paying fan base is not an either-or proposition. A fairly meaningful number of people bounce back and forth, casually following both MMA and wrestling. Whether or not they buy an event from either entertainment is almost surely driven by the dynamics of a rivalry, the context of the entire promotion, and/or the personalities of the combatants. The performers' abilities and charisma, along with how they are promoted, becomes the crucial consideration. That means the pressure is on, for both disciplines, to continually develop fresh faces, because few will ever crack the golden circle of feature events to become formidable drawing cards.

Ultimately, MMA may pose yet another problem for WWE (and it is a headache for TNA as well). Recruiting new ring talent has always been a priority. Sam Muchnick and the NWA, despite the fact that amateur coaches in the 1950s and 1960s always publically demeaned the pros, donated money to amateur wrestling programs, even sponsored Olympic athletes. A not insignificant number of amateur grapplers found their way into the play-for-pay ranks, making the investment worthwhile. Even then the industry understood that new blood was the key to its longevity, and promoters complained constantly that not enough young guys were coming into the sport.

Virtually every NWA convention, well into the 1970s, included a speech from Sam or some other prominent promoter about the importance of finding new talent. During that era, wrestling also picked up many top-line grapplers from the ranks of those who could not quite get over the hump to play in the National Football League, or whose gridiron careers had ended. From Ernie Ladd to Wahoo McDaniel, from Bruiser Brody to Butch Reed, from Stan Hansen to Dick the Bruiser to Nick Bockwinkel, many of the sport's biggest names had football backgrounds. Although it has become less common in recent years, the tradition dates back to the likes of Bronko Nagurski!

Top professionals like Jack Brisco, Dan Hodge, Ali Vaziri (the Iron Sheik), and Bob Roop are just a few of many who could boast excellent amateur credentials. Baron Von Raschke wrestled and played college football at Nebraska. Big Bill Miller did both at Ohio State, as did Cowboy Bill Watts at Oklahoma. Ken Patera came from college track and field, weight lifting, and the Olympics.

Just as important was the fact that with all of those small businesses scattered throughout the continent, athletes looking for another chance had somewhere to go, someone to talk with, and an experienced hand to train them. There were places to break in everywhere (some better than others, naturally) and learn the ins and outs of a difficult, demanding art.

Verne Gagne, for one, fails to get anywhere near the credit he deserves for churning out top-level talent like Patera, Raschke, Iron Sheik, Jim Brunzell, Jesse Ventura, Sgt. Slaughter, Curt Hennig, Ricky Steamboat, Playboy Buddy Rose, his own son Greg, and many others including, of course, Ric Flair. Gagne turned an old farm into a training school that was rigorous and efficient in making, or breaking, prospective pros. He earmarked high-level athletes who had excelled in wrestling or some other sport, who at least appeared to have the kind of drive necessary for entering a brutally demanding business like pro wrestling. Obviously, his graduates were superb.

When each of a couple dozen promotions were finding one, two, or three guys on a regular basis, wrestling had a feeder line of new talent, no matter how much promoters moaned and groaned that there were not enough prospects. Compared to today, there was a veritable flood of fresh blood. But how many of those just mentioned would be inclined to gravitate to MMA rather than wrestling as the second decade of the 21st century dawns?

As the territories disappeared, so did the many jobs available for new wrestlers. Eventually, it was almost impossible to earn a decent living while honing the mechanics that could lead to bigger and better things. Vince finally recognized this problem as well, and at different times has made attempts to develop training locations in Louisville, Atlanta, and Tampa. Overall, the projects have not been terribly productive, although the likes of John Cena, Dave Batista, and Randy Orton were early successes. Still, nothing has been able to surpass the larger number of athletes getting a taste of wrestling when territories existed, nor has any training been better than working night after night against different opponents before live crowds, large or small.

Even if many failed and dropped by the wayside, since the pool was so much bigger, more also broke through, at various levels, including into main events. They got to the top, in addition to becoming an important part of what Lou Thesz called "the base of the pyramid."

At one point, when Jim Ross was influential in the process, WWE focused more on finding good athletes to train. The pendulum has swung toward seeking people who resemble television stars and teaching them to wrestle (if it were only so easy!), rather than discovering people who can wrestle and turning them into television stars.

Today, the offspring of a former grappler already has a leg up. The theory is "second generation stars" will understand the culture and better handle the demands of the lifestyle. Unfortunately, however, there's not exactly a large number of potential candidates — more than a few children of wrestlers have heard (and experienced) the horror stories of the business from their fathers.

Recently, because the likes of Brock Lesnar and Bobby Lashley earned big bucks for a while and then unceremoniously left WWE on their own accord (after the company had invested so much into making them stars) the concentration has been on finding those who have always wanted to be pro wrestlers, particularly if they have what WWE deems is the right look. The fear seems to be that those more competitively oriented, like Lesnar, Lashley, and Bill Goldberg, will bail out as soon as they earn some real money. Even Kurt Angle, an Olympic gold medalist, ended up with TNA — and it's in part due to Kurt's troubles with the demands of the WWE life, physically, mentally, and politically.

During the late 1980s, a theory making the rounds behind the scenes was that Vince was trying to devalue the good workers and the legitimate tough guys. The thinking was that if somebody who qualified under those standards became a star and decided to "hold up" the promotion for more money or about finishes, he was almost impossible to replace. Therefore, there were those who felt — rightly or wrongly — that Vince preferred to put body builder types on top, because they could be trained and brainwashed in the then-WWF mindset.

Of course, exceptional workers have since demonstrated their value time and again, if for no other reason than to help make someone less talented into a star. While the odds of a real "shoot" ever happening in wrestling today are virtually nonexistent (insider knowledge of who was in fact the toughest used to matter when it came to main-event booking and championship reigns), the ability to handle oneself in the ring and to grasp the fundamentals of working are as important as ever.

The problem is that those who have those gifts, or whose skills could be developed, are now looking at alternatives. One recent criterion for getting onto WWE's radar was growing up as a fan and wanting to be a wrestler. Well, just wanting to be a professional wrestler is not nearly enough to make it at the upper echelons, especially not when so much money is at stake.

Here's where MMA bites a chunk out of wrestling. It's clearly a viable alternative, and perhaps even preferable, for those who believe they are athletic, tough, competitive, and smart enough to make serious money. The lucrative top positions in WWE are limited, both in number and, often, by politics. With MMA, a promoter is not making as many backroom decisions about who gets pushed (at least not blatantly); in MMA it's relatively simple, if you're good, your opportunity will come. There's also time to train and heal. Winning, which is in the competitor's hands completely, will provide upward mobility.

Only a few have what it takes, both in ability and charisma, to become a star that drives business no matter which direction they choose. If wrestling loses just a couple of those to MMA, the product is hurt.

Brock Lesnar has become the poster boy for this new development. An NCAA wrestling champion, a legitimate pro football prospect, and a hot main-event resident on WWE blockbusters, Lesnar generated an earthquake in his move to UFC. Granted, he catapulted to the top of the UFC's contenders' list almost overnight because of his WWE fame. Brock is a drawing card, a charismatic tough guy who has genuine credentials. He has "the look" — and he has the goods.

If Lesnar couldn't fight, if he was not the real deal, his tenure as a top MMA attraction would be short. (Consider Kimbo Slice —

although UFC is making an effort to resurrect him.) When Lesnar flattened UFC hero Randy Couture in November 2008, the stars aligned. Couture was on the downward slide of a great career, while Lesnar was just building toward his peak. Nonetheless, Lesnar whipped a legend, solidifying his position in MMA. Even a loss, now, will not seriously hurt his box office appeal. More to the point? Brock Lesnar is going to be making money and producing publicity for UFC . . . *not* for WWE. And don't underestimate Bobby Lashley's potential to eventually become an important player in MMA as well.

When Lesnar defeated Couture, WWE briefly became its own worst enemy, publishing an article on its website that was tinged with jealousy — congratulating Lesnar on his victory, but criticizing the fact that in MMA there is no way to know whether a headline bout might end quickly in unexpected fashion. The piece was deleted quickly. Perhaps somebody recognized that it actually called attention to one of the strengths of MMA — the sport's unpredictability. Quick and explosive or long and grueling, its real plot emphasizes overcoming obstacles. They're qualities WWE and pro wrestling could utilize as well, especially because their battles are pre-determined. They were missing the boat.

When more of the legitimate "studs" go to MMA rather than WWE, wrestling must increasingly rely on shallow skits and gimmicks rather than the guys who can deliver thrilling in-ring action. Depth on any lineup, MMA or pro wrestling, matters. Not everyone is a star, and there is clearly a place for role players. The more prospects choose MMA, the more wrestling is hurt.

Without question, this is an issue that must be addressed. But despite these incursions onto wrestling's turf, do not expect the business to go away quietly. Thanks to new technologies of mass communication, more people have access to it. Still, the name of the game is hold an audience, and build it. It can be done, but not without the most nimble and imaginative effort possible. Ignoring the foundation of your fanbase could spell disaster, but so could neglecting the hunger for change as well. It's no easy juggling act, but it's not a challenge for which Vince McMahon's WWE is unprepared.

So, what *will* wrestling be like when the day comes, as it surely will, that Vince McMahon is no longer dominant?

Forgive me, but once more I must return to one of the central themes of this book. For me, there is no way to dissect what wrestling has been, is, or will be without comparing Vince McMahon and Sam Muchnick. It's unavoidable — each man defined wrestling when they were its representative. In different eras, with totally diverse styles and personalities, they were the most powerful individuals in the game. They directed the ship like polar opposites, both in tone and tactic. Sam was *not* the *face* of wrestling, however, nor did he care to be. Vince is, and he likes it that way.

Wrestling is a malleable beast. The temperate Muchnick coerced, massaged, manipulated, persuaded, and enticed wrestling into a loosely cooperative alliance with many independent pieces. In Sam's time, wrestling was a splintered, many-pronged monster; Muchnick was the patient caretaker, the protector, the mediator, and the conscience. He was a philosophical man, searching for honesty in a corrupt wrestling environment. His power and influence, while often unsung and usually discreet, was tremendous.

The bombastic McMahon twisted, turned, poked, prodded, and pummeled wrestling into virtually one giant corporation of his own design. He alone governed. McMahon filled a vacuum with his energy, motivation, and hunger when the business was going to be buffeted by changes out of its control. Sam was a man for his time, just as Vince is a man for *his* time; both were exactly what the deviant sport needed at the particular moment.

Ironically, Sam and Vince share more traits than either would likely care to admit. To understand, and perhaps even adore wrestling without grasping how two such opposite outlooks could prosper is impossible. That their conquests were achieved differently has little to do with "old" or "new." Their differences prove that wrestling, in all its grime or all its brilliance (and usually a mixture of both), can fascinate and entertain a huge audience.

A foundation has to be poured before a mansion can be built. Muchnick and the NWA did that, in the process securing the Northeast for Vince Sr.'s son. Vinnie Mac is the culmination of all the industry's spadework, controversial though much of it may have been.

But what if?

Even had there been no Vince to crush them, the NWA would have collapsed. Look at the wrestling landscape at the dawn of the mid-1980s. Verne Gagne was most certainly sniffing around, looking for ways to expand. Even after Vince's early success, Gagne was able to land a deal with ESPN. If the WWF had not been stampeding, would Verne have been able to build something national?

Fritz Von Erich (Jack Adkisson) was on fire with his syndicated *World Class Championship Wrestling* program, setting new standards for production values and spectacular choreographed ring entrances. Rest assured that Fritz would have tried to use his syndication success to land a network deal and branch out across the country — at least until all the brutal drug tragedies took their toll on his family.

Best positioned was Jim Barnett and WTBS. Folks all over the nation were already talking about their Saturday afternoon wrestling show. Barnett and his Atlanta partners, however, were heading for a messy break-up under the best of circumstances. Even though the promotion would have likely disintegrated, rest assured Ted Turner and WTBS would have made an attempt to do something nationally.

Cowboy Bill Watts with Mid-South Wrestling was smart and ambitious. His promotion was a favorite among many hard-core fans. At one point during the various political intrigues involving McMahon and Turner, Watts actually landed a spot on WTBS. The pieces never fit together, though, for Watts to make inroads nationally.

What about Jim Crockett Jr. in the Carolinas? He was another ambitious fellow who would have, in some way, responded to the changing scene. Eventually, his company used WTBS to tangle with McMahon in the mid-1980s.

And just suppose Vince *had* failed the first time. Does anyone really think he wouldn't have tried again? Based in the media capitol of New York and entrenched in lucrative Northeast markets, he probably would still have had the wherewithal — and even more desire — to make another run at becoming omnipotent.

Age would have taken a toll on the likes of Gagne and Barnett. Shifting power within ownership structures would have altered the playing field. Would the successors have been as smart, smarter, or more foolish, than those they replaced? Who would have had or been able to develop contacts with key power-brokers in the new age of television and communications? Could anyone have developed the marketing that tidied up wrestling's image at different times over two decades and made wrestling the *hot* item for the larger, casual audience?

The most likely result? Chaos. Complete and total chaos — a melee unlike any other in the history of wrestling. Predicting the outcome of such confusion is impossible, but one thing, perhaps, is clear: most of the territorial promotions would still have collapsed, though a few would have survived, at least for a while, in altered form. Cable channels were burgeoning and becoming accessible to a greater percentage of the population; and all the new outlets were seeking products that were, like wrestling, relatively cheap to produce. Pay-per-view would have, or at least could have, enticed the surviving companies away from house shows, although none of the ppvs, in a more scrambled industry, would have had the WWE's drawing power. A TNA type of sales level might be distributed among three, four, or five survivors.

Today, those three or four remaining promotions could possibly turn a profit — although, again, hardly at WWE's level. Each might have their loyal followings — their own little fiefdom — but they'd be nothing like the *kingdom* WWE is now. They'd have trouble generating a response from the mass media, good or bad, and certainly never could come close to what WWE can ignite when it is on its game. They'd fiddle with merchandising and other revenue streams, but never approach what WWE achieves with so much material under its control.

The hard reality is, like it or not, Vince correctly anticipated what type of wrestling company would thrive in the 21st century marketplace. Once he dodged the early financial and competitive bullets, his triumph was assured.

This does not necessarily mean Vince's style of booking and wrestling was responsible for WWE's success; instead, the way Vince structured his company to take advantage of the world as it is today made the difference. WWE is a highly efficient marketing and promotion conglomerate — one that just happens to concentrate on wrestling.

MMA, over a relatively short period of time, has grown into the perfect parallel universe. That sport burned through gobs of money and almost crashed until UFC, under the skillful, McMahon–like direction of Dana White, finally figured out how to market what they had. Vince McMahon was miles ahead of the likes of Crockett or Gagne, but even he had to learn lessons as he moved forward. WTBS, with Turner's backing, had deep pockets, but nowhere near enough knowledge about wrestling to understand how to merge it and marketing into a promotional giant.

So is this the way wrestling will always be, a dominant and regal WWE with a scrappy but stumbling TNA yapping at its heels, and MMA making inroads into, but not taking all of its base? A few tiny independent operations paying guys $25 or $50 a night, sprinkled around North America?

Unlikely. More change is inevitable. TNA could finally show some significant profit, or it might trip and lose its deal with television. Currently, the operation is pretty much kept alive by Spike TV. It might start losing buckets of money again. Or it might be swallowed by Vince — remember, a wrestling promoter does not own TNA; Panda Energy does. TNA's president Dixie Carter is the daughter of the Texas company's owner. They're business people first, and business people buy, sell, and fold, just as they did at WTBS when Ted Turner removed himself from power.

Assuming it survives the inevitable overexposure as television rushes to get on the bandwagon, MMA has a splendid opportunity to entrench itself further — UFC will be there certainly, and maybe a competitor or two — as a profitable player with a different product whose roots are still deep in pro wrestling.

If anyone new wants to play the fight-entertainment game, deep pockets will be the first requirement. Very deep pockets. They'll need to pony up for quality television production, find an appropriate, worthwhile broadcast vehicle, and spend an absurd amount of money. In retrospect, perhaps the most important factor in Vince McMahon's conquest has been his expert assimilation of new technology. It allowed him to take televised wrestling from the small studio set-up of yesteryear to today's sizzling circus of fireworks, music, blinding hi-def colors, and various degrees of freaks, athletes, violence, drama, and, maybe, even a very tiny bit of competitive sport.

The truth is, *Raw* and *Smackdown* are actually *Wrestling at the Chase* on massive amounts of steroids, the magnificent chandeliers of the Khorassan Room pumped full of television growth hormone.

The intense, psychological, and stiff work has mostly been converted into a cartoonish, acrobatic soap opera, except for rare moments when the most exceptional performers collide. But those are issues of taste and education, subject to the whims of booking and society. What really counts in this game of how best to utilize television is money. Lots and lots of money. WWE lays out almost two million to produce each PPV spectacular. High Definition means each television taping now costs more than $750,000. That's $750,000 *per* week, and the figure does not include what's being spent on talent or promotion.

Poor TNA, the token opposition. No matter how noble the effort, it still looks like a cheaper imitation, even with its six-sided ring, thanks to its production and booking. Sadly, TNA has spent a small fortune just to get where it is.

Then there's Ring of Honor, tip-toeing at the edge, eager and hungry as it dives in with a new deal on HDNet. Can a small, independent, cult operation not called ECW grab a meaningful following? Respected by serious insiders for their philosophy, ROH apparently intends to feature much less talking, less lame comedy, a lot of hard-hitting wrestling within a competitive atmosphere, updated television production techniques, and — bless them — not cutting away to commercials in the middle of a match. Doesn't that sound like the territorial formula of the 1960s and 1970s? Still, even if their ideas are solid — and somewhat novel for wrestling in today's marketplace — they'll need a fat wallet and good political connections to stay alive. To fight *this* war at *this* level, to gain a spot on the national stage, you better plan on spending serious money and having friends in the right places. Thanks to outside pressures, things that had little or nothing to do with wrestling, they began to struggle almost as soon as it looked like they were making headway.

No less important for any group hoping to crack the current market is *patience*. Be consistent. The product has to be good, yes, but an audience has to be built and taught. If your philosophy is going to change with every bump in the road, failure is guaranteed.

At a 2008 stockholders conference, Vince McMahon said WWE needed to move away from focusing on . . . Vince McMahon. He praised others within the company, saying talented people would keep WWE vital and, naturally, profitable for stockholders long into the future. It was a wise move, and Vince is nothing if not very intelligent. Perhaps any future WWE announcements need to be considered in this context, that even Vince McMahon recognizes things must change, and that plans are being made to deal with that eventuality.

But, bless him, despite admitting his mortality, he's still Vince — he also argued that WWE, and by extension wrestling, did not need mainstream media in order to be successful, that with the direct contact of television and the Internet, WWE could always be profitable. Sure, there was some pandering: he mentioned the need to be more media-friendly to encourage sympathetic understanding of the business. Does anyone believe, however, that Vince wouldn't jump through hoops to get the esteem of the establishment? He's certainly done it in the past.

Was this actually news? Hell, Sam Muchnick and his associates knew wrestling could survive quite nicely without the approval of the upper crust, even in the 1960s, when the spectacle was built around local television and direct mail. Wrestling might have been "in the closet," so to speak, but it was incredibly lucrative.

Positive attention from the mainstream media was just a bonus, a significant one, but a bonus all the same. Muchnick sought out and cultivated that bonus. And Vince does too, whether he admits it or not. How did Sam go about it? He kept a tight handle on the baser instincts of the sport. Muchnick realized that in addition to selling some extra tickets, a considerate nod from the mainstream also brought respect both to wrestling and, in particular, to *him* personally. He liked that — being recognized as a reputable and powerful operator who elevated pro wrestling to a better level. Rest assured, Vince has hungered for the same recognition as he has tried to get the business acknowledged as an art form.

Wrestling has generally been its own worst enemy when it comes to mainstream media and culture. The steroid controversies alone have established WWE as a less-than-trustworthy operation. Media and public distaste for the product has been brought on by the promoters themselves. It's not just McMahon: many, many promoters have crossed the line between tolerable and absurd — or worse. In the course of wrestling's history, every social sore, from sex to the bizarre, from the threat of foreign menaces to race bating to extreme, senseless violence, and every variation thereof, has been used to generate heat with the intent of drawing money or garnering publicity.

Today, however, WWE wants absolution. It wants to once more become family entertainment, smoothing over the realities of wrestling to become more cartoonish and "kid friendly." A cynical lot anyway, with their own agendas, the media mavens will be all too happy to do softball features with wrestling figures. But when controversy develops, or if the content strays toward the edges of respectability (it's happened before and it'll happen again when declining revenues make bookers desperate to try anything to fire fans' imaginations), expect the media to pounce. Either way, too much water has passed under the bridge for the media to ever treat pro wrestling with respect and deference.

The day when WWE will mean something other than Vince McMahon approaches, and the Wall Street types who are currently tolerant might become uneasy. Going public with a portion of his company was an absolute masterstroke. Bluntly, it made the McMahon family a fabulous amount of money — which is the idea of running any business, including wrestling. Yet the move also opened the door to a different kind of public scrutiny.

Whether investors would be as confident in wwe without Vince at the helm is uncharted territory. Far bigger conglomerates and personalities on the financial scene have come — and gone. But a century of wrestling history tells us one thing: wrestling will find a way to survive.

In *The Audacity of Hope*, President Barack Obama tells a story about former vice president Al Gore that explains how transient power can be — in essence cautioning those who have power (including, apparently, himself) to always remember that circumstances change. Obama writes about a "big steep cliff, the precipitous fall." Power is temporary, fleeting. Presidents, politicians, executives, entertainers, and even the wealthy have taken falls. Why in the world would a professional wrestling promoter be exempt?

With all due respect to Vince's children, would they stay deeply involved without Dad's guiding hand? Would they be as effective? Vince is a once-in-a-lifetime personality. Do his children have the unquenchable fire their father has? (Some insiders have speculated that Stephanie might — *might* — have inherited the passion.) At some point, though, wouldn't making a mountain of money by selling off assets make more sense than staying the course to deal with the unending stress? Think about it: who might buy wwe? *What* would they be buying without Vince's vision?

Would the executives Vince recently praised be as eager to stay with someone else's wwe? Or might they leverage their successful tenure in the hope of moving to another big company?

I know one thing with certainty: If Vince were gone, all the sharks would smell blood and begin to circle. That includes those within his own organization. Does anyone seriously believe there are not those quietly plotting for a future without Vince? World Championship Wrestling had Ted Turner's fortune, but without a visionary, it was rudderless and eventually engulfed by wwe's wake. There are still those with grievances, and they might try to exact their revenge on Vince's children. In wwe, Vince is God. When he's gone, well-financed challengers will smell opportunity because, let's face it, greed and often stupidity are not in short supply.

Compare McMahon and Muchnick yet again. The St. Louis operation was miniscule compared to WWE. It's David and Goliath, certainly, but as much as they are different, they are alike. After all, both Muchnick and McMahon had children.

Why didn't Sam groom his offspring, especially his two sons, to become wrestling promoters? He told me several times that he feared the reprisals his sons Dick and Dan might face from a nasty, cruel business. "I had to do things over the years a lot of people didn't like," Sam stressed to me. "I was afraid some of those who secretly held grudges against me would try to get even by hurting my children if they were in the business after I was gone."

Even more instructive was Sam's take on selling the St. Louis Wrestling Club to Bob Geigel, Harley Race, Pat O'Connor, and Verne Gagne. One day he listed for me what his minority partners were really buying: "A couple of typewriters, some filing cabinets and desks, a couch, a bunch of photos, a lease on the office at the Chase Hotel, a contract to produce wrestling programs for a television station, a good reputation for the promotion, and you as an employee," Sam enumerated. "They are not buying future success."

Muchnick felt what made St. Louis profitable was the way he operated, the knowledge he had about the enterprise and his market. I clearly remember him saying, "I cannot sell them the people." It was why he told me not to put up my own money to buy into the new partnership, but rather to let the new owners make it worth my while to stay.

What Sam was saying, discreetly covering his unmistakable pride in what he had built, was that a promotion was the person or people who had the dream and understood the concept and could make everything work together successfully. The company was about the leader. Isn't that also true of WWE and Vince?

Muchnick retired from promoting on January 1, 1982. Dismayed about the direction his former company was taking, he resigned as consultant on December 31, 1982. Frustrated and discouraged, I quit as general manager on February 28, 1983. The St. Louis Wrestling Club contract with KPLR-TV was cancelled at the end of 1983. The newcomers simply did not understand why wrestling had worked in St. Louis. In little more than a year, the model franchise was in complete disarray.

Certainly, WWE has far more things to sell — plenty more desks and lots of computers and even real estate. They have a state-of-the-art television production facility. Licensing deals, television contracts, talented employees. A gigantic video library with hours of potential programming. WWE has a huge footprint in the business world. Regardless, can the corporation be as successful and nimble when the Vince-less era dawns?

Isn't it interesting, and somewhat disconcerting, that the talent hasn't factored into this? While wrestler contracts would undoubtedly be involved in any sale, it's a safe bet that this "overhead" would be relatively easy to manage and manipulate from a financial standpoint. Shouldn't wrestlers be more highly valued? Well, the philosophy has always been that talent can be replaced. If wrestlers had a union, it might be a different story. Rest assured that if a Major League Baseball or National Football League franchise were sold, the monetary valuation of talent would be a major negotiating point in any deal.

All things considered, the pressure on Stephanie and Shane will be incredible. And as much as WWE is structured as a massive marketing machine, its roots and its heritage are still . . . wrestling. The future is not a lock.

If television turns a cold shoulder — and look at the struggle WWE's had in finding the right home for *Smackdown* — the business could end up on the endangered species list. Television masterminds would not hesitate to turn their backs on *Raw* if a once-stable corporation becomes a liability. Time and time again, TV has proven itself to be a fickle monarch that, on a whole, is not a fan of wrestling. Anyone remember what happened to Westerns? When a type of programming runs its course, television is not at all squeamish about pulling the plug.

Perhaps old school Sam Muchnick was right to be content with wrestling known as a minor, cult, but comfortably profitable operation; something television always found a spot for because it was cheap to produce. Sam presented wrestling's need for television politely, quietly, and respectfully.

Today, wrestling *needs* television, and TV knows it. At Vince's level and in Vince's terms, wrestling's need for television is loud and obvious. Television, however, does not need wrestling . . . or, for that matter, Vince.

Ratings provide a last line of defense. Because there will always be viewers who love to watch wrestling, and there will always be stations with time to fill, wrestling in some form should survive. Maybe it won't be prime time — the interested networks may not be prestigious, and the stations may not be able to charge as much for advertising, but it should be enough to keep wrestling on the air.

Vince McMahon's greatest challenge may be his last. More than changing the wrestling world, or becoming its czar, wouldn't a company that thrived without him be an even more momentous accomplishment?

In the unlikely, worst-case scenario for the future, the wrestling business would implode and collapse. For a while. Wrestling is a survivor. It went on without Sam Muchnick, just as it will without Vince McMahon. Nobody owns wrestling. No matter the flaws, the magic will live — if only at the grassroots.

And then some television producer will rediscover the excitement, take a chance, and put wrestling on at midnight, on Saturdays. People will slowly re-discover the fun. A smart, imaginative, eager promoter will find the right way to position the product. Hungry talent will sense opportunity. The audience will grow.

The time will be right, and the cycle will begin again.

I hope.

CHAPTER THIRTEEN

GO HOME

Whenever Bruiser Brody comes to mind, I cannot help but think of an airplane trip my old buddy told me about, and how it relates to everything that has happened in wrestling over the years.

His outrageous appearance, the long hair and beard, plus the patchwork of ugly scars on his forehead meant Brody, standing 6'6" and weighing 285 pounds at the time, could hardly travel incognito, especially when he was wearing an expensive sweat suit with the pants rolled up to his knees and had his wild hair pulled back in a bushy ponytail. Nonetheless, being a serious and capable student of the financial markets, he liked to settle into his seat and study various stock prospectuses or business commentaries. He rarely looked for company — at least not more than usual when in transit.

On this particular journey, the gentleman next to Brody could not help repeatedly glancing at his quiet, polite, but scary-looking fellow traveler. Dressed in a conservative coat and tie, obviously a respectable businessman, he finally had to ask: "Just curious: what do you do for a living?"

Brody answered, "Professional wrestler," but kept on reading.

Haltingly trying to start a conversation, the gentleman acknowledged having watched a few wrestling shows. "Looks pretty rough," he noted.

Brody grunted assent.

Finally, though, the question had to come . . . ever so carefully: "It's all fake, right?"

Brody might have argued the point in all its idiosyncrasies. He might have feigned anger. He might have tried to change the subject. Instead, because he just wanted to read, Bruiser Brody answered gently, "Yeah, it's fake."

After a rather lengthy and surprised silence, the fellow said, "Oh, I don't know. Look how banged up your head is. You guys really get hurt." And he began defending the exact position Brody might have been expected to take had he not been seeking solitude.

With a reluctant smile, Brody surrendered to the moment. The two talked wrestling for the entire flight, and Brody later admitted enjoying discussing his business with the intelligent guy.

The scene is perfect. Frank Goodish, in the persona of Bruiser Brody, is professional wrestling in all its contradictions. His seatmate, polite and cautious, is society with all its curiosity.

Brody projected an image of wrestling that both scares and intrigues: athletic, untamed, violent in appearance and reputation, exciting, entertaining, flamboyant, dangerous.

Society is fascinated by these diverse elements and has to inspect what all the turmoil is about. Not surprisingly, an incredibly large portion discovers just how much enjoyment, despite the numerous defects, wrestling can provide.

Whatever it does, wherever it has been, however it evolves, wrestling has a deliciously naughty and therefore timeless appeal.

Many rip wrestling apart, even as they watch and delight in every bit of action. They insult it, degrade it, publish its flaws. Some only want what they enjoy to be better. Others want to hear themselves talk. They all condemn, indict, judge and — often with good reason — find guilty a most incendiary endeavor.

But despite it all, I want to hug wrestling, the ugly old brute. And I am not alone, not by a long shot. Wrestling is not evil. People who are involved with it can be, in many instances. Maybe I unconsciously romanticize the dark corners of wrestling, hoping to make the jagged edges of a hard business easier to accept. But maybe I also understand that wrestling's biggest problem is what wrestling people do to it.

There's so much about wrestling to love. It doesn't care how old you are or how young, how handsome or how disabled, how rich or how poor. It doesn't care if you are white, black, Asian, Hispanic, or green. The more wrestling gets bashed, the more people — lots and lots of people — want to delight in it and understand it.

At its best, wrestling wants to mesmerize and delight, fascinate and entertain. Wrestling wants you to forget your troubles, your fears, your past, and your future. Wrestling wants you to exult in the passion and the fun. Do not confuse wrestling *in its heart* with the ways in which it is often twisted.

Wrestling is like an energetic little boy you can't stop watching and even laughing about. He grabs a piece of chocolate cake and eats it in the backyard. Mischievous kid! But he's smiling and the icing is smeared all over his face. He plays in the mud, but helps his elderly neighbor pick up trash. He hugs his baby sister, but hides her beloved toy monkey. Good, bad, and undeniably human.

Sometimes, however, like wrestling, he is more than bad. He steals coins, throws rocks at the dog, and bullies weaker classmates. Maybe part of him is almost evil. So what is this kid, good or evil?

Well, we cannot stop watching, enjoying, detesting, and loving this thing called wrestling. The same culture that may have helped destroy Chris Benoit made millions cheer Hulk Hogan and John Cena, Lou Thesz and Ric Flair. That isn't wrong.

Maybe this reveals more about us as a society than it does about professional wrestling — an unsettling proposition. Wrestling is like us: many good things, some bad parts, and always seeking escapism. Great memories, strong emotions. Highs and lows.

So, does wrestling, with all its faults, deserve to be treated with respect and affection?

Wrestling is a work. And, thanks to the great entertainment it can offer, it doesn't matter one damn bit.

***

The pretty, pleasant lady asked me, "Is it real?"

Yes, my dear, it is.

Wrestling is more real than anyone dare imagine. That's why countless millions, for almost a century, have been trapped in its bearhug.

ACKNOWLEDGMENTS

Thanks must go to the following stalwarts:

My wife Pat. She recognizes when to puncture my ego with an incisive critique, and when to ease my frustration with a hug. But there are more laughs than anything. (It still isn't dull, is it?) And my daughter Kelly. She loves to give me her opinion, and it's always right on target.

Michael Holmes, my editor at ECW Press. His love of wrestling makes the entire process of writing a book like this satisfying. Amy and Logan are lucky to have him as a husband and a father, plus he is a pretty good speller.

Mel Hutnick, the distinguished attorney who enjoys making me do mental gymnastics about what and how to write. Luckily, Mel hasn't (yet) gone on the attack when I've borrowed his intellectual property.

The wise and helpful gang of critics and collaborators that includes Dave Meltzer, Bob Costas, Irvin Muchnick, Terry Funk, Buck Robley, Bob Orton, Jim Raschke, Nick Bockwinkel, Doug Dahm, Tim Shifflet, Keith Schildroth, Herb Simmons, and a mysterious masked man or two.

And to friends like Darla Taylor and Cathy Jackson who reminded me that, no matter how cynical this business can make you at times, I'm still a fan myself.